GUARDIANS OF YELLOWSTONE

GUARDIANS OF YELLOWSTONE

*An Intimate Look at the Challenges of Protecting
America's Foremost Wilderness Park*

Dan R. Sholly, Chief Ranger
with
Steven M. Newman

WILLIAM MORROW AND COMPANY, INC.
NEW YORK

It is the policy of William Morrow and Company, Inc., and its imprints and affiliates, recognizing the importance of preserving what has been written, to print the books we publish on acid-free paper, and we exert our best efforts to that end.

Library of Congress Cataloging-in-Publication Data

Sholly, Dan R.
    Guardians of Yellowstone / by Dan R. Sholly, chief ranger, with
Steven M. Newman.
        p.   cm.
    ISBN 0-688-09213-6
    1. Forest fire fighters—Yellowstone National Park.   2. Forest
fires—Yellowstone National Park.   3. Yellowstone National Park.
I. Newman, Steven M.   II. Title.
SD421.32.Y45S53   1991
634.9′618′0978752—dc20   90-48529
                                                                    CIP

Printed in the United States of America

First Edition

1 2 3 4 5 6 7 8 9 10

BOOK DESIGN BY A. DE MAIO

ENDPAPER MAP BY JEFFREY L. WARD C D S

To the Yellowstone Rangers
and their partners,
the Naturalists, Scientists, Administrative and Maintenance staffs,
who all make it happen

Acknowledgments

I am grateful to all those who contributed to my journey to Yellowstone: my dad, George, the epitome of a ranger, who laid the foundation of my life; my mother, Maurice, who nourished my love for the out-of-doors; my Park Service mentors: Lee Shackelton, Jim Brady, Jack Morehead, Walt Dabney, Rick Smith, Roger Rudolph, Butch Farabee and the rest of the Yosemite mafia; Frank Betts at Crater Lake; Dave Ames at Hawaii Volcanoes; Tom Ritter, Stan Albright, and Mike Finley at Washington, D.C.; and at Yellowstone, the incredible Bob Barbee, a friend and great leader who has delicately balanced the direction of Yellowstone as we approach the twenty-first century.

I want to thank everyone in Yellowstone who contributed stories and information that helped make this book possible, especially Steve Frye, Jerry Mernin, Norm Bishop, Terry McEneaney, Tom Tankersley, Joan Anzelmo, Janet Fay, Barbara Zafft, and Bev Whitman.

A big thank-you goes to Sandy Redmond for the hundreds of hours she spent transcribing Steve Newman's tape-recorded interviews and observations. And certainly never enough credit can be given to Suzi, Steve's lovely wife, for giving him up for yet another year to his word processor, and to editor Jeanne Bernkopf, a lady whose talents are as big as her heart, and whose own love of nature helped make this book all the more alive.

My special appreciation to my wife, Tana, for her continual support of my dreams, and to my children, Cameron, Alexandra, Brooke, and Trevor, the next generation of the guardians of Yellowstone.

7

GUARDIANS OF YELLOWSTONE

1

I felt as though I were a part of Armageddon. Yellowstone National Park was black and smoking.

Over my head, the helicopter's blades tore swiftly at the afternoon sky. I rubbed my one good eye long and hard.

It's like a battleground, I thought as I gazed at the patchwork of black, gray, and green stretching to an enormous mushroom-shaped smoke pillar. Seen from four thousand feet in the air there were many similarities between the forest fire's destruction and that of the napalm attacks I had witnessed in Vietnam. Both left the same impression: *Horror has passed this way.*

The razor-edged mountain ridges were shrouded in a thick gray haze. The late August sun was as red as blood, reflecting off the pilot's dark-glassed face visor.

The desolation we were passing over seemed surrealistic. In place after place smoldering trees lay as if a giant sickle had swept through their ranks. Those two-hundred-year-old trees had been ripped from the earth by the firestorm's howling winds and then slammed back onto it even more violently. It was as if hell itself had spilled from the earth's bowels.

I couldn't close my eyes anymore without seeing endless black, endless burn. I'd seen it so many times these past two months, there was more soot than blood lately in my veins. And I had a foreboding sense that the worst was still just ahead.

Ashes flew past like a swarm of ghostly insects. The air suddenly seemed hot, almost suffocating.

There was a massive convection cloud just ahead, so huge it resembled a thunderhead. It extended higher into the sky than even our helicopter could venture.

The flames at ground zero were rolling over the thickly wooded earth with the mercilessness of a three-hundred-foot-high tidal wave. Sucked along by trees so dry they might as well have been matches, it looked unstoppable. Watching the basketball-sized fireballs being flung into the thin mountain air, I felt as though I were in the middle of something mythical.

I knew fire, but this Clover-Mist monster was making no sense. Last night's increased humidity and lower temperatures should have at least slowed its advance. But they hadn't. Not at all.

I stared numbly at the spreading flames. This was a barbarian of a forest fire: ruthless and unpredictable. Like the five others in the park, it had been born of violence—in this case the result of a lightning strike tearing into the heart of a tree.

I believed in fire. I liked it. I knew, as did most of my rangers, that the ecology of Yellowstone needed it desperately. Needed it to supply the soil beneath the trees with nutrient-rich ash. Needed it to allow the sun's rays to reach the earth. It was a way for nature to renew itself.

But unfortunately what the American public saw was only death and destruction. They saw in Yellowstone's fires the end of America's greatest natural treasure. They saw those flames, the enveloping smoke, and in their minds and in their headlines, hell had indeed come to Yellowstone.

I tapped the pilot's shoulder. He turned his mirrored face to me.

"Eric, I've seen enough. Let's get to Silver Gate," I said through the ship's intercom.

He nodded and steered the helicopter away from the battling elements.

As we skimmed over a huge and nasty mountain ridge called "The Thunderer," I thought of what was ahead.

Silver Gate is a tiny tourist community in Montana that lies just a couple of miles outside the park's Northeast Entrance. Its 170 or so summer residents and those of the slightly larger neighboring community of Cooke City had called a town meeting to discuss the forest fires burning all around them. I had no doubt that they feared the Clover-Mist fire would soon be at their very doors.

I could understand their being angry since they, like so many, believed the Park Service should have—could have—put the fires out as soon as they started. I could also understand their being suspicious, since none of the experts' predictions about the behavior of the fires had proven anywhere near correct. But I also knew their anger was mixed with hatred.

People in Silver Gate and Cooke City had long been leery of the Park Service. Though we provided—at the federal government's expense—law enforcement, fire protection, road maintenance, and medical services to their isolated communities, theirs had always been a "we versus Big Brother" attitude. Those who depend on guided hunting and fishing, logging, and mining activities for their livelihoods are a highly independent breed, and many of them had never quite accepted the fact that nearby was a vast wilderness they couldn't simply utilize for themselves.

A few of the rumors that had come back to me from their neck of the woods the past days were especially disturbing. The Park Service, according to one, was actually hoping the Clover-Mist fire heading northeast from Yellowstone Park would destroy their communities. The reasoning, as I understood it, was that once their dwellings were destroyed, the park would then be rid of its most annoying neighbors.

I glanced at the gold nameplate on my flight suit: DAN SHOLLY, Chief Ranger. The way some people were acting lately, it should have read: DAN SHOLLY, Stormtrooper.

Just ahead a barren gray peak loomed. I glanced at the pilot. We seemed to be on a collision course. But at the last second Eric yanked us up and over the mass of cracks and scree.

We were over a seemingly endless panorama of mountains and valleys. We descended into a deep valley in the shadow of the mountain's north precipice; there was still some snow clinging to its sheer heights.

Through the dense forest we saw a cluster of wooden rooftops along a blacktop road. Closer, closer Eric angled the chopper's skids.

With a rapidity that made me catch my breath, the ground rose to us. The wood-shingled rooftops became motel cabins, a general store, a gas station, a cafe—all made of neatly fitted pine logs. Then bodies became distinct faces: the tired ones of yellow-jacketed firefighters, the grimacing ones of idled tourists, the red leathery one of a Stetson-topped lawman.

We had landed in a field next to the road, where a ranger patrol was waiting to escort me.

I took off my helmet, pushed open the side door, and stepped down to the grass. The smoke cloud from the Clover-Mist was blocking the sun so thoroughly that the yard lamps around me were on, even though it was hours before nightfall. As I strode toward the building where the meeting was being held, all about me were the signs of imminent battle: fire engines, hoses, hard hats, rucksacks, shovels, flashing lights, and still more ashes on the wind.

Outside the two-story Range Riders Lodge I paused in the dust of the parking lot to pull my portable radio from its holster on my waist. I pressed the call button and asked for 700-Fox, the dispatcher at the fire command post in Mammoth Hot Springs, the park headquarters. I knew the meeting inside the Range Riders had already started, but I didn't want to face that crowd without the latest on the Clover-Mist fire's size, perimeters, and projected behavior, and the weather forecasts.

The locals knew their mountains. If they thought for one second that I was not being truthful about the advancing fire's movements and speed, all hell could break loose.

"Dan! There you are!"

Coming down the lodge's cement steps was one of the naturalist rangers, a bearded young fellow named Tom Tankersley. He looked frazzled but was still managing a smile.

"Dan, you better get in there. We've been telling them all day everything's going to be fine, that we don't think they are in danger. But now others are telling them the opposite."

"Any troubles?"

"Well, nothing like murder," he answered with a laugh. "But that's not to say they aren't fightin' mad either."

That I could have guessed. Only a week before I'd been at the first of the daily fire meetings, in the lodge's cavernous dining hall. And I'd been lambasted. One older merchant lady from Cooke City had been particularly harsh: "Why in the hell don't you put the fires out! Why don't you just put them out!" she'd screamed again and again down at me from the open balcony that went around the hall's second floor. Her words had resonated through the dark ceiling beams.

"What are you going to do—let it burn to here and then try to stop it?" she'd cried as the jammed hall let loose with waves of thunderous applause and shouting.

I'd really felt lucky to get out in one piece. And here I was going right back into the same crowd with no better news to offer, and with the Clover-Mist fire now so close that it was raining ash onto their properties.

My radio crackled to life. It was Mammoth.

"I'll be right in," I assured Tom.

He went back through the lodge's front doors, but was out again barely a minute later.

"Dan, I think you better hurry. It's getting nasty."

I signed off and followed him. Inside the dark, cool lodge was a sign tacked to a stout support beam: NO GUNS ALLOWED.

"By God you can bet I will do something about this terrible tragedy!" railed a voice at my left.

I whirled to see one of the most ardent opponents of wilderness areas striding toward me across the lodge. His green Park Service–issued flight suit was unzipped to the middle of his large chest, displaying an expensive designer shirt. His thick gray hair was brushed back sternly.

"All of you know how much I am against all this wilderness craze!" the congressman boomed, his thick fists striking out at imaginary foes. "And all this 'let burn' stuff that is gonna end up burning you out of your homes is exactly why!"

The huge old room, which had once been a gambling hall, was crammed from its sooty brick fireplace and hanging moose antlers to its long bar with more people than I thought lived in the whole county. Some wore the droopy, stained cowboy hats and even droopier mustaches of outfitters and ranch hands. Several had beards. Nearly all—men and women—were nodding their heads and shouting. It was as though I'd arrived just in time for a revival meeting, or a lynching.

Across the room, just below the moose antlers, I could see Bob Barbee, the park superintendent and one of the tallest persons in the room. I squeezed my way past one scowl after another to get to him. All the while, the congressman kept on about how he was going to return to Washington at once and bring punishment upon those who'd allowed such a catastrophe to occur.

"Thank God you are here!" whispered Barbee in a way that hinted he had reached the end of his patience and probably very nearly his sanity. He looked perfectly calm, but I knew that inside he was anything but. His forte was charming dignitaries and journalists, not dealing with enraged citizens.

Unfortunately, I felt about as helpless as Barbee did, as I listened to the rising tumult. It was easy to see that the congressman, who had arrived with Barbee in another helicopter, was casting doubt on virtually every bit of information Tom, Barbee, and the assistant superintendent, Ben Clary, had handed over to the two towns' permanent and seasonal residents. I would have given anything to be allowed to put a gag over the grandstanding politician's mouth, but I didn't dare to rebuke him openly. Certainly not with newspaper and television reporters looking on. There were already enough sensational stories on the news wires about the fires to give any administrator migraines for a year. There was simply no need to be adding fuel to what was already being called by the media the worst disaster in the 116-year history of Yellowstone Park. And what irritated me all the more was that the park wasn't even in the congressman's district.

I was wondering what I might do to "politely" stem his rhetoric when suddenly from a table near the front windows came an unexpectedly shrill shout.

"What are *you* going to do about these fires coming at us!" demanded the voice, so sharply that everyone, including the congressman, looked to see where it had come from.

It belonged to a little old lady in a flower print dress and straw sun hat. She was so frail it hardly seemed possible such a loud sound could have come from her. I guessed that she and the two elderly lady friends beside her were probably retirees with a summer cottage in the area.

"Well, Mister Politician, just what *are* you going to do? Answer me!" she repeated with a mighty bang of her fist against the pine table's thickly branded cowhide top.

The congressman's jaw squared angrily, but only for a second. He was a highly experienced speaker. In less time than it took to flash her an irritated glance he also evidently dismissed her as a flake. He again started pacing across the floor's worn and gouged boards. His litany against the dangers of too much wilderness and too many liberals spilled forth with ever greater flourish.

But the lady would have nothing of such a brush-off. Once more a very arresting screech came from her blue lips.

This time the congressman whirled and charged her, his finger pointing at her so sternly that it seemed he might gore her right between the eyes with it.

"Now see here!" he said sharply. "Don't you turn on me. I am here to help you people."

A hush fell over the crowd at once. It was as if they suddenly realized *he* wasn't one of them after all. His eyes flickered nervously at the bodies now crowded against him.

"Help *us? Hah!*" taunted still another voice.

This time every head turned toward the doorway. There stood a short wiry man in a rumpled aviator's jacket, his hands on his hips and a mocking look on his small crinkled face.

I recognized him instantly. He was Hayes Kirby, Silver Gate's most independent and mysterious resident.

He was a master of energy; it was almost as if he had sugar for blood. I had had to listen to Kirby's anger about something or other more than once over the telephone or at other town meetings. I was convinced he just plain loved to raise tempers. He could have inflamed the emotions of a dead man, given enough time.

Hayes was a former jet fighter pilot, and so he had just enough mystique about him to make everyone believe that maybe he ac-

17

tually was a war hero, a mercenary, and a CIA employee, and that
he had a lot of money tucked away. It wasn't that he necessarily
went around saying such things, but he sure could leave one with
those impressions from his stories of going to Iran and Turkey and
Africa to rescue businessmen and deliver arms for the government.
I wasn't sure anyone, even his girlfriend, who helped him run his
local motel, knew just exactly what it was that Kirby was up to half
the time. But he did have a plane, and did have a way of sounding
as fearless as a man with an ace hidden somewhere up his sleeve.
And that was plenty good enough for the locals, since like them
he was no fan of the Park Service.

"And just what is that supposed to mean?" the congressman
huffed at Kirby.

Kirby swaggered in as if he were a foot taller and two feet wider
at the shoulders.

"It means we're going to burn. It means we're going to lose it
all. It's time we got some action. Time we had less talk, more
results."

He scanned the crowd with confidence. They loved it! More
voices began to shout out.

"Damned right!"

"More action!"

"Talk ain't gonna save our homes!"

"Make them sons of bitches put out those fires—now!"

I looked at Barbee. The bags under his eyes seemed even larger.
I worked my way to the bar to see if I could get a Coke. Something
told me this could be a long meeting.

I took a deep breath, let it out slowly, and leaned against the
bar counter.

They never taught me anything about this at ranger school, I
thought, as voices shot back and forth behind me. The books
contained everything I'd ever want to know about splinting a broken
bone or rappelling down a cliff to get to a stranded climber. But
how about calming an angry town-meeting crowd?

My father had been a chief ranger too. For the first ten years
of my life I'd watched him run the new Big Bend National Park in

Texas, and his rangering life had been an inspiration to me. I thought it romantic and heroic. He had spent time almost every day riding horses or hiking, and weekends fishing. There had always been time in his week for him to take my brother and me on some fantastic ranger adventure. We went rafting down the Rio Grande with him and his boss, Mr. Garrison, the park's superintendent, as they searched for illegal Mexican crossings and smuggling. Or on a horse patrol to look for mountain lions or to survey archaeological sites.

But I didn't remember his ever having to try to calm down a hateful crowd, or being ridiculed by headline-hungry journalists who came in droves and demanded answers to absolutely mindless questions and then sped away to cover in six inches of print, or one minute of television, a subject that had taken a whole day to explain properly. Perhaps he had, and I had just never been aware. But then again, he always told Mom everything, good and bad. And given the tiny huts we lived in in those early years I couldn't have missed his complaints about such things.

My father had always been respected and looked up to by everyone, even in the toughest of times. He had been the lord of his wilderness domain.

I finished off the Coke. Through the upturned glass the distorted form of an enormous animal skull leered at me grotesquely. I set the glass down slowly on the counter and studied the horse skull on top of the tall freezer. It was almost as long as my arm and seemed to have a thousand teeth.

There was a local legend that the skull was that of Chief Joseph's favorite horse. I rather doubted that, but if it was true then that skull had seen a lot of changes in the area since the handsome Nez Perce chief had led his people on their tragic retreat across Yellowstone from northeastern Oregon, not the least of which was how a part of America that at the time had been mostly unknown, inaccessible, and unwanted was now visited by millions from around the world each year, and wanted so badly by some that it had to be protected like the priceless and irreplaceable treasure it had become.

"Well, all I can tell you is what I know to be true from what I've seen," said the congressman's voice above everyone else's. "And by God I know that fire is running out of control."

I turned around. He was still arguing with Kirby, his nose now to Kirby's forehead.

The two were basically in total agreement about everything. But apparently that was not about to satisfy Kirby. I had a feeling the only thing that was going to satisfy him was for someone from the government to jump up and proclaim: "Yes, we have done absolutely wrong! This fire is exactly where Mr. Kirby says it is, and by golly it is going to do exactly as he says it will!"

Barbee raised his large hands into the air and cleared his throat.

"Gentlemen. We're here today to update you on the fire situation. Can we *please* get on with it?" he said.

He looked my way.

"Chief Ranger Dan Sholly will update you with what he has."

I strode to a map of the park hanging on a wall between the room and the dining hall.

"As I'm sure all of you know, the Clover-Mist has extended its front since I was last here. However, we are still confident it will *not* reach Silver Gate or Cooke City," I said calmly.

A murmur of disagreement and distrust rippled through the crowd.

"I've done a fly-by of the fire this afternoon, and have received the latest update from the fire command center. The fire is still south and west of Cache Creek. It is very unlikely that it will jump Cache Creek or these ridges. If it goes anywhere, it should move off to the east, where we are building lines on the Divide right now to keep it inside the park."

"Bull!" shouted Kirby from a few steps away.

"Kirby, I was just up there. I know what I'm talking about," I challenged.

"And so do I!" he shot right back. "*I* was just up there. Flew over in my plane, checked it out firsthand. That fire's gotten so big it ain't going to stop till it's burned everything. Maybe if you'd gotten off your rear ends and fought it when it was still possible to put it out with a bucket and a shovel, we wouldn't be here now!

Fact is—" He turned to the crowd. "Fact is I heard from sources that they plan to have the fire burn right to the northeast corner of the park before they address it."

Another roar erupted. Whereupon Kirby continued passionately: "Well that, you might like to know, happens to be where we're standing!"

I frowned. Kirby was stirring up everyone's emotions with bad information. If he had in fact flown up there, he would have flown into closed airspace, thereby jeopardizing other official aircraft, including the flight I had just arrived on. But that, I decided reluctantly, would be an issue for another time and place.

"The Cache Creek area is so smoky, Kirby, I doubt you knew exactly where you were," I pointed out.

He threw up his hands and rolled his eyes as if he couldn't possibly be in error.

I waved for order. "Again, I'm telling you the Clover-Mist fire is not going to burn down your towns. And even if it got as far as the top of the west side of Amphitheater Mountain there's no way it could jump all that bare rock." The thought of the huge bald peak and the snowy precipices flashed through my head. Surely to God *they* would stop the flames.

"Liar!" shouted a female's voice.

"How's that?" I asked.

A mother with her child in her lap shook a fist at me. "Every time you guarantee us the fire can't go past this or that, you come right back two days later to say it has! How can you expect us to believe you when you're one hundred percent wrong one hundred percent of the time?"

"That's right!" roared a man.

I felt more than a little embarrassed. They were right when they said every single prediction made about the fires had turned out to be wrong. Not just my predictions, but those of five of the top fire behavior specialists in the world. The problem was that *no one* had ever seen fire behavior like this before. The book on projecting wildfire movements was seemingly being rewritten by Satan himself.

All the land features—rivers, canyons, meadows—that usually

guaranteed the end of a forest fire's progression were proving to be worthless. Fires that in any normal year would have petered out after a dozen acres were still raging hundreds of thousands of acres later. It really did seem that the park was going to be totally consumed by flames.

This summer's fire behavior was straight out of science fiction—the sort none of us had ever witnessed before. And most frightening of all, the official fire season was a long way from being over. In all likelihood the worst was still ahead.

"You've declared martial law on that park and aren't going to let the truth be known," charged a grizzled cowboy. "You can feed us all that propaganda you want, but we ain't swallowing it. We know you're not doing anything to put them fires out, that you're just paying men to stand around and watch Yellowstone be destroyed! Why . . . ." His face was so red with anger he could hardly get the rest of his words out. "You're nothing but a bunch of communists."

"I assure you we've not been letting any new fires burn since the middle of July. We've suspended the natural-burn policy and have been aggressively suppressing all new fires with everything we can muster. And as for the big fires, if you saw firefighters standing around doing nothing, it's not because they've been told just to watch it. Truth is in many places they *can't* do anything! It'd be suicidal to put men in front of those fires. With such powerful winds pushing the fire fronts and the fires spitting embers miles ahead and making new fires all the time, we'd have dead men in no time," I countered.

"Well let them bring in the bulldozers!"

"Bulldozers are totally worthless when you've got fires spotting two to three miles ahead of themselves," I countered, for what seemed the thousandth time in the past several weeks.

By the time I finally left the meeting I felt as if I'd been on trial. And I knew that plenty of new emergencies had sprung up in the hour-plus I'd been in that room.

It certainly did seem that we were fighting a losing battle, I thought, looking up at the mushroom cloud hanging over Amphitheater Mountain. How could we keep asking them to believe everything was going to be okay, when all they saw every day was that huge expanding beast over their heads?

On the way to the helicopter I couldn't help noticing how much darker it was. The smell of smoke in the hot air was very strong. It even stung my eye.

I stopped and looked up and down the narrow valley in which Silver Gate sat. Solid trees. There was talk of building a six-blade-wide bulldozer break line across the slopes behind the Range Riders, to deter the Storm Creek fire that was advancing from the national forest in the north.

But since the fires were jumping river valleys one mile wide, how could any fire line constructed by man through those trees be effective? It was like expecting a plow's furrow to turn back a legion of starving ants.

Still, something needed to be done, if only to ease the residents' minds. It was never easy to think that you'd lost all control.

One of the other fire-incident commanders had remarked that if the Clover-Mist or the fires on the surrounding national forest lands ever did reach this valley, they would race down its steep sides and bottom like the flame of a blowtorch.

He was probably right. As dry as everything was from the drought and as steep as the valley was, the flames would be so intense and the winds they would suck in so violent that it would all be over in a matter of hours.

But the fires weren't going to get here, were they?

No, of course not, I sought to reassure myself as I headed back to the helicopter.

. . . Of course not.

Even though it was close to dark, and it would be dangerously smoky, I was determined to fly back over Cache Creek on the way home. I wanted to verify what I had told everyone at the meeting about that fire's whereabouts. It was very important to me that I not mislead them. I had also promised Tankersley and another ranger, Bill Schreier, who were informing the local people of the fire situation in the park, to let them know just exactly where the Clover-Mist fire's edge was.

At the helicopter, I turned to ranger Brian O'Dea. He almost looked apologetic for the way the meeting had gone. It was his area of responsibility, the Northeast Entrance, that bordered the Silver Gate–Cooke City area. He personally knew many of the people at the meeting.

"What do you think, Dan?" he asked.

"About it getting to here?" I pulled on my helmet and scooted back onto the seat while he held the side door open. I looked him in the eyes. "I don't think it can make it over that ridge. Still . . ." I gazed up at the ridge's imposing form. ". . . Keep your eyes on it all the time. If the fires make an all-out run, the first thing you'll notice will be spot fires up there." I gave him a firm handshake. "Take care. And good luck."

I pulled the side closed and latched it shut, then looked at Eric. His visor was up and his face said it all: He was tired and he wanted to get the hell home.

So did I. But first there was that one last look at the fire in the Cache Creek drainage.

We circled Silver Gate and Cooke City to gain altitude. The sun had set, and the smoke from the 200,000-acre fire was thick. But once over the ridge, we found ourselves above the smoke for the most part. The cooler evening air was pushing most of it into the valleys, creating a collage of soft smoke rolls and jagged island peaks. It would have been beautiful, if not for what the smoke was hiding.

To my relief I saw the fire in the Cache Creek drainage was still to the south and west of where I had said it was. There were no new advances on its front. Most of the blazes were in areas that hadn't burned during the fire's initial sweep into the drainage.

I radioed the information to Silver Gate, then turned to Eric.

"What do you say we head to Mammoth?"

He didn't waste a second in getting the craft turned around and heading to where the sun's glow was still barely visible.

It was thirty miles to Mammoth, and darkness came swiftly.

As the helicopter's outside strobe pulsated light and darkness through the cabin, I stared ahead. Sometimes I thought back on the meeting. Mostly, though, I thought about all that had happened to me those past two months. Enough drama to fill a lifetime.

And yet something told me that the "Fires of '88," as they were being called, were only just starting.

2

M y back wanted to mutiny, and the Saab seemed to be getting smaller with every mile. It was November 1985, and we were on our way to my new job in Yellowstone. We had left Virginia three days before and were *almost* there. Would the prairie between Billings and Livingston, Montana, *never* end?

I watched a tumbleweed skipping from one barbed wire fence to another. It was like a weightless round sprite that delighted in teasing the frozen landscape.

I pried my hand from its perch on the steering wheel and straightened the rearview mirror. I studied the blue minivan behind me and smiled. Tana, my wife, was driving it as steadily and effortlessly as she had every one of the last two thousand miles. She hardly complained, though she certainly had plenty of good reasons.

She had been very surprised, to say the least, when I told her I was considering applying for the vacant chief ranger job in Yellowstone National Park. Not two years had passed since our move from the Hawaii Volcanoes National Park to my new job in Washington, D.C., and we had planned to stay for four or five years.

Tana was no more ready to be on the move again than she had been to leave Hawaii.

Tana develops strong personal attachments. There is a brightness about her that quickly makes her friends. And she had plans in Washington to take Brooke to piano lessons with the minister's girls, to participate more in her aerobics classes at the community center, and to go back to work. In short, my pretty, brunette wife was putting down roots again. But then . . .

My own obsession with moving to Yellowstone had made no sense to her. I can't say I blamed her. By transferring from the National Park Service's headquarters in Washington to the office of the chief ranger of Yellowstone Park, I was not only stepping *down* in my job ranking, from a GM-14 to a GM-13, but, worse, I was also taking a cut in pay and forgoing a sure promotion within weeks to a GM-15 with its six-thousand-dollar pay hike. And even more daunting was the thought that no chief ranger could ever hold a higher ranking than a GM-13. In effect, I was putting myself in a position where I might never again receive a pay raise—at least not while I remained a chief ranger.

How foolish could I be? I was trading a sensible and fairly manageable workload for one that every Park Service ranger knew was a real backbreaker. In Washington I had been the chief of ranger activities for the entire National Park Service. I was only thirty-nine years old and had reached headquarters, the base of power. I had overseen a headquarters staff of seventeen and had been responsible for formulating and defining the policies and regulations governing the Service's 2,400 rangers. It had been a semi-predictable seven-to-five job that—unlike that of chief rangers out in the field—didn't involve being on call at all times. To Tana's joy I had been able, for the first time in our seven years of marriage, to go to bed without worrying if the phone was going to ring.

The chief ranger job in Yellowstone, however, had a list of responsibilities as long as my arm. And with good reason. Yellowstone is the largest American national park outside of Alaska. It has over 2.2 million acres of everything from grizzly bears to mosquitoes—along with over two million visitors each summer with all their zillions of problems.

I rubbed the deep cleft in my chin. Try as I might, I couldn't rid my mind of the two-story brick home we'd left in Virginia. After years of living in little government plyboard rentals—in Yosemite, Crater Lake, and Hawaii Volcanoes—that house had seemed a castle. It was the only house Tana and I had ever owned. The only one we'd ever been able to say was ours, not the government's.

I took a deep breath. I knew from experience that the residence awaiting us in Yellowstone was going to be one huge step down from what we'd had in Virginia. I just hoped Tana would learn to understand, and forgive.

She was a ranger, too. While my expertise was in management and emergency operations, such as law enforcement, firefighting, and resource protection, hers was in interpretation. Or, in layman's terms, she was a naturalist and I was a cop and a bureaucrat.

When asked why they became rangers, naturalists almost always answer that they did so because they liked teaching others about nature. In many ways the interpretive rangers are the heirs of the wilderness philosophers of old. They keep alive the philosophies of the John Muirs, Henry David Thoreaus, and Rachel Carsons of our society. Through the dispensing of knowledge they strengthen the wall against those who would argue that wilderness has no practical use in a modern world.

Tana understood that I would rather chase a dream any day than live solely for the sake of money and promotions. The letter informing me I had been accepted for the chief ranger's job in Yellowstone Park was out of a dream.

I was six when I first visited Yellowstone. Until then my world had been the deserts and mesas of Big Bend in southernmost Texas, where my father was the first chief ranger.

Compared to the moonscape of Big Bend, Yellowstone had seemed a carnival of color, sparkle, and movement: Old Faithful shooting to the sky; the Lower Falls of the Yellowstone River's Grand Canyon roaring like a thousand dragons; and Yellowstone Lake looking as large and blue and pretty as the sky. Big Bend had the lazy mud flow of the Rio Grande and the occasional flash flood, but in Yellowstone the rivers and streams virtually exploded from their ravines and canyons.

And those animals! Some I could have sworn were right out of my picture books. Never again would rattlesnakes and mountain lions seem quite so incredible—not with snorting mastodonlike bison and elk with antlers as tall as trees trampling through my dreams.

A sound of cloth rustling in the backseat snapped my thoughts back to the present. I tilted the mirror further down to watch Trevor stirring in his sleep. His little two-year-old body was nearly invisible in the mass of household gear stuffed around his baby seat.

I wondered if he was dreaming of his mother and five-year-old sister, Brooke, in the van, or of his playmates back in Virginia. Being the child of a ranger wasn't the easiest of lives. I too had been what was fondly called a Park Service brat. While my childhood had been filled with things like the red skies of Texas, the tall oaks and crab apple blossoms of the Shenandoah Valley, and the cute prairie dogs of the Dakotas, it had also had too many sad goodbyes to too many close friends.

Though Yellowstone would be a new experience for the rest of the family, to me it was a homecoming of sorts. In the summers of 1963 and 1964 I had worked there as a teenager on what were called "blister rust crews." Blister rust is a fungus disease that kills white pine trees, the nuts of which are a favorite food source for grizzly bears. My job had been to help control it by cutting away the currant bushes that hosted the fungus.

Though those summers of hacking away with a picklike tool called a hodag had had their share of sweat, bug bites, and sore muscles, the thing I remembered the most was the exhilarating sense of freedom and belonging. For the first time since Big Bend I had found wildness—not just wilderness—where the animals and the land were as near to harmony as anything on earth could be.

My childhood had been spent moving with Dad from one part of the country to another, but he died when I was only fourteen, and Mom remarried shortly after I got out of high school. She moved to my stepfather's ranch in New Mexico, and for the next four years *home* for me was usually a college dormitory room.

Then came those last two summers of my boyhood in Yellowstone.

At first I was still Mr. Cool, enjoying my brawn and a bubble-topped Corvette, and "jungle juice" parties on moonlit beaches beside the grand old Yellowstone Lake Hotel. Searching perhaps for adventures and girls, not for much else.

Slowly, though, Yellowstone spoke to me. And so subtly I didn't even know my heart was being captured. Times like when

I strolled under a full moon with a girl to the Lower Falls of the Yellowstone River and saw its cold thunder dancing in an eerie rainbow of color and night. The lacy spray of that waterfall danced upon the canyon's breath, and I fancied I saw the moon reflected in each droplet. Those droplets of sparkle and color swirled and wove their magic so deeply into me that I would always remember them, but not whether I ever did kiss the head resting on my shoulder.

I felt on some of those long hikes I took into the backcountry that I was not far removed from something holy, sacred. I was a visitor walking back countless years, yet never stepping out of the present. Calendars and clocks seemed unimportant amid such natural grandeur.

My father had talked often about how few who visited his parks had any idea of the true value of wilderness. Or of leaving parts of this nation untrammeled by man. So few, he pointed out, realized that such areas were as much for the soul as for the eyes.

How tiny Yellowstone was in comparison to those forces of change and greed that my father had lamented; I had worried that its magic was perhaps doomed. And I decided that those rangers who worked to keep Yellowstone intact against such tremendous odds had to be a special breed.

And in time I realized that to become a guardian of something so precious was what I wanted.

Now, in only a few hours, I would start to live my dream.

LIVINGSTON DOWNTOWN read the green and white exit sign I was approaching. I moved my hand to the turn-signal lever, then decided against it.

If I remembered, there was another exit to Livingston in about half a mile or so. That second exit came out on the road to Yellowstone Park's north entrance, still some fifty-six miles south. It also came out near a supermarket.

I had returned to Yellowstone on business in the past year. While there I had sized up what living inside the park would be like for my family. Mammoth Hot Springs, the park's headquarters, had struck me as more of a college green than any kind of settlement, given its population of four hundred. There was a tiny general store and a dining room run by the concessionaire there, but the food selection was limited. And as for the little town called Gardiner, five miles north of Mammoth near the park entrance, I supposed that on a good day, when the ranchers and their wives came in to do their shopping, there might be four hundred or five hundred people there. Gardiner did somehow manage to support a small supermarket, but with not nearly enough variety in it to keep a serious housewife from pulling out her hair after a few months. If we wanted the kind of shopping and prices we were used to back East, it would mean driving fifty-six miles to Livingston or ninety to Bozeman.

After all the shopping malls and supermarkets of the Washington, D.C. area, I hoped we hadn't been *too* spoiled. Luxuries were not often a part of the usual ranger's life. And I was sure that could be said double for a place as isolated as Yellowstone. We would be going back to basics there.

In the parking lot of the big IGA supermarket near the exit, I roused Trevor. It wasn't easy to extricate him from the baby seat when he was still so sleepy. But once he saw we had parked in front of a store, he quickly perked up. No doubt M&M's and cookies were dancing in his head as I bundled him into his coat, locked the car, and hurried him through the bitterly cold afternoon winds.

"That'll be $432.66 . . . sir," sighed the baggy-eyed lady behind the checkout counter.

I didn't want to look at her, let alone at the six tangled carts spilling over with what I hoped were a few months' worth of staples. Tana coughed nervously behind my shoulder. I put a big friendly smile on my lips.

"H'm, we're new here," I said nicely. "We haven't had a chance to open an account at any of the banks in town. We have only our out-of-town checks, and also I—I don't have a check-cashing card with me."

I waited for a snicker, then for a disgusted huff and an angry shout across the store to a manager who would come over to inform us our checks were as welcome in his store as a rabid pit bull.

She leaned toward me. My smile shortened.

"Whatever is a 'check-cashing card'?"

I couldn't believe my ears. To try to cash even a local check back in Virginia without identification *and* that check-cashing card was asking to be tarred and feathered. Suddenly, I was feeling a lot better.

"You'll take our out-of-town check?"

She bulged her right cheek with her tongue, cocked a brow, and looked me in the eyes.

"Is it good?"

"Sure." Very grandly I pointed to the large, flowing blue script atop the check that said *First Bank of Northern Virginia,* as if that were some kind of magic phrase.

"Looks okay to me," she said.

I quickly penned in the sum and my signature and handed it to her. She simply jammed it into the cash register's drawer as she would have a food coupon. She didn't even ask to see so much as a driver's license.

Somehow we crammed all the food into the vehicles, despite the wind and our stinging fingers and ears. Someday I would tell Tana that Livingston was the second windiest place in America, right behind Chicago. But not now. Not when I could hear her teeth chattering.

Like a pair of bear cubs, Trevor and Brooke were quite glad to snuggle in among so much food. Tana, though, looked as if her shoulders were slumping wearily. When we were about to pull out of the parking lot, I motioned to her to roll her window down.

"Just one more stop, honey," I said cheerfully.

"Where?" she almost whispered.

I winked. "Yellowstone."

I tooted the car horn for no specific reason other than I was feeling happy. We were quickly back on the road, heading south toward the mountains and forests and, I was positive, many great adventures.

3

*F*or the Benefit and Enjoyment of
the People.

The inscription on the massive dark stone arch at the north entrance to Yellowstone stood out very clearly through the snowflakes piling against the windshield. For me, about to pass through that arch as the park's chief ranger, those words were no longer a phrase out of a 113-year-old act of Congress, but a commandment.

I turned and woke the sleeping Trevor.

"Trevor! Trevor, do you know where we are?"

He looked around confused.

"Trevor, we're at our new home."

I pointed out the windshield. "This is Yellowstone Park."

His eyes widened as he stared out at the treeless snowy hummocks and the hulking stone arch which, even on the best of days, looked like a remnant from some medieval castle.

I smiled and drove on. "Don't worry, Trevor. This is just the yard."

With pride and some nervousness I realized I was crossing the threshold into the one place I had always wanted to say was my home. I sat straighter and raked my fingers through my thinning brown hair. Slowly we drove through the arch. Along the narrow lane to the little brown entrance booth, we passed tall and skinny red snow poles marking the road's edges. In the gusting wind each pole rocked and bowed low, first to the car, then to the horizons.

The entrance booth was a half mile from the arch. As my car neared its sliding side window, I could hardly wait for the ranger to poke his head out, flash a big grin from beneath his flat hat, and say proudly: "Welcome to Yellowstone Park, sir."

But, it was not to be. Instead there was a sign taped to the window that said Yellowstone National Park was closed. And that tire chains were required over the next five miles to the head-quarters.

I looked at the light frescoes the wind had made on the road's powdery shoulders. I knew this road was the only one plowed during the winter. It had to be. The Montana villages of Silver Gate and Cooke City were at its other end. They had no other way to the outside world in the winter except for this road through the park.

I decided it was unlikely there were any deep drifts or difficult road problems ahead. The road was, despite the warning, actually fairly dry. I nudged the gearshift and waved Tana to follow.

It wasn't like me to disregard a regulation, but the tire chains were buried under a ton of junk, including all those groceries. Besides, I did have snow radials on the car and van. And something told me a ranger had forgotten to take down an old sign. I made a mental note that if that was correct I would get someone to take that sign down very soon. If visitors drove five miles with their chains on and the road was bare pavement, not only would they ruin their chains, but they might also doubt the park's credibility. It was essential that park signs be accurate, because visitors had to be able to depend on them.

Through a narrow river canyon, then in and out of curve after curve after curve I encouraged the car. The road was in good shape and mostly dry as I had guessed, though I was not without some concern, for we were climbing.

Steadily, slowly we gained in altitude as we neared the plateau upon which Mammoth Hot Springs was located. Glancing at a map I saw Gardiner was about 5,300 feet above sea level and Mammoth was just around 6,400. If I was going to drive on past Mammoth, to the other plateaus upon which most of the park's interior lands rested, I would have to go up still another thousand feet. In effect I was heading up a sort of gigantic set of steps.

Past gnarled junipers with shoulders of white, sign poles with flaky wizard caps, and a dark river with granite boulders and up-rooted trees guarding its trout, the car whined and hummed.

I eased the car into another sharp curl. My adrenaline rushed again. We had reached *Yellowstone Park*—the first, the oldest, the most famous, the most respected, and certainly the most treasured of the world's national parks.

Yellowstone wasn't just any park: It was *the* park. America's cathedral to Mother Nature. The very birthplace of the philosophy of preservation as a national goal.

And here I was—I squeezed the steering wheel—responsible for keeping its magical wilderness intact.

"The park is full of exciting wonders," the naturalist John Muir had written after a visit to Yellowstone in 1885. "The wildest geysers in the world . . . hills of sparkling crystals, hills of glass, hills of cinders and ashes, mountains of every style of architecture, icy or forested . . . mountains boiled soft like potatoes and colored like a sunset sky. Therefore it is called Wonderland, and thousands of tourists and travelers stream into it every summer, and wander about in it enchanted."

I steered into a series of steep switchbacks, smiling broadly. Somehow after all those years, the park was still as wild and virtually undeveloped as ever. In an age rampant with road building and real estate developments, Yellowstone's 3,500 square miles were still 99 percent *untouched*. Surely that had to be something of a miracle. And a credit to the men and women who had been its guardians those 113 years since its formation.

I found myself staring out over a sweeping panorama of white peaks biting sharply into a blue sky. Then just as suddenly the car was crunching down a wide white boulevard of deep snow banks. Ahead were some high massive buildings of cut gray stone. At last I was at my destination.

I knew exactly where to go, because the assistant chief ranger, Gary Brown, had mailed me a map to my new home. As instructed, I turned down a small lane between the post office and the back of the visitor center. I drove past the administration office where I would be working, past the superintendent's huge stone residence, past a row of three-story employee apartments which had once been

U.S. Army officers' quarters, up to a row of very simple wood-frame duplexes that had been storage sheds in the days when Mammoth was a fort. I eased the front of the car into a parking spot and shut its engine off for, I hoped, the last time that day.

Tana and Brooke, Trevor and I made our way to the screen door at the back of what was to be our house. It was located at the farthest end of the middle duplex building. The outside of the building was not comforting: dagger-shaped icicles hung thickly from a rusty tin roof and the drab tan paint was peeling everywhere. And then the door wouldn't budge. When at last it yielded, we spilled into a tiny unheated laundry room, then through the main door into a kitchen crowded with cupboards, counters, and mountains of the cardboard boxes that held our dishes and counter appliances.

"Well, at least the moving van's been here," Tana said. "But what's the freezer doing in here?"

I'd been wondering the same thing. I had been sent a floor plan and snapshots of the house's interior before our move, and I had returned them with explicit instructions that the freezer was to be put in the basement.

While the children clattered up the skinny stairwell to the second floor in search of their bedrooms, Tana and I looked for the stairwell to the basement. We planned to make it into a family room; it had looked quite large in the photos.

But every door kept leading into a closet. Totally confused, I decided to look outside. At last, at the bottom of a trap door beside the woodpile, I found our basement. It was cramped and dark— little more than a root cellar. Only a vampire could have envisioned it being a family room. When I rose from its musty rock walls and dank floor back into the dusk, there were goosebumps on me that weren't necessarily from the cold.

While Tana and the children put away the groceries, I made a hasty dash through the sharp air to the administration building, to see my boss the superintendent. I wanted to let Mr. Barbee, whom I had met at Yosemite and then had seen off and on over the past fifteen years, know I had made it okay to the park.

I breathed deeply of the dry thin air as I strode down the shoveled sidewalk alongside the former canteen and barracks. Hardly an hour had passed since I had turned that last curve in the road to Mammoth Hot Springs, yet already I was certain I was going to be extremely happy here. How pure was the air. And how wonderful the silence! No rumbling of pistons here! No screeching of horns! At least not today. Only the voices of the mountains.

Anyone passing me on foot could have heard my very innermost thoughts, I told myself and smiled.

As I stared up at the three-story wooden buildings that nearly a century ago had been officers' quarters, I knew I was home. I couldn't quite put my finger on it, this strange and insistent sense of belonging. It loomed there deep inside me, solid as the dark red Dickensian chimneys on those quarters.

There were four of the old quarters, now employees' apartments and duplexes. Each stood as straight and neat and evenly spaced apart as proud veterans on a parade grounds. From between two of the homes a mist on the side of Sepulcher Mountain snared my attention. It was caused by the hot springs from which Mammoth got its official name, as well as its sulfur smells. The springs were only a quarter of a mile away at most. Their algae-streaked terraces of bumps and lumps, and steamy scalloped limestone, resembled a gargantuan melting marshmallow. It was easy to see why the Indians had never told the white man of such spectacles. They looked supernatural, especially with their vapors writhing so thickly in the cold.

I reached for the door handle, looked up at the redwood sign that said in large yellow letters OFFICE OF THE SUPERINTENDENT, and swallowed noisily. Not from nervousness, though. From pure and simple excitement.

4

Ahead of me on his snowmobile, Gary Brown was adjusting his helmet's visor. I pulled at the thick collar around my neck to keep out the dawn's freezing breeze, wriggled my toes, and flexed each finger further into its insulated cocoon. I revved my snowmobile's engine. Its long and heavy roar reassured me that it was ready for the long trip ahead.

Swirls of snow danced in the narrow halogen beams of our headlamps. The lumpy white ground reminded me of a sunless sea floor. I shivered and tried not to think about how cold the air was outside my snowmobile suit and bubble helmet.

Gary turned to me, flashing a thumb up. I did the same, then crouched lower on the seat and squeezed the throttle. Away we shot into the pine forest, where we followed an old service road. Plumes of snow trailed us like errant blizzards. Gary, older and more winter-seasoned, led the way. I hung behind at varying distances as if connected to his buzzing steed by an invisible rubber band.

The last time I had gone snowmobiling had been five years before in Oregon's Crater Lake National Park. It took a few minutes for me to get the hang of navigating the bumps and tight turns that kept appearing unexpectedly in the deep powder. Weaving and bouncing over the long leathery seat of the machine, I felt like a bull rider in a rodeo.

Nearly a month had passed since my move to Yellowstone. My trip now into the park's snowbound and still closed interior was being made for two reasons: to meet with those rangers and maintenance workers who watched over the park's abandoned interior,

38

and to experience the park itself before it was reopened around the middle of December to snowmobilers and cross-country skiers. So many of my colleagues had told me that it was during the months of December to May that Yellowstone was at its most peaceful, pristine, and haunting.

We zipped through the trees, then onto the main road going south from Mammoth. Though it was winding and steep beneath deep and ungroomed snow, at least the road held few of the bumpy surprises of the service road. And so I tempted fate by edging a little closer to a small canyon at my left to peek down and back toward the plateau upon which Mammoth sat. From far away the teeny lights of the still sleepy community twinkled like the stars of a constellation.

Carefully we skirted ghostly bands of cliffs, wound through a chaotic belt of limestone boulders called the Hoodoos, plowed past snow-heavy aspens, then zoomed up and onto a wide open plain called Swan Lake Flat. There Gary suddenly eased up on his throttle and halted his machine. He pointed its nose to the east. I pulled alongside, realized his engine was turned off, and did the same. The silence that swept in to replace the noise was swift and complete. It was as if we were on a planet that had never known any cries of life.

With the fat stubs of my gloves I brushed the snow dust off my visor. Through the streaks poured a sky ripening with a glorious dawn and the promise of another of those perfect white-and-blue days that the Rocky Mountain region has in abundance each winter. There were no clouds in the sky. Ever so slowly at first, then quite feverishly, shades of blue and pink oozed across the gray and black undercoatings of the night.

"Look behind you," said Gary in a voice soft even for him.

I turned to the west and whistled. The sun's rays were being snared by a pack of lordly summits. One by one they were bursting into glowing islands against the night shadow. Beginning with the jagged crown of Electric Peak, the snow-mantled mountains awoke in order of importance.

So beautiful and so magnificent were the peaks that I wished to spend more than just a few minutes in their company. So out

39

of the small day packs lashed to the rears of our seats we took our Thermoses of coffee.

The heat of the black liquid helped to thaw me. I sat straighter and tried to imagine a ranger working in the park in the winters before things like snowmobiles.

I had read that the high-altitude plateaus upon which Yellowstone is situated trap some of the coldest and whitest winters anywhere in the United States. The average year-round temperature of the park is only 35 degrees, and I'd read that if that dropped by only three degrees the glacial buildup that once covered the area for hundreds of thousands of years would return. In one place, Pelican Valley, readings of 50 below were said to be common. I shook to my very hair roots. God only knew how fiercely cold those peaks must have been at night. Many of them were well over ten thousand feet in elevation.

While such coldness and deep snows could be a curse for the animals that wintered in the park, they were also a blessing in other ways. At least for a few months the trample of visitors was stilled. Even in the age of snowmobiles, most people were reluctant to go off into such an intimidating setting.

Indeed, without its formidable walls of snow-covered peaks, Yellowstone Park might never have been possible. While the rest of America was being tamed or beaten into submission by the railroads, the cattlemen, and the farmers, Yellowstone had remained unexplored and unexplorable just long enough for people to realize its value as a reserve of nature and peace.

"What are you thinking?" Gary asked.

"I'm thinking I can't wait to see more," I replied with a twist of the Thermos's stopper. "What do you say we take a look?"

He was all for it. Gary loved being out with the park's animals as much as an eagle loved the winds. Soon we were off again to the south, still hoping to finish all 150 miles of the park's "Grand Loop."

From Mammoth to where we had watched the sunrise, we had covered perhaps a total of five miles. So it was clear that we were not going to be able to stop in any one place for very long. Not if we hoped to be back in Mammoth before dark. I eased back on the throttle at those spots where the trees and drifts squeezed the road, but then sped along more daringly at the occasional breaks of the meadows and old beaver lakes. Skimming so close to the ground, even at forty miles an hour, was exhilarating. Still, I looked away more than I should have from the white snake of the road. I wanted so much to pull over and venture out on foot into the deceptively gentle-looking terrain, to see up close how the animals were surviving such cold.

So few people ever had the whole park to themselves, as Gary and I did on this day.

A great forest of lodgepole pines closed in around us. By the thousands the straight skinny trees poked from the waist-deep snow. Each trunk was barely wider than my arm and around one hundred feet high. They were the same lodgepoles that covered over 60 percent of the park. In many places there seemed to be more dead than live ones. So thickly were the dead and live trees jumbled together that they looked like pick-up sticks left behind by some slobbish giant.

Grotesquely sculptured snow gnomes with bent skeletons of young pines and willows were the only inhabitants for the longest time. So deeply were the earth and its pelage covered that I wondered how anything of flesh and blood could survive in such a setting for one week, let alone six months.

Just before the turnoff to Sheepeater Cliffs, the forest took on a darker and more impenetrable look. Here the early explorers had found the loneliest and most wretched Indians in the West. Called the Sheepeaters, the small band was said to be so afraid of outsiders that it shunned any contact with them. Scorned by both the whites and the other Indians for their ragged dress and filthy hair, they were doomed to perish in a reservation far away from and far less bountiful than their Yellowstone hermitage.

After twenty-one miles we descended from the trees to a broad, open, foggy plain. Eerie and largely barren of trees, its skyline was dominated by countless billowy pillars of steam. At first glance I thought of the campfires of a massive army. Then of the spewings of an industrial city.

The plain was the Norris Geyser Basin. Its ground is the hottest and most tremorous in the park, and the boiling spillovers from its subterranean kitchens some of the most acidic. The snowdrifts that so dominated the rest of the Yellowstone world had been soundly defeated here.

Just as the first white explorers had, I wanted to compare it to hell, the sulfur odors the breath of the devil himself. Yet another part of me remembered how playful those geysers had seemed to my teenage mind, how even their names had been so entertaining: Splutter, Whirligig, and Fireball; Medusa, Dark Cavern, Arsenic, and Orbicular; Feisty, Ragged, Dabble, and Puff-N-Stuff.

I had a lot to learn about the park's thermal features, but what I did know awed me. There are over ten thousand thermal features in the park. They range from simple steam vents and burbling mud pots to the famous geysers. Some of the blue-green algae in the park's thermal pools live in temperatures up to 165 degrees. With three hundred geysers, Yellowstone contains over 60 percent of those on the planet. And those fountains of nature come in just about every shape and size imaginable.

Old Faithful, in another area of the park, is unquestionably the most famous. Its predictable, almost hourly eruptions have made it the easiest to know. But it is hardly the most spectacular when compared to others like Steamboat Geyser, the world's largest. Sometimes when Steamboat erupts, it roars like a tornado for hours and throws up a boiling plume over 380 feet—three times the height of Old Faithful! Well over a million gallons of water can be expelled from it. Very few people are ever around when Steamboat puts on one of its awesome shows, but in 1963 I was lucky enough to be one of those. I was working on one of the blister rust crews about a mile away in the forest when suddenly it sounded as if a 747 jet were passing right above my head, and the ground shook violently.

"Ready to go on?" asked Gary now.

"Sure," I said reluctantly.

We gunned our engines. Their purple exhaust drifted off to mingle with that of the steam clouds above the basin. We raced to the east, toward the Grand Canyon of the Yellowstone River. Gary took the lead again. I stayed right behind, lost in thought.

The geyser basin stayed in my mind for most of the twelve

miles to the next road junction at Canyon Village. Beneath where we were riding the earth's molten interior was only half a mile down. Yellowstone was born from volcanism and is still being shaped by its forces. About two million years ago, then one million years ago, then again six hundred thousand years ago, tremendously destructive volcanic eruptions occurred right where I was now half freezing. The latest alone supposedly spewed out nearly 240 cubic miles of debris. The 28-by-47-mile caldera, or basin, which dominates much of the park's interior, was the result of the earth collapsing from losing so much lava.

The massive magmatic heat that forced those explosions still powers the park's thermal features, as well as the thousands of small earthquakes that shake the park's basement each year. And on an even more ominous note, some scientists say the park is due for another cataclysmic eruption. Studies of some of the old benchmarks in the park show that its terrain has risen over the past century by as much as three feet! To think that just below my snowmobile was a bubble of molten terror as big as a small moon!

At the empty snow-blanketed tourist complex that in the summer was Canyon Village, we paused long enough to go to the canyon to see the Lower Falls. There we saw something I had never seen before: a one-hundred-foot-high ice cone at the bottom of the falls. The falling water disappeared into a hole in the top of the cone, only to come out below with a wildness that turned it as white as the snow.

Once more we headed south. Our next goal, Yellowstone Lake, was sixteen miles away. As the pine forests rolled away again just south of Canyon, we seemed to shrink into mere dots in the enormous Hayden Valley. In the warm months Hayden is one of the world's most scenic and wildlife-rich valleys. Then in its river meadows are the park's largest herds of free-roaming bison, as well as elk, coyotes, and grizzly bear. In the sedge of the slow-moving Yellowstone River are trumpeter swans, pelicans, otters, and moose.

It seems appropriate that the greatest concentration of wildlife is to be found at the park's heart. To see hundreds of the darkly brown bison speckling the valley floor on a summer's evening, their beards dragging over the ground as they fed, is like looking at a living painting. Listening to their sneezes and snorts and bellows on the winds, I almost expect to hear, too, the sudden whooping of an Indian hunting party or the crack of a Union Pacific Railroad buffalo hunter's carbine.

But on this day there were no bison. Nor even a single blade of grass. The meadows were as shiny white as a sea of cumulus clouds. And the oxbow bends in the river were empty of the bobbing pelicans and ever-hungry moose.

How still it all was. So crystallized was the dream valley that it might have been sculpted from finely ground glass.

About two thirds of the way to Yellowstone Lake a rancid fog suddenly enveloped us, and as we started to climb out of the valley and slip into more forest, the smell of rotten eggs pinched my nostrils. We slowed to pierce the breath of a seething monster known as the Dragon's Mouth. At the steamy feet of that natural bogeyman there boiled, hissed, and gurgled craters of gray witch's brew known as mud pots. Ugly stepsisters to the geysers, those pots belched and regurgitated their slimy messes all over themselves as if they were incessantly sick drunkards.

The Dragon's Mouth presented its own fearsome scene. It growled and grumbled and seemed to want to escape its rocky prison. In the past I had always felt rather lucky to have escaped it and this time was no different. It seemed that any moment it might explode like a volcano.

At last we dipped out of the trees and came to the shores of Yellowstone Lake. As we dismounted to stretch and refuel at a maintenance shop, I looked at the wide expanse of ice. It was as if I had come upon Antarctica itself; a white void stretched almost as far as I could see. It was, I realized, probably the largest ice sheet in the continental United States. Over 136 square miles!

If Yellowstone Park is the crown jewel of the world's national parks, then surely the lake is that to the park. Everything that is Yellowstone—water, freedom, flowers, adventure, peaks, wildlife, color, mystery, danger—is concentrated in and around the lake to such a degree in the summer that I think even God would have to be pleased. In some parts of the world the lake on its own would have been highly adored as a wonder. Yet in Yellowstone Park it is only another attraction. That is perhaps as good an indication as any of how unique the park is.

I'd spent enough time on the lake when it wasn't frozen to know that beneath that ice was another wilderness every bit as intriguing as the one at my back. Drifting along in a canoe I'd seen beneath me trout dressed in princely speckles and every color of the rainbow. And I'd spied the faint burps of submerged thermal vents and felt in their ripples a warmth that was foreign to the water. When the lake shed its ice, back would come the cormorants and terns and skinny-legged avocets. Back would come the eagles and ospreys and moose.

On the ocean off Hawaii I had learned to sail, and ever since I could hardly look at a large body of water without imagining myself on it beneath a set of billowing sails. There was more than enough room here for a thousand sails. I resolved that in the coming summers I would somehow buy a sailboat with which to seek out the lake's Shangri-las.

Time was growing very short when we steered away to the west. Half of our journey was still ahead, but less than a third of the daylight remained. And we could hardly throw caution to the wind: In the seventeen miles between Grant Village and our next destination, Old Faithful, the snow was its deepest yet.

Twice we plowed our way to the top of the Continental Divide and ran into walls of snow that seemed to sweep away the ragged lodgepole forests in that stretch of America's backbone. Progress was slow, arduous. We butted the machines into more than they could handle at times. In some places we had to add our own muscle power.

At one point, on 8,262-foot-high Craig Pass, we paused to catch our breath. A coyote loped across a meadow walled in by pine. Whatever could he find to eat way up here, I wondered. And what must he be thinking of us and our sudden roaring intrusion into his peaceful world?

We were much further along, and the light was fading rapidly, when Gary came to a stop in the middle of the road. I pulled alongside and cautiously rose from my idling snowmobile's seat, my

45

boots firmly planted on the running boards. Through my visor I peered to my right, then to my left. Huge shaggy mounds of humps and horns were blocking the road. And to each side were impossibly deep snowbanks, a jumbled pine forest, and a dark steam-shrouded river with a backdrop of geysers and thermal vents.

The hugest of the bull bison snorted suddenly through cavernous nostrils, causing a small avalanche to tumble off the mountain that was his back. I swallowed hard. This was my first face-off with a bison while I was on a snowmobile. Would he charge? If he did, there was no way I could get my machine turned around in time. He weighed easily close to a ton. I would be trampled like an insect.

I flicked up my visor and looked over at Gary. We still had at least fifty miles to cover before we would be back in Mammoth. It was not the time of the year to be out in the park after dark, far from warm shelter and food. Yet with the wall of stubbornness we had run into, it looked as if we might be considerably delayed.

"Do you think they'll ever move?" I shouted above the complaining engines.

Gary's cheekbones rose behind the portal in his helmet. I knew one of his big boyish grins must have broken across his lips. He was something of an expert on the park's bears and bison, and he was obviously enjoying this encounter. Even if he hadn't smiled, the gleam in his eyes would have said as much.

"You can never tell with these guys. They could start moving any second for no reason, or they may decide to stay put until tomorrow morning. One thing I do know, though, is they don't want to go off into the deeper snow," he replied.

I couldn't say I blamed them. There was at least a good four feet of the fluffy stuff off to the sides of us. And from the amount of compacted snow still stuck against the bison's foreheads, it was obvious they had spent the better part of the day pushing aside tons of it with their broad heads, trying to nibble on the grass underneath. They had to be extremely tired.

I supposed we could have jumped up and down and yelled, maybe thrown snowballs. But we wanted to avoid such fright tactics. In such a harsh winter setting, every calorie saved by an animal is important in its struggle to stay alive. Many of the larger animals like the bison might spend more time standing still than anything else. Somehow they know they shouldn't waste any of the fat and muscle they've built up during the summer and fall. They have to save that energy for digging their way to what scraps of grass they can find. Theirs is a long, cruel odyssey of survival. Even without man's interference only the strongest ever make it to the spring thaw.

I wondered if we should just try easing up to them. Or if we should gun the engines and pretend to charge them. I discussed the options with Gary. He mulled them over as I pulled at the thick collar around my neck, wriggled my toes, and flexed each finger once more. There was no feeling in them. The temperature had to be around 10 below zero and dropping quickly. I shivered to my toes: I knew I could easily become a human ice cube.

We decided we had no choice but to rev the engines and dart toward the glossy-eyed roadblocks. We did so, and in a flash the bison sprang upright with amazing speed and dexterity. As if it were a cattle roundup, they stampeded further along the road. For at least a hundred yards they refused to yield the right of way to us. I felt terrible at the thought of all the energy they were burning. When they finally plunged, like small humpbacked whales, into the deep snow, I breathed a little easier.

Gary sped ahead. On the way back to Mammoth, I almost didn't notice the celestial show that came into view overhead as I thought about how the snarling and whining B-flat noise of a snowmobile engine had to be one of the most unpleasant sounds anywhere. I detested the brutal intrusion it made into the solitude of this winter paradise. But at the same time I knew I could never have seen all I had without the aid of such a machine.

To cross-country ski this loop would take a week instead of one day. And even then I would be fortunate if I didn't become trapped in one of the sudden blizzards for which the region was infamous. I would prefer that there were no loud engines or vehicles of any kind in the park in the winter, for snow and quiet seem to be as much a part one of the other as a flower and color. To truly experience the magic of a winter scene it is necessary to be out in it with only the light crunching of flakes underneath one's boots or skis. But what can be done in a place as huge as Yellowstone: Turn its millions of acres into a kind of forbidden land for over half the year? There were many inside and outside the Park Service who had proposed as much.

There is no easy answer to the problem of the increasing winter visitation of the park. Once the public was allowed in and discovered what an incredible fairytale land it was, there was no turning back the tide. The park belongs to the American public as much in the winter as it does in the summer. And what the public demands they are probably going to get, as long as it isn't too unreasonable. The snowmobile groups in the western states surrounding Yellowstone are very powerful politically. They would not meekly accept being told their machines were no longer welcome past the park's boundaries.

In another week the winter tourist season officially started. From then on, there would no longer be only the occasional ranger passing along these roads. Instead there would be dozens of the big dark machines snaking into the park's body from its border towns. Hunched over like trolls on machines trailing smelly fumes of black and purple, the cowboys among those snowmobilers would be hooting and screaming across the once-calm setting. In the beginning there had been only a few thousand visitors to the park over the winter. Many of them were content to lurch and sway from Mammoth to Old Faithful in the tank-tracked snow coaches. Now there were over a hundred thousand visitors in the winter, most of them on snowmobiles.

While the number of winter visitors seemed minuscule in comparison to the millions who came in the summer months, it really wasn't to our budget. I had learned that it cost the park four dollars per summer visitor to keep them and their facilities healthy, while it cost *thirty dollars* per winter visitor. Quite simply, our resources and manpower were being badly overstretched by the rocketing numbers of snowmobilers in a season in which it was never easy to keep a man or a machine running properly.

Nor was the number very small in terms of the animals' nerves.

The one time of the year they had always previously depended upon for some solitude and peace was being increasingly denied them.

So why not outlaw the noisemakers and allow only cross-country skiing? asked some people. I sighed. Like most of the rangers I loved to ski. But the maddening fact was that, overall, the skiers probably displaced the wildlife more than did the snowmobilers. As were the autos in the summer, the snowmobiles were restricted to the roadways, and studies on the elk and bison had shown that those animals came to recognize the sounds of the machines and ignored their passing, learning over time that the sound, as ominous as it was, would not injure them.

The cross-country skiers, however, could go anywhere they liked. And unfortunately many of them were as pesky about getting close-up shots of the animals as so many of the summer visitors were. The animals, it seemed, knew little respite from the eye of the camera. And they had come to dread all the skiing about in their space. Some, I had read, were even said to be suffering stress from all the intrusions. In one experiment, listening devices placed over a number of elk's hearts had registered barely any difference in the animals' heartbeats when a snowmobile buzzed past. But when a skier slooshed past, the animals' hearts went crazy.

Mammoth had never looked so good as when Gary and I finally dropped back off Swan Lake Flat and saw its lights below. I was like a Popsicle when I returned to Tana and the warmth of our home. And late that night as I crawled under the covers and put my arm around Tana, my body was still lightly buzzing from all that riding—but my heart was playing in the park's inexhaustible wonders.

5

I rapped my knuckles against the front door of the park minister's home, and instantly the chill of the late December dusk was warmed by cries of welcome. Tana, the children, and I entered a small living room cheery with ornaments and cards. The heat from a wood-burning stove together with the smiles of at least a dozen rosy faces made me feel as if I were at a family reunion.

"Merry Christmas!" cried out several whom I immediately recognized as my peers in the park chapel's choir.

"Merry Christmas to you, too!" I replied, even though it was still a couple of days away.

The Reverend Young and his wife, Debbie, hurried out from the kitchen to join the revelry. He was strongly built, in his early thirties, and sported a thick dark beard that would have made a mountain man proud. She was dark-haired and pretty, and quick to smile and shake my hand.

"Bill and I are so glad you're going caroling. The more voices we have the more glorious we'll sound," kidded Debbie.

"And now we've got someone who can even sing!" added Reverend Young with an evangelical lilt to his voice.

I blushed at the compliment. It was true that some said I had a nice singing voice. But it had been too many years since my college choir days for me to feel confident of its quality.

"I'll be lucky if my tonsils don't freeze before I get ten words out," I joked.

Everyone laughed but nodded. It was nearly as cold as Santa's own home place. I didn't know what the temperature was at the moment—if it was below or above zero. But it had nipped at my nose and ears more than at any time since my move to Mammoth.

The Reverend grinned at the little boy hugging my legs.

In return, Trevor stared long and wide-eyed at the bearded giant.

The Reverend bent over and placed an arm around the boy's shoulders. "You know you have many gifts coming in a few nights from dear Santa. I'm sure he thinks you're very special, because everyone else does."

The Reverend winked at me, and I nodded back.

"Debbie, isn't that hot cocoa I smell?" asked Tana.

"Why yes! What do you say we go get ourselves a cup?"

Debbie and Tana practically raced to the tract house's kitchen, laughing and talking and gesturing like best friends who hadn't seen each other in years. Debbie was truly a godsend in the way she had helped Tana feel welcome in Mammoth. They had met our first Sunday at church services and hit it off right away. Both were not only mothers of young children, but also lovers of the outdoors.

I lost myself in the hospitality and merriment. The children darted and shouted throughout the house with a small legion of other youngsters. It was impossible to tell we were of many different denominations. There was a strong sense of togetherness.

"Is everyone ready to get out and *sing?*" boomed the Reverend's voice after a few minutes.

There was a sudden flurry as body parts were rammed into sleeves, gloves, and hats. I helped Tana tighten the drawstrings on the children's hoods. We made sure everything but their eyes was snuggled beneath wool or down. In their oversized coats and mittens and snow boots, Brooke and Trevor looked swollen to twice their normal size. They made me think of helium-filled parade floats.

"Here you go now. You'll need this," offered Debbie. She pressed a mimeographed sheet with Christmas songs on it into my hand. "At every stop we'll start with one of the songs, do maybe another one or two, and then end by singing 'We Wish You a Merry Christmas.'"

Out into the pitch-black night went all of us but the Reverend's shaggy springer spaniel. He looked up wide-eyed from his spot near the stove as if he were thinking we had lost our minds. *Why would you go out to play now?* asked his eyes.

I pulled Trevor on a sled. At least a dozen of Mammoth's other little ones, including Brooke, tried to keep up with their shivering parents. Our boots crunched along the narrow unlit streets of what was called "lower Mammoth," one-story wooden tract houses built in the early 1960s. Beneath their snow-mantled roofs and smoking tin-pipe chimneys, colorful streams of lights cheered us on. An occasional elk watched us from its bed of snow.

At a house where a front light was blazing, some of the older children raced across the tiny front yard to ring the doorbell. The rest of us tried to read our song sheets with our flashlights and lanterns.

The house's inner door flew open. Several pale faces pressed against its storm door. The looks of delight in their eyes as we tried to brighten the night's darkness made us forget that we were half frozen. As more front lights clicked on all across the little "suburb" of lower Mammoth, the songs on our crumpled sheets seemed too few.

As we shuffled from house to house, so thickly and brightly did the stars sparkle that it was as if a million angels were just above our heads with lit candles in their hands.

Though they were invisible now, I felt that the trees and peaks and the animals they sheltered were looking down across the huge darkness to the little nest of lights that was Mammoth. While many in the cities and towns beyond the ridges had festivities and great shopping bazaars in which to lose their thoughts on this evening, we few had but our families and God to embrace. But wasn't that what Christmas was supposed to be about? That, and brotherhood?

All I had to do was look about me at the faces shining in the lanterns' glow to know that I had a lot to be thankful for. It took a special kind of person to leave behind the excitement of the outside world and settle into such a bastion of peace and tradition. Such was my good fortune that I had them as my coworkers, neighbors, and everyday friends.

On one side of me I saw Dennis and Barbara Zafft, my next-door neighbors. They were a kindly couple who had told me that every summer they searched out the park's wildflower patches and picnicked beside them. And just behind them were Steve and Kim, parents of twin girls and foster parents to children in need of their love. Steve had twelve students in his classes at the headquarters' little elementary school.

Those who lived and worked in Yellowstone came from many backgrounds—from the shadows of New York City to the open farmland of the Midwest. And they had equally diverse temperaments, too. For every one who liked his beer and hunting and *Monday Night Football,* there was another who stitched quilts, or played the violin, or simply relished curling up with a good book.

Among them was Ted, the old Mormon bachelor at the Hamilton General Store beside the Mammoth hotel and dining hall. He seemed perfectly willing to spend another thirty years quietly keeping the stock in order, helping out at the checkout registers from time to time, and answering countless questions about Spam and postcards each summer.

But on the other hand there were the rangers who lived alone in the remote backcountry areas, and who frowned at any uninvited intrusions into their privacy. Some even actively participated in environmental groups that advocated closing Yellowstone to any and all humans.

All of them, happily, had realized that the preservation of the park was too important to be upstaged by their personal beliefs. Conservative and liberal, young and old, evangelist and atheist, each seemed more than willing to put aside his or her opinions for the sake of the park. When they came together it was almost always to plan and solve, not to bicker. More than any other community I'd lived in, Yellowstone's had a purpose.

"Even people who have no religious side to them find themselves unconsciously asking spiritual questions when they explore

Yellowstone's grandeur," the Reverend once said. "How did all this come about? *How* is it possible? What is behind this grand scheme of things, and where do I fit in?"

The Reverend Young was in many ways typical of the sacrifice and quiet individualism that characterized the park's residents. He and Debbie had been high school sweethearts, and in the move to Yellowstone they had left behind in West Virginia a fancy thirteen-room parsonage and a much, much larger salary. Their residence now had only three bedrooms, a living room, a tiny dining room, and the kitchen for them and their four rapidly growing Tom Sawyers.

Bill, as the Reverend insisted on being called, was not an employee of the National Park Service. On his own he had volunteered to come to Yellowstone to be its pastor. He had been smitten with its beauty in the summers of 1975 and 1976 while working on a trail maintenance crew. He was a civilian, even though he was living in government housing. Like everyone else, he had to pay rent and utilities. The money to pay his salary, run the park chapel and another small nondenominational church in Gardiner, and administer social services to the many troubled who were steered to him every year by the rangers in the park and by the sheriff's deputy in Gardiner came entirely from the Sunday collection basket. Bill didn't get a dime from the government to keep the spiritual and emotional end of the community in order. Yet he wouldn't have had it otherwise.

"The National Park Service is a civilian service, so I think a civilian pastor is much more appropriate," he would say. "And, besides, I just am so thankful I have had the privilege of working in such a paradise."

Debbie did occasional clerical work for the park offices, sold cosmetics to the park rangers' wives in their homes, and worked part-time for a travel agency.

"I didn't come here to get rich monetarily," Bill sometimes said. "To me being rich is flipping off the suit as soon as church is over, sliding into my jeans, pulling on my black Stetson, leaping up into the saddle, and riding off into the mountains.

"I like to tell Debbie that spending time like that gives a man

54

the chance to think about his sins a lot. But mostly I'm just soaking in the sights and sounds and thinking what a privilege it is to be working in such a country as America, where we still have places like this."

By the time we reached old Mammoth every lip and nose was badgering its owner for someplace warmer. Still we wandered on a while longer. The evening wouldn't be complete without spreading some Christmas song to the families in the old officers' quarters.

Standing on the sidewalk in the glow of the old-fashioned glass-topped lamps along the homes' front yards, I could feel the history of the place as much as I did the air's sting. There was something humbling about the thought that, except for the height of the old cottonwood trees along the lane, the scenery was very little changed from a hundred years ago. The timelessness of Yellowstone still dominated over all.

Our singing done, we retreated as a merry herd to the little stone chapel at the end of the lane. Tradition decreed that on the night of the caroling there was also the decorating of a freshly cut pine tree inside the chapel. Then after that, hot chocolate and more singing around a piano at someone's home.

The chapel was the last building constructed by the Scottish masons the army had hired to build the settlement's stone buildings. It fit right in with its gray slate roof, squat buttresses, colorless translucent windowpanes, and plain Celtic stone cross above the entrance, but the snow that had for weeks been piling upon the buttresses and eaves had turned it into a master baker's finest confection.

The buttresses and steeply slanted roof slates whispered of horse-pulled wagons and black-clothed elders.

And the chapel itself was so clean and well kept that it looked as if it had hardly been used during the past century. Yet as I passed the long, narrow, dark pews, I could see where the bodies of the worshipers had over the years worn the wood's varnish.

At the front of the church I joined the laughter and gaiety about the base of a tall pine. Ornaments of all kinds—some very old, some very new—were pulled by eager fingers from the boxes they had been hibernating in since last January. Ornaments and tinsel and gold bows, strings of tiny white lights, and small white hand-stitched crosses were hung among glistening needles.

At last it was decorated. Gleaming and gay it stood as a fine tribute to the joy of the Savior's birth.

6

"Busy day again?"

I looked up from the potted plants I was watering. A short woman with gray-pepper hair and Irish eyes whom we all knew simply as "Janet the Janitor" was standing in the open doorway of my office. She was wearing her usual yellow Playtex gloves and a very disapproving look. Normally by the time she reached my doorway I was on my way home.

"I was just getting ready to call it quits and go for a jog," I replied.

She cast a shriveling look at the water can in my right hand. I shifted the toe of my left boot over a fresh water spot on the carpet.

"Why do you want to mess up your office with those plants?" she asked dryly.

"Don't you think they make the place look a lot more comfortable?" I said with my best smile.

She marched over to the wastepaper basket, shook it vigorously upside down over a white plastic trash bag, set it back down and returned to the doorway. There she folded her arms and gave me a frown. She was not about to forgive my latest attempt at humanizing the horrid crypt I'd inherited from the last chief ranger.

"You know what I think?" she asked with enough Puritanism in her low New England voice to make me squirm.

I had to fight a sudden impulse to straighten my badge.

"I think those plants are just plain terrible-looking," she said, while thumping wastebaskets in the otherwise empty front waiting room. "A few plants would be fine. But just to bring in a mess of

57

them and put them all around and try to make it look like they fit or belong—" Her head poked around the doorjamb. "Dan, there just is no continuity to the scene."

I shrugged and went back to my watering. She was right in that the plants, which I'd bought one or two at a time while in Bozeman on other errands, weren't arranged as in a magazine photo. All the same I wouldn't have gotten rid of a single one. They were alive and made me think of the outdoors. Which was a lot more than could be said about the room I'd moved into three months ago.

I'd thought then that it was the most depressing spot in the park. The walls hadn't been painted in fifteen or twenty years, I decided almost immediately. They were a filthy white that showed where every painting and poster had been hung during that period. Even all the old nail holes were everywhere, like a bad case of the measles. And the pictures still on the walls—I shivered just thinking about them. In what gloomy, musty museum had they been found?

I'd seen better waiting rooms in garages. The old gray radiators and exposed pipes looked like a bad afterthought. The carpet had to have been around as long as the park, if the number of stains on its green stubble was any indication. And then there was the desk—an old standard government-issue metal thing with a laminated top that was peeling up at the corners. Scrooge himself couldn't have chosen an uglier place to do his paperwork.

As quickly as possible I had the room repainted and the carpet replaced. The park's carpenters were busy for days replacing anything gray and metal with bright wood. To me wood was soft and human; it was real, about the environment, and had an atmosphere to it. Metal was cold, sterile.

Out had gone the two-seater sofa that would have been avoided in a yard sale. Same with the musty books, outdated manuals, and the black-and-white photos with their gaudy frames. In had come the fresh-smelling wood, bright paint, and some semblance of organization. For just $160 worth of wood and a few days' work, the room had blossomed. Dressed in new carpet, brass desk lamps for both myself and my secretary, Jean, an old oak desk, and even wooden cases in which to hide the filing cabinets, it had finally begun to look like a place I'd be proud to come to each day.

I try to be at my office—clean-shaven and fresh and ready to go—by five A.M., no later than six. That way, by eight o'clock I have all of the leftover paperwork from the day before completed and a fresh new slate in front of me, so to speak. I regard the office as my home away from home. It is where I do most of my thinking, organizing, and decision-making. It is of the utmost importance that it be attractive to work in.

I believe deeply in the importance of first impressions. I wear a crisply pressed uniform and polished boots to work each day. I want my office to exude that same sort of professionalism, while letting my visitors know that I am very much a ranger with his heart in the outdoors, and not just another paper-pushing bureaucrat.

Two things I have never been accused of: lacking in pride at being a ranger, and not enjoying my work. Admittedly I am a bit gung ho and quick to action. There were some raised eyebrows when my staff found out I started working every morning long before they were even out of bed. But I couldn't do otherwise, even if I wanted to; I love so much being a chief ranger.

To me being a ranger has *meaning*. It leaves me at the end of each day feeling I have made a definite contribution toward bettering the world.

When I look at my office, I see not only a command post from which I send out the orders and priorities for a very large and complex work force, but also a part of a deeply satisfying role in life.

I know that to most visitors anyone in a gray shirt and green slacks and the famous Smokey the Bear hat is simply a ranger. They aren't aware that there are two different divisions with completely diverse functions and training backgrounds. Or that those two kinds of rangers have long been highly competitive rivals.

With the ranger profession becoming, out of necessity and public demand, more and more specialized by the year, it is increasingly asked by all in it which type—the Protectives or the Interpretives—is the *true* ranger. Is it, some joke, the sissy and professorial "fern feelers," or the overmuscled and thick-skulled "pine pigs"?

I suppose that as long as the responsibilities of one are mostly of the physical sort—making arrests, riding patrol, rescuing stranded climbers, trapping errant bears—and of the other mostly mental, there will always be more than enough debate to go around. Thankfully, most rangers—male and female, naturalist and protectionist—find the rivalry a source of amusement. And there is even a degree of envy on both sides. The perfect ranger, they all know, has the qualities of both sides.

I am sure there still exist a few rangers who can easily switch from one side to the other, who can saddle a horse and track a bear as handily as they can write a research paper and deal with congressional task forces. I myself try as best as I can to be in that mold —constantly honing my rescue skills and going camping as much as my office chores permit. But I would be lying to say I spend even one tenth the time in the field that I hanker for. Even the most optimistic have to admit that kind of ranger is a dying breed. Quite frankly there are too many visitors in America's parks, placing too many highly complex demands upon the usually understaffed ranger corps, to allow any one ranger the luxury of being a jack-of-all-trades on any normal workday.

But that there are rangers at all is still plenty of reason to celebrate, in my opinion. While the world around us is making the cowboy into something of a rodeo showman, the ranger still stands as solid, and liked, and needed by society and nature as ever.

I crossed the room to the wall opposite the windows and stared at a large organizational chart drawn in grease pen on a Plexiglas board. Hundreds of neatly handwritten names rested on the trunks and branches of the chart's tree. Yellowstone is not just pretty scenery and wild animals; it is also people. To keep ahead of their problems and their needs, to fulfill the demands of the park's people—workers and visitors alike—requires a tremendous amount of time and energy.

Now that it was the dead of winter, there weren't all that many people in the park: a little over sixty full-time rangers and perhaps some two thousand cross-country skiers and snowmobilers each day—about one fifteenth the crowd on a slow summer day. But that certainly didn't mean this was a time of rest for my office and staff. In reality, there are no slow periods for the administrators.

Formally, I am the park's chief of resource management and visitor protection. Historically and functionally I am simply the chief ranger. In the grand scheme of overall responsibility for the management of the park, the superintendent, of course, is number one. He is responsible for overseeing the Maintenance, Administrative, Interpretive, Research, Concessions, and Ranger divisions. He reports to the regional director, who works for the director of the National Park Service in Washington, D.C. In turn, the director reports to the assistant secretary of the interior, who is a political appointee. The very top man, the secretary of the interior, is appointed by the President.

As the chief ranger I am responsible for all management and operational aspects of law enforcement, fires, the search-and-rescues, the emergency medical services, the resources management, and the resources protection. Or, put another way: The rangers do anything and everything they can to help the visitors and to protect the park's features.

The ranger's duties do not come to a halt in the winter. There are still numerous daily operational matters because of the thousands of skiers and snowmobilers. It is not at all unusual, I was told, for a Yellowstone ranger to have to go out in the middle of a winter's day to help a heart attack victim at Old Faithful, to rescue someone who had ventured too far out onto the snow overlooking the waterfalls or the thermal pools, to assist after the collision of snowmobiles, or to arrest a drunken snowmobiler. Not long ago there had been an accident involving a semi truck loaded with toxic materials. It was on U.S. Highway 191, which traversed the northwest corner of the park. The spill had to be dammed up before it could spread.

And, of course, there were the poachers. They never rested, and it wasn't just meat or game heads they wanted. Among the most sought-after items were elk antlers. The antlers were ground and sold as aphrodisiac powder in the Far East: They were worth hundreds of dollars each to those who slinked into the border towns to purchase them from the locals.

Winter was the season to do the paperwork that had been set aside during the hecticness of the summer and fall. A time for reviewing job applications, selecting the coming summer's seasonal rangers, placing orders for such critical supplies as ropes and boat motors and canoes, setting the goals for each of the park's four districts, deciding which of the campsites and trails were in need of major maintenance work, familiarizing ourselves with the new policy changes and bills out of Washington, going over the past year's successes and failures, writing out recommendations for those deserving promotions and raises, continuing the never-ending search for more funding, and somehow upgrading our own training and taking all the required tests.

The ranger division budget had never been adequately funded. Even though the budget exceeded three million dollars, I could tell already there wouldn't be enough to go around. And of course there was no such thing as simple government paperwork; the government processes were cumbersome at best.

My reduced staff was spending a considerable time just interviewing and hiring the over two hundred summer workers. In addition, there was the ordering and purchasing of the gear needed by that summer staff—from horses to fly spray.

I had started work in the off-season, but the schedule I already had to maintain each week was not for the weak of heart. The meetings, phone calls, forms, reports, and inspections were seemingly endless. It was amazing, too, how many senators and congressmen felt—even in the dead of winter—that there was something they should go to Yellowstone to check up on.

I was never far from a telephone or radio, even on my days off and at home after I left the office. If I didn't have a walkie-talkie radio hooked to my belt or sitting beside me in my car or house, I was sure to have a pager. Tana grew tired at times of all the radio crackling, but it was essential that I be readily available for consultation by the other rangers. The scope and complexity of the problems and situations that could hit the park's personnel at any time were awesome: everything from earthquakes, fires, and avalanches to homicides, bison gorings, poachers—even childbirth!

I sat down at my desk and pulled out a four-page report listing the statistics of the park and the duties of myself and the rangers of Yellowstone. In the coming summer season, there would be over 300 employees, seasonal and permanent, in the ranger division, in addition to some 30 volunteers. They would be spread out over 15 ranger stations, 5 entrance stations, 13 widely spaced campgrounds with over 2,000 sites, 3 fire lookouts, 36 picnic areas, 7 visitor centers, 1 marina, and 370 miles of paved road. And in the back-country, which was the vast bulk of the park, we had to watch over 1,200 miles of trails, almost 300 campsites, 600 streams and rivers totaling 3,000 miles, 130 lakes larger than 10 acres, 300 miles of highly rugged park boundary, and 10,000 thermal features.

In the Visitor Services and Fee Collections office alone, they had in the past year answered over 15,000 requests for written information about the park, sent out 36,000 information packets, and answered over 17,000 informational calls. They'd also found time to process 100 commercial-use permits, over 4,000 lost-and-found items, 800 park vehicle registrations, and over 100 other kinds of permits for such people as contractors. Also, they oversaw the collection of almost $4 million in fees from the campgrounds and entrance gates, kept all the entrance stations and visitor centers supplied with park information materials, and supervised 40 Youth Conservation Corps workers. Yet that little office next to mine had but a couple of workers.

In the Law Enforcement section we had 120 rangers in the summer. Since Yellowstone is exclusively under federal jurisdiction, the surrounding states have no authority for any law enforcement activities inside it. The rangers have all 2.5 million visitors to themselves, in other words. We also have to conduct mandatory training sessions, maintain liaison with the U.S. attorney in Wyoming and the sheriff's and police departments of the surrounding five counties in three states, and supervise twenty-four hours a day, every day of the year, a communications center that handles nearly 200,000 calls and 10,000 teletype messages annually. Also, Yellowstone has a permanent U.S. magistrate and a jail.

The tiny communications center is just down the hall from my office, in what used to be the bathroom when the historic administration building was a barracks. It has to be a zoo in there at times. Not only do they have all the telephone calls and teletypes to deal with, but also an average of some 480 radio transmissions and 18 emergency 911 calls *daily*. They also somehow monitor dozens of fire alarm systems, four radio channels, the air net frequencies, the Civil Defense, and the neighboring sheriff's departments. How, I marveled, did the two to four people who were usually crammed in behind all those wires, lights, and speakers each shift manage to keep their sanity?

And what about the animals? After all, they are as much our responsibility as all those people. How many of them are out there?

I swung around in my chair, ran my fingers through another short stack beside my coffee pot, and pulled out a "Yellowstone Fact Sheet." And I read that Yellowstone has the largest concentration of large and small mammals in the lower forty-eight states. There were over 30,000 elk, 2,200 bison, nearly 1,000 mule deer, almost 700 moose, around 400 antelope, maybe 600 black bear, a like number of bighorn sheep, an estimated 200 grizzlies, and many hundreds of coyotes and otters and beavers, as well as tens of thousands of pikas, marmots, squirrels, chipmunks, and mice.

Such a plethora of animal life to have management responsibilities for! And I had not even touched upon the birds, including such special and fragile species as the bald eagle, trumpeter swan, loon, osprey, and peregrine falcon. Or the millions upon millions of fish. And the billions of insects.

And what about human life? There were over 20,000 visitors a day in the summer, plus some 5,000 employees. Surely it is a miracle of sorts that in one area we could have so many people and vehicles—2,000 buildings of every sort, too!—and still have so much wildlife grazing, swimming, crawling, leaping, and flying about in good health and freedom.

Yellowstone is definitely not a place anymore for the simple ranger of old. These days a ranger needs to be a psychologist, policeman, firefighter, animal handler, naturalist, medic, parent, guide, scholar, clerk, and cowboy all in one day.

Not just in Yellowstone but in most parks in America, the new breed of ranger is probably not so much a naturalist as a policeman and responder to emergencies. Most of the up-and-coming generation of rangers know more about firearms, legal rights, criminal investigations, and firefighting than they do about plants and animals.

Americans in the past four decades have come to love their national parks *too* much, coming to them in such huge numbers that they are inadvertently bringing to many of the nation's parks the very things they had hoped to leave behind: mile-long traffic jams, horrific auto accidents, overflowing parking lots, temper flare-ups, smog, litter, crime, and noise. The chief priority of a ranger is no longer protecting the land from the people, but protecting the people from the people. And if anyone has any doubts, they need only look at the arsenal of weapons the law enforcement rangers have.

Thankfully Yellowstone is both large and isolated. Most of its visitors have to come such long distances to visit it that they cannot stay for more than a day or two. Even with the over two million visitors each year, Yellowstone—unlike many of the other parks—has kept its wilderness. Still, even Yellowstone has its limitations. And it wasn't all that many decades ago that the annual visitor count in Yellowstone was only in the tens of thousands.

I switched off the desk lamp and headed toward the doorway, but paused again at the organizational chart. There were a few names there of people I had not met. I hoped to do so before too long. Those I had already talked with had struck me as highly educated and committed to their respective positions. There were, as Barbee had said, lots of excellent people running Yellowstone.

But, as Barbee had also pointed out, morale had been steadily eroding over the years. And the reasons were the same as throughout the entire Park Service: bad housing, low wages, and politics. Whatever else I did, it was imperative that I bring the morale back up among the rangers. They needed to realize that their long hours and personal sacrifices were not going unnoticed.

In checking into the records of the Yellowstone rangers, I had been appalled to learn that many of them had gone for years without a raise or a decent promotion. We had low-graded employees who worked extremely hard and should by all rights have been a GS-9, or a GS-11, or even a GS-12, but were still at the GS-5 and -7 levels. Those rangers had been slighted terribly. Yet they had to work so hard and go home to places that were oftentimes little better built than shacks. No wonder the Park Service was losing a lot of its best people to the private sector and to such governmental agencies as the FBI and the DEA, where they could automatically double their wages, work half the hours, and get a lot more respect.

My expertise was in management of park operations. I knew the dangers of allowing even one part of a team to become dissatisfied or uncaring.

Neither the superintendent nor I was going to make this park tick on our own. It was simply too enormous. But if we could make all our people work together, give them the resources they needed, and head the whole into one direction, I knew with every fiber of my body that Yellowstone could survive anything the world threw at it.

I also knew from experience that I had a long and extremely frustrating battle ahead of me to get the raises and promotions the rangers deserved. Somehow I was going to see that those who were GS-7s got promoted to 9s, the 9s to 11s, and the four district supervisors up to GS-12.

One of the most difficult facts of life in the park system career ladder is that a ranger usually has to move to another park to get to the next highest position. But with decent wages maybe Yellowstone's district supervisors would be willing to stay around a few extra years. Then when they did leave, we could attract equally qualified and skilled people to come and take their places. Surely Yellowstone deserved as much.

In the hallway I decided to take a detour before heading downstairs. I turned to my right and pushed on the thick door that emptied onto the second-floor porch. Turning up the collar of my coat, I strolled across its painted planks to the corner where the plain wood railing met the building. The night air hinted ever so faintly that a chinook wind might be coming. It had just enough zest in it to make my skin tingle.

I planted both hands on the railing and looked at the moon peering over the top of Mount Everts. The extreme clarity of its light was matched only by the extreme stillness of the world beneath us. Over at the stone fire cache building, which had been the cavalry's horse stable in the old days, the snow was piled on the long roof. Above the potholes and the tire tracks in the parking lot below a couple of lamps shone softly on nearly invisible supports.

A secret part of me told me to tilt my ears—first one way, then the other—and listen as an owl might. I was certain I'd hear something—a motor humming, a voice, a door creaking. But nothing stirred the stillness.

So peaceful. Nothing in this moment held even the slightest hint of despair or fear.

The freshness of the air and the snow tufts on the village's roofs swept me back many years to a faraway ski retreat hidden in the Italian Alps. I had been a young marine officer on leave then, and in love with the cheese, the long loaves of bread, the wine, the skiing, and—well, everything! It had seemed I couldn't get enough of life's sights and sounds and smells.

I had drunk of the days, and of the nights, and of the people and the food and the cobblestones. And then I had stood on the balcony of my tiny room in my little hotel on its narrow side street and let my eyes leap from one gabled roof to another, to another, then to the Matterhorn . . . and had paused and listened to the distant church bells, and thought a man could live out his life there.

I exulted in the language of life then, because only a few years before I had learned how fragile life was. The sickle of death had swung savagely at me one hot and sticky morning on a Vietnam field, left me facedown and imbedded in the bottom of a deep hole, shredded and dripping with pieces not only of myself but of two comrades who had been only inches from me when the antitank mine exploded. One had been left with no head. The other, a giant of a black man, had simply been vaporized. Fortunately for me, my flak-jacket vest had stopped most of the shrapnel that flew my way.

* * *

A piece of wind groaned through the porch's rafters. The tendons around my right eye socket quivered. I rubbed the rough skin around the socket and brushed away the grains of dried mucus that clung to its bottom edge. The glass eye turning cold inside my skull reminded me, like the fragments of shrapnel still buried in my flesh, that all we held precious could be destroyed before we even knew what had happened.

Being so close to death had taught me that nothing should ever be taken for granted. I could understand a man's being frustrated by his job or pay, but I could not imagine looking at a place like Yellowstone as anything other than a great blessing.

The rangers and the park are a team. Just as the land and animals need the rangers to keep greed and abuse away, so the rangers look to the park's wilderness for food for their souls.

I bid the old man in the moon a good night and headed home, feeling more committed than ever to the park and my rangers. And thankful that Yellowstone had let me be one of its players.

7

Spring had truly returned, and there was a decided change of rhythm.

According to the calendar, it had arrived weeks ago. But calendar to the contrary, every morning had found the air as full of bite as before. Now—I smiled at the sounds of honking close overhead in the afternoon sky—it *was* back. No doubt about it.

Gently I spurred the muscles along the sides of my horse, Shibida. It shook its mane and continued us on our circuit around lower Mammoth's homes, up from the valley of the Gardner River, through a wind-beaten field of buffalo grass, and around aging snowdrifts that clung like discarded scarves to the rocks.

At the edge of a tall lone hill that rose from the field like a watchtower, several resting antelope does suddenly took notice of our approach. They sprang onto skinny legs with the quickness of targets in a shooting gallery. But rather than flee, they stood still and faced me.

With mouths agape, ears erect, and black eyes almost comically intense, they looked as if they couldn't decide whether to turn away or charge.

I reached the Mammoth campground, the only one in the park that remained open all year, and directed Shibida into it. Its looping service road and foot paths would afford a bit more riding time before I headed to home and supper.

In two months there would be tent fabrics and motor home walls where now were melting patches of snow and deepening shadows. Spears of cottonwood leaves poked through the snow. In the summer they would be fodder for boot cleats and tire treads as this campground and all the others in the park would be FULL night after night.

What would most of those travelers to Yellowstone be like? And what was it they wanted the most out of Yellowstone?

Some would be returning with their children, to see again after many years—decades?—the park that their parents had brought them to. Would they be disappointed that the black bears were no longer begging along the roadsides? And that many more of the rangers now wore firearms and patrolled in cars? Or would they be more impressed than ever with the scenery and wildlife?

And what about those who were coming for the first time? What would they be expecting? Some sort of Wild West Disneyland, complete with high adventure each day—and cowboys and mountain men? Or would they know it was a constantly changing *nature* sanctuary where things like contemplation and peace of mind were of great importance?

How many of those 2.5 million incoming people would be potential troublemakers? Even if all but one half of one percent were totally law-abiding, that would still leave thousands in conflict with us and each other, thousands who probably had no respect for what Yellowstone was about. And I knew there would also be those few who came solely to take advantage of the trusting nature of most of the visitors.

I had been taught early in my ranger career never to call anyone who came to the national parks a "tourist." Supposedly that term connoted loud, potbellied men in floral print shirts, platinum-haired widows with big teeth and horn-rimmed glasses, and screaming kids who always had their fingers up their noses. Instead I was to refer to them always as "visitors." But there was not a ranger alive who didn't know that many "tourists" lurked in those visitors.

Visitor, tourist, whatever, in Yellowstone they would be coming into a setting most of them were unfamiliar with. Understandably many would find the huge wilderness intimidating. Every ranger was bound to get his or her fill of worried inquiries, frantic looks, and just plain discouraged sighs.

At the visitor center in Mammoth, one of those who would be having his hands full during the next several months was ranger Tom Tankersley. The year he'd already put in at the visitor center had taught him so much about the ways of the traveling public's mind. There was almost no need for him to go seek out the world; it came to him by the thousands each year dressed in everything from saris to Bermuda shorts to bib overalls.

Tom had developed from his encounters at the information desk a deep understanding of why some of the park's visitors seemed much more tourists than visitors.

"The average visit in the summer is, I believe, less than a day and a half," he said. "There is too much hurrying in the way many people try to experience the park. It's as if they want it to come to them, rather than they to go after it.

"I don't know how many times a day I am sitting at the desk when visitors who have just come in the north entrance, five miles away, come up to me and say they haven't the foggiest idea where they are. 'I have just arrived,' they will say. 'Can I have a map?' And I will look them in the eye and ask them if they were handed a newspaper by the ranger at the entrance. Whereupon they inevitably say they were, and I have to point out that had they bothered to take a minute to pause in their drive and look at that newspaper they would have found not only *three* kinds of park maps on its pages, but also a folded road map.

"Whereas the visitor fifty years ago came for a week and went away with a lot of intimate encounters with the park, today's visitor has been conditioned by such things as television to expect everything instantly and quickly. Before, you had to really work to get to the park. It was normally the destination of the vacation. Today, however, it is so much easier to get anywhere that the park has become but another 'stop' on the vacationers' itinerary."

Tom told of a time when he was driving through the park and found himself following a man driving with a video camera mounted on the passenger seat.

"The man was recording the park as he rushed from one side of it to the other, never bothering to take time to pull over and look closely at it. I believe he intended to pause and 'experience' the park only when he got home and could sit back and watch it on a screen."

It was not at all unusual, he said, for someone to come to the information desk and ask where was the best place to camp for television reception. Recreational vehicles—or "pig rigs" and "land whales," as they were referred to by some rangers—with satellite dishes on top were becoming more and more common.

"It is a frustrating thing, because there is no way those visitors are going to truly know Yellowstone, when all they are worrying about is what television programs are coming on that night," he lamented.

Many visitors to Yellowstone, he added, became strangely disoriented almost at once by the sheer size and distances in the park.

"I don't know that we need to have more roads in the park. So many people can't seem to handle the few we do have. They act afraid when you tell them the next intersection in the park after Mammoth is twenty-one miles away. That seems incomprehensible to a lot of people. And it is amazing to hear how many *missed* that intersection, even though there are stop signs there! I mean"—he gave his full brown beard a good scratch—"they had to have stopped. Didn't they?"

It amazed me, too, that anyone could come to a place like Yellowstone, scan it for but a few hours, and then return home satisfied that they had seen all they wanted to. I had explored the park as much as I could in those summers on the blister rust crews and in the past several months, and I still felt I was but a freshman in one of the world's most resplendent classrooms. And though I hoped to, I knew I would probably never know all of it; there were simply too many places and things in the park for one person to become intimate with even in a lifetime.

And even if I *had* been able to visit every meadow or mountain, walk every trail, and fish every stream and lake, I knew I still couldn't really claim to "know" Yellowstone. For even as I was trying to discover all its characteristics, it would have been changing dramatically right alongside me. Unlike what some visitors think, especially those from foreign countries where there is no wilderness,

Yellowstone was not meant to be a regulated collection of animals or plants like those in a conservatory or ranch. Instead it was supposed to be more of a preserve, where nature's players could interact undisturbed. And because nature is never still, is forever evolving, it is foolish to suppose a place as large and rich in life as Yellowstone can stay the same from year to year. Given time, and in spite of man's best efforts, all sorts of species of plants and animals will come and go; mountains will surrender to gravity; streams will change their courses; even the most faithful and most powerful of geysers will become dormant pools, while others are being born.

People have to realize, just as the Park Service learned to, that in nature there are no such things as right and wrong or good and bad. There is only birth and death and evolution. Nature never stands still. The forces that have pushed it along into each epoch are too powerful to behave for very long according to man's whims and fancies.

While it disturbed me to read of those times in Yellowstone's past when, for the sake of attracting visitors and appeasing politicians, the park administration had allowed and even encouraged such things as hunting, predator extermination, bison roundups, bear-feeding arenas complete with huge grandstands, bath houses fed by the hot springs, and massive releases of nonnative fish in seemingly every lake and stream, I was encouraged by the fact that for over a decade now the park administration had had a mostly hands-off policy in regards to the wilderness area. Of course there could never be a total abstention, because of the use of the back-country by the public. But still such things as clearing deadfalls from hiking trails were not nearly as impactive as the forced elimination of a whole animal species, as had happened to the wolf in Yellowstone.

It seemed arrogant of man to think that he could play God with the course of nature. I was glad I had come onto the scene when Yellowstone's animals and land were once again being allowed to be their own bosses.

It was folly to keep trying to make Yellowstone into something of an "ideal" vacation spot. The public's ideas of what was fun or amusing or inspiring were just too numerous and too varied. Some visitors would have probably liked the park to have amusement rides; others would have loved to come and find trams and skiing and motels; still others might have craved more museums. To keep compromising for the sake of man would only turn the park into another cheap diversion.

What Yellowstone had to teach me was just as important as what it had to show me. And to be a proper student I knew I had to take the time in my own rushing about to *feel* what the gurgling of a hot spring or the shaking of a wildflower's petals were trying to tell me about my world. Just as a book's cover could merely hint at what was inside, so it was that those who rushed through the park and merely glanced at its major spectacles not only never got to know the park, but also hadn't really seen it. They could never know just how exciting Yellowstone actually was.

Back in 1826 Henry David Thoreau had penned: "It is true, we are but faint-hearted crusaders . . . who undertake no persevering, never-ending enterprises. Our expeditions are but tours. . . ."

Why, I wondered as I turned the horse back toward its corral below lower Mammoth, was there the inability in so many to relax and, as Thoreau put it, "saunter"?

Such a shame to think that amid such splendor some people's eyes never focused on the grandness in that very moment, but were always looking ahead to some other thing or place. Yellowstone is a perfect place for discovery of both the world around us and our own selves.

I put the horse into a gallop but just as quickly had to slow it down. A rattling old pickup truck was turning into the campground's entrance. A Dodge that had seen far too much of the road, and probably a few ditches, too, it had a homemade camper spilling over its rusted sides. I directed the horse to the sage along the dirt road's shoulder, to let the truck pass. As it pulled alongside, it slowed, coughed, sputtered, and died.

"Howdy, Mr. Ranger!"

"Howdy to you, sir."

They were an elderly couple and they were smiling from one ear to the next. I couldn't help noticing they had more gum than teeth in those smiles.

"Is this where we camp, sir?" asked the woman, who was leaning over the driver and threatening to squash his skinny frame with her considerable bulk.

"Yes, ma'am. In fact this is the only camp open right now."

The man coughed. It sounded as if he had emphysema.

"Where you from?" I asked.

"Ohio!" they both replied at the same time, very proudly.

"Oh, Cleveland? Dayton?"

The man's crooked back straightened, as if suddenly he felt important. The woman, however, only leaned closer to the driver's window and bent him back with her enormous chest.

"Oh no, we're not from the city. We're from down near the river, across from Kentucky."

"We're hillbillies is what she's saying," her husband mumbled with embarrassed laughter.

I smiled and patted the side of Shibida's neck. "Been to Yellowstone before?"

They shook their heads, even as the twinkle in their eyes grew larger. They hadn't, but had wanted to for so many years. In fact, they were on their first "real" vacation ever. He'd only just retired after a life of coal mining.

"Well, I hope you have a nice time while you're here," I said.

"Oh we will, sir!" she replied at once, adding: "This is so beautiful out here, it's like being on our honeymoon."

He turned a little red. Something told me it *was* their honeymoon.

I clicked my tongue against the inside of my cheek and started to move on with a friendly wave goodbye.

"Oh! Oh!" cried out the woman. I stopped the horse.

"Stop by and have some coffee tomorrow. Please, we'd love to talk with you," she yelled through the window.

"Maybe I will," I said with a tip of my hat.

"Oooooh!" she cried aloud in her poor spouse's right ear. Someone would have thought she'd just seen a movie star.

I continued on with a warm chuckle.

8

"Dad, I thought you said there had been a forest fire through here."

I looked at the strong blond sixteen-year-old boy, my son from an earlier marriage. He had been visiting his mother and his sister, Alexandra, when we moved to Yellowstone and had come back to us in January.

"Can't you tell, Cam? The signs are all around you."

He pursed his lips. His blue eyes flicked from the richly pink meadow that our hiking trail bordered to the forest wall on its other side. He eased a hand underneath his large nylon backpack and shifted it higher on his shoulders. A bead of sweat trickled down his temple. He had never cared to be stumped.

I motioned for him to follow me through the fireweed and red Indian paintbrush.

Suddenly we heard a crashing sound just inside the forest. Something very large was scrambling through the heavily tangled trees and deadfall. I froze, then crouched. My right hand gripped the waist buckle of my backpack, ready to throw it off, my heart pounded loudly in my ears.

"What is it?" Cameron whispered.

"Probably just a mule deer or an elk," I shouted without looking back.

When I did turn around, he was giving me a look that said: *You don't have to yell at me.*

"Remember what I said about hiking in bear country? Always

talk loudly, make a lot of noise. So you don't surprise any," I explained in a more normal voice, as the crashing sound grew fainter.

"Yeah, but you just said it wasn't a bear."

I frowned. "I said it *probably* wasn't a bear. Never, Cam, be anything less than cautious in such circumstances. You know they're in this area."

His jaw stuck out a little more sharply, but he acknowledged through his silence that perhaps I was right.

"Here. I'll show you how I know there's been a fire here in the last few years," I offered.

We waded through the rest of the mountain flowers to the trees. I pointed to a pine that had a trunk darker than the others.

"Rub it with your hand," I instructed.

He did so and his fingers turned black, as if he'd handled a lump of coal.

"That's from a fire that swept through here years ago," I said. "You can tell from the distance up the tree that it was probably just a ground fire. And"—I leaned over and picked at the scaly bark to show it was still mostly brown a quarter of an inch below —"it must have been a pretty cool fire at that, because it only barely scorched this."

I looked at him with a big smile, pleased with myself at having passed on a grain of woodsman lore. But he wasn't impressed.

"Dad, I already knew all that. Don't you remember telling me that when we lived at Crater Lake?"

"Oh . . . Well, did you notice what kind of flowers we were walking thr   "

He threw up his hands. "I know. Fireweed. We learned about it at school. It likes to grow wherever there's been a fire. But I thought you meant there had been a fire through here in the past couple of weeks, not years ago."

I laughed. "Guess it'll take me a little while longer to get used to the idea that you know a few things, too," I kidded.

He looked down shyly. "C'mon. Let's see if you can keep up with me the rest of the way to the lake." He quickly returned to the trail. "Don't get lost back there!" he taunted just before being swallowed up by a crowd of trees.

"Ho, boy! Listen to you. We'll see, we'll see."

As Cameron and I made our way further along the narrow dirt path, it rose steeply through a series of switchbacks to a narrow tree-choked ridge. My steps grew a little more heavy than his, I noticed, but I didn't mind in the least. The treasure at the end was going to be a very, very special one indeed. It had been years since I'd been back to Grizzly Lake, but I still remembered how spectacular its scenery had been. I was sure it would be a perfect spot to spend some quality time with my son.

The last half mile to the narrow lake's north end was downhill, through more cool pine forest. The footing was firm and dry, a hiker's dream.

As so often when I went on a hike, I found myself wondering why I didn't get out into the park more, solely for pleasure or relaxation.

But there had been so much to learn and organize in the six months since my arrival. I'd really not had a fraction of the time I'd wanted to do outdoor things with the family. We'd gotten in some skiing, some snowmobiling, and had splashed around in the Gardner River below Mammoth, where a boiling hot underground stream emptied out into it. But Tana and the three kids were still waiting for me to show them the unpublicized wonders of the park that I remembered from my younger days. Of course I couldn't have done much about the snow and the cold. But summer was here now. Had been for over a month.

Sometimes at the office, I felt as restless as a corralled horse in a storm. So much spectacular scenery right at my door and there I was looking at reports and sitting in meetings nonstop! I wanted to know Yellowstone better than anyplace I'd ever lived. But that meant getting out into it as much as possible.

This little overnight camping trip was as much for Cameron as it was for me. I wanted my oldest child to have the same sense of the park that I have.

I caught up with him at the lake's tree-lined shore. Cameron was staring at the deep blue water as if mesmerized. It was as pure a scene as was imaginable. All I could hear was an occasional sigh in the boughs, a lapping of water against polished stones, and somewhere near the clouds—which weren't that far away—the thin screech of what might have been an eagle.

We filled our lungs with the sweet piney air.

"Just think, this is only one of hundreds of lakes and ponds in Yellowstone. And there're some even prettier," I teased.

He glanced at me out the side of his eyes, as if he didn't quite know what to make of my boast.

He slipped his backpack off. I did, too. We sat and looked at the rich mix of water and trees and snow-capped peaks.

"Dad, how many people do you think will see this over the summer?"

"Oh, not very many. Most people won't go anywhere they can't drive."

"So you think we're the only ones here right now?"

"Well, I don't remember the ranger at the backcountry desk saying there was anyone else staying back here tonight. So, I bet you this is all yours and mine."

"Would be neat, wouldn't it, if we owned a lake like this."

"Well, in a sense we do own this. Yellowstone and everything in it, even this lake and big old Mount Holmes there, are the property of all the American people."

He nodded and looked very pleased. I studied his rugged profile for a few seconds. It was uncanny how much Cameron looked like I did when I was sixteen. And then there was Trevor. He was, I swore, the spitting image of Cameron at his age. It almost made me think there was a mold somewhere up there being used to turn out Sholly boys. Maybe I wasn't so crazy to feel my father was still alive, somehow, inside of me.

A trout rose to nip an insect on the water, not far from where we were sitting.

"Say. What do you think about fishing for that trout's bigger cousins?"

"You bet!"

We leaped to our feet and set out to find our assigned camping spot. From the crumpled map I yanked out of my shirt pocket, the clearing where we were to stay was just a couple hundred yards away.

"This way," I said, heading north along the shore.

"See anything?" Cameron was soon asking over and over.

"Nope, not a thing," I was still replying half an hour later.

Finally we found it, a mile away and not alongside the lake, but near a creek that ran out of it. I frowned and Cameron asked me what was wrong.

"Oh, this is okay," I answered cautiously. "But . . ."

"But what?"

"Well, I don't like how close it is to the trees and this trail along the creek."

"Looks pretty good to me."

"Might look pretty good to a bear, too. They like to use the trails to get around. And they especially like to travel along the lush brush of the streams—fish or no fish."

Cameron's eyes grew wider. He'd never been backpacking overnight in grizzly bear country before.

"You mean you think a bear might come through our camp tonight?"

I nodded. "I have a bad feeling about this spot. You?"

"Think we could try another campsite closer to the lake?"

"No, this is the closest campsite to the lake."

We made camp. It was after all a lovely place where the view of the stream and the small canyon it poured through was priceless. We'd have the cascading water as a serenade, I noted with much satisfaction. In no time we had our gear piled around our packs and were setting up the camp. I did the tent, while Cameron searched out firewood. There was a lot; the weight of the snows over the winter had broken off many branches. When he returned, it was with a large armful. Immediately he wanted to go after the deep lake's trout.

"Not yet." I pointed to his pack. "Make sure you've got all your fishing gear out of it."

Heaving my own pack over one shoulder and carrying a rope

in my free hand, I ventured about one hundred yards into the trees. There I found a pine tree with especially thick limbs. I dropped the pack and heaved one end of the rope over a limb about twenty feet off the ground.

"We'll hang our packs and the food up there. That way no bear can get to them."

As we walked back to the lake, Cameron was overflowing with questions.

"Why didn't you hang the packs closer to the campsite? I mean if a bear wants to try to get into them, he's gonna try no matter if it's fifty feet or a hundred yards from the camp. Right?"

I picked up my spinning rod and a small lure box from a tree stump beside the tent.

"Up until about 1970 that probably was a proper observation. Before then the bears in Yellowstone were used to eating people food and going into the campgrounds to search for it."

"Like the roadside beggars I saw the pictures of?"

"Yes. Like them and like the garbage dump bears."

"Garbage dump bears?"

"Sure. Before they were stopped in the early 1940s, the park had 'bear feeding shows' that were actually run by the rangers. I've been told—have seen pictures, too—of traffic jams stretching for miles of people coming to the shows.

"They had an open dump or wooden stages out in a field where they would dump fresh garbage each evening, when the bears came wandering in to scavenge. There were rows of bleachers for the people to sit on and watch from."

"Like at a baseball game?"

"Right."

"That's weird. Imagine people going to watch bears stuffing themselves with stinky garbage."

"The people loved it. Sometimes they'd even have the rangers make some of the bears do tricks, like sit or beg, for a piece of the garbage."

Cameron looked at me suspiciously. "What kept the grizzlies from just going up in the stands and eating the people?"

"Well, grizzlies are not man-eaters to begin with. Sure, I know people get killed, and eaten, by grizzlies every once in a while. But they're not all that interested in chomping down one of us."

"The garbage probably tastes better."

"Probably does. Just to be safe, though, the rangers down at the feeding stage or dump pit carried high-powered rifles."

"So why did they stop the shows?"

"Same reason they stopped the bears begging by the road and why we now haul all the garbage out of the park, as well as why no food is ever allowed in the open overnight at a campsite: Bears that get accustomed to human food are too likely to depend solely on that, and will always go where there are people to get more. And you know what that means?"

"The bears get bolder and try to take it away by force sometimes?"

"Right. People are going to get hurt, some very seriously. After all, if you weighed six hundred pounds and had claws several inches long, would you let some puny human stand between you and your dinner?"

"No way."

"So now we finally have a Yellowstone that's almost free of bears that know about eating people food. For the first time in over half a century, nearly every bear in the park is truly wild and natural. It's not so much like a zoo here anymore, which is what Yellowstone was never meant to be. But if we start hanging our food by our camps again, and any of the bears start figuring that out and get into it, they'll start coming back. And I don't know about you, Cam, but I don't care for a grizzly prowling around my tent in the middle of the night. They might just come inside!"

"Aw, a grizzly isn't going to come inside a tent when they know there's people inside. Right?"

"Wrong. It's happened several times. Only they don't bother with the door. They just come right through the wall. The bear smells the food and may not even be aware there's anyone in the tent. And then when the person in the tent makes a commotion, the bear thinks it's being challenged for the food and so instinctively strikes out."

Cameron was unusually quiet for a minute, then asked in a low voice: "Dad, you don't think we really will have any grizzlies coming to our tent tonight, do you?"

"Never can tell. Remember the sign at the trailhead that said our safety was not guaranteed if we went on the trail? Well, that's a pretty strong statement to make to somebody. There has got to be a reason for the park to imply you could be hurt badly, even killed, if you go any further."

"They're talking about running into bears?"

"They are saying that in Yellowstone's backcountry man is no longer Number One. That out there are things a lot more powerful, and he had better respect that, if he wants to stay in one piece."

Cameron shrugged as if a chill had run through him. "Don't you think that's scary?"

I looked up from the Mepps spinner I was tying to my line.

"Yeah, I do. But I also feel good, too. It means there is still wilderness in this country outside of Alaska, for grizzlies can only thrive where there is true wilderness. If the grizzlies are thriving, then it means I'm doing my job well."

I saw he had his rod assembled and a lure on his line.

"What do you say we catch some dinner, build a nice campfire, then talk some more about bears and maybe what you want to do when you grow up?" I teased.

He smiled and ambled off to the south, while I stayed near the creek. I wasn't the most skilled of fishermen when it came to trout. I was a little impatient with their general fickleness. But with the ice having been off the lake only a few weeks and with us being some of the first fishermen back here, I figured I should have my dinner in no time.

An hour later I was still wondering why my lures couldn't get even a look from all the trout I saw below the crystal clear water. At sunset I slumped into camp as empty-handed as when I'd left it. Cameron came sauntering in with his limit of five.

I sat back against the tree stump, feeling as if I were the richest man in all the world and still holding a ticket to heaven. The aroma of the trout we'd sizzled in a pan lingered deliciously in the cool, still air, and there was just enough warmth emanating from the fire to make my eyelids heavy but my mind contemplative.

A sharp *pop* in the fire sent a yellow ember streaking into the darkness. I watched it die almost as soon as it hit the black of the night.

I looked at Cameron and saw how the glare from the fire made his face look older, sharper than I'd ever seen it. I saw something else, too. I saw my own painful memory of growing up into a man without the father I loved being there to share in it. Dad had always been my hero; constantly in charge, forever defending firmly the land and animals placed under his protection. Going horseback riding with him through the strange and impressive maze of canyons, buttes, hills, cliffs, and gullies that was Big Bend had always made me feel like I was part of a grand adventure.

But then in virtually the blink of an eye, my father was gone. Dead of a heart attack just when our adventures were getting to be the best ever. Like his father before him, he had passed away at what seemed to me a cruelly young age: only a few years older than I presently was. It didn't take a genius to figure out that perhaps there was a biological clock built into me that was set to run down around the same age. I didn't think so. I ran every day and ate so much more sensibly than they had. But one could never be sure.

Few things are as special to me as sharing my love of the outdoors with my children. If I could leave but one part of me in my children, it would be my belief that everything in life is part of a miraculous but fragile oneness that needs much more harmony among its parts.

The ability to clear from my mind the clatter and distractions of everyday life and to see the beauty of nature is as important to my well-being as anything. In my hikes with the children I was reminded again and again that the key to their and my happiness was feeling a reverence for all life.

And if my father's sudden passing had taught me anything it was that I had to make the most of what time I did have with my kids.

"Have you ever seen anyone who had been attacked by a bear?" Cameron asked calmly.

"Yes," I replied just as calmly. "It's not a pretty sight. There's a lot of power in a bear's jaws and legs. Usually with a black bear there'll be mostly puncture wounds. A grizzly, however, will do a lot of slashing and tearing."

"Well, if I was ever attacked I'd make sure I had a big knife or"—he glanced at my pack where I kept my work pistol—"I'd make sure I had a gun. I'd do anything I could to kill the bear."

"How can you know when it's going to happen? You can't go around with a big hunting knife or a gun in your hands all the time. If a grizzly did attack, you'd probably have no time to get a weapon out of your pack. Even the biggest of them can run twice as fast as you. And remember that firearms aren't allowed in the backcountry except on rangers."

"What can you do, then?"

"A lot of people have survived by curling up into a ball, clasping their hands behind their neck, and pretending they were dead, like a possum. Then the bear usually comes up and sees you're no threat and leaves or takes a few curious bites to test you."

"I couldn't take some grizzly nibbling on me without wanting to scream."

"You'd be surprised how many people have kept still while a bear was sinking its teeth into them. It's gonna hurt, but then look at what might happen if you don't stay quiet."

"Are there any other ways of saving yourself?"

"Sure. Some people have made loud noises, such as clapping their hands or shouting or banging things together. I've even read where some people have scared away bears by growling right back and pretending *they* were a bear! I don't think that's such a good idea, though. That bear might just happen to be smarter than you think."

"I guess you could climb a tree."

"That usually works, since a grizzly is too heavy and his claws are too long to pull himself very far up a tree. I even did that once myself."

"You had a grizzly come after you?" He was leaning forward as if all of a sudden I wasn't just good ol' dad, but a real storybook adventurer.

I sat up straight. "Oh yeah. I was about your age when it happened."

He wriggled on his log seat and inched closer. "What happened?"

"Now if I tell you, you won't be too scared to go to sleep," I teased.

"Heck, I already am!"

"Well, it goes like this: I had a buddy named Woody. He was from Texas and red-haired, freckled, real tall, and older than I. We were working here in Yellowstone on the old blister rust crews—the summer of 1963, in fact. It was around mid-June, and we decided to go camping in the backcountry on our days off. We had weekends off, and since we were both about as poor as you could get, we thought it'd be a good idea to catch a lot of fish at one of the mountain lakes and stuff ourselves. We were growing like weeds and it seemed to us we never had enough to eat. We were always hearing how easy it was to catch big trout in the mountain lakes, because supposedly they didn't see lures as often as the fish in the rivers.

"So we scrounged up some old sleeping bags from our supervisor—they must have weighed twelve pounds and were as big around as pigs—then 'borrowed' a big skillet from the mess hall kitchen and stuffed it and some potatoes, marshmallows, and coffee into two ancient canvas army rucksacks we checked out of the canteen. God they weighed a ton! But, we were young and strong, we thought."

"You mean they were heavier than what we brought today?"

I laughed. "Oh much! And that was just the beginning of our troubles."

I went on. "We were so anxious to get going that we skipped breakfast and took right off in Woody's old Ford contraption to the Pelican Valley on the northeast side of Yellowstone Lake. There we started on the ten-mile-long hike to a lake that a new ranger who had issued our permits had picked out on a map for us. But the tundralike ground had only recently thawed, and it sucked on our boots almost every step of the way. We were famished before we had gotten halfway up the valley, and we had eaten most of the marshmallows by the time the lake appeared.

"Yet even with all our crushed vertebrae, blisters, holes in our stomachs, headaches from the 8,200-foot-high thin air—a lot different from Texas!—the tons of mud on our new boots, and the rain that was starting to fall, we rejoiced. We were practically salivating with the thought of all the plump trout that were as good as ours. In a clearing on the eastern side of the lake we set up a tarp, since we had no tent, and tossed everything under it except the fishing gear. And without further delay we set out. The fact that it was almost dark and that the rain was changing to snow did nothing to dent our enthusiasm.

"But by the time we crawled into our sleeping bags, you couldn't have found two more miserable people in the park. We'd caught no fish, had had merely a potato and leftover marshmallows for dinner beside a most miserable fire, and were so soaked and cold we might as well have been in the arctic. I didn't think I'd ever get warmed. Then just when I finally did, guess what?"

"A bear!"

"Uh-hmm," I agreed, tossing another log on the fire. "We were in bed in our underwear, semiasleep, when we heard some mighty loud splashing in the marshes around our camp. We both sort of sat up at the same time.

"Sure enough, there it stood not seventy-five feet away at the edge of our little clearing—the most humongous grizzly in all of the world. I'm not sure who was out of his bag first, but I do know I was up my tree for at least a minute before I realized that the white knobby tree limbs I was seeing in the tree next to mine were Woody's arms and legs.

"That bear came right up to our camp to look for food. All it found was the coffee, and he gave it a good sniff and then threw it everywhere, as if he was more than a little disgusted."

"Did he see you and Woody up in the trees?"

"Oh yeah. Soon as he saw there wasn't much in our camp, he came to the bottom of the trees and started growling and hinting that he was going to come up and introduce himself. Woody was about to squeeze his tree in half. He'd left his eyeglasses down at his sleeping bag and had no way of telling how close the bear was getting to his bare feet."

"Did the bear just go away?"

"That we couldn't tell. It was spitting snow so thickly, and the campfire had burned so low it didn't put out enough light. We didn't know if he was waiting for us to come down or had gone on."

"What did you do?"

"We waited, and waited, and waited. Neither one of us wanted to be the first to go below. But around two in the morning Woody's teeth were chattering so loudly I thought we'd better get down before we fell out of the trees. Luckily, the bear was gone. Or so we hoped. It seemed to take forever, but eventually we got a big fire going and somehow dozed off around dawn."

"Bet you left as soon as you got up."

I shook my head. "No, we were young and foolish, and awfully weak from all that shivering and no food. We *had* to catch some fish. So, believe it or not, we tried again. Nothing, though." I shook my head even more as I added: "I tell you it just about drove us into fits. How could anyone be so unlucky? For the first time in my life I actually started thinking about all those stories I'd read in *Sports Afield* and *Outdoor Life* about the skeletons of people found in the wilderness.

"After a while we simply gave up and started back to the car. When we were almost halfway, we crossed Pelican Creek on an old service road bridge, and as I looked at its wide deep flow I got the idea to try floating down it to near where the car was. I thought that would be much easier than carrying our heavy backpacks all the way. We were in such a weakened state.

"Using the straps from our backpacks, our canteen belts, and even our fish stringers, we lashed together several eight-inch-wide ties left over from when the bridge had been constructed and made a sort of crude raft."

"That sounds like a great idea."

"It was, until the current got hold of us. With no oars or a pole to steer with, we were at the mercy of the wide stream's fast flow. And the raft was only four ties wide and very unstable with Woody and me and our packs piled atop it.

"We slammed into the bank at the first curve. Immediately the raft came apart and dumped everything, including Woody and me, into the icy water. Woody ended up half on the bank and I went under the water. Somehow we managed to hold on to the packs and sleeping bags, as well the bridge ties. When we lashed the ties back together, we tried from there on to hold them together by stretching our arms across the ends while we hung in the water from the chest down."

"You must have been freezing."

"Try numbed. That water was colder than ice, I swore. But actually that worked real well. Except for the fact that with so many bends in it the creek was taking us twice as far as we would have walked. However, we toughed it out for several miles. Then when we hiked again, we found those god-awful huge sleeping bags had soaked up what felt like fifty pounds of water. I tell you our noses were practically in the mud as we stumbled onward toward the car. It was about a mile back to the trail from the creek, and on every step we sank several inches into the ground. And in the meantime the sun sank lower and lower, and the wind grew ever chillier.

"It was almost dark and Woody's blisters had nearly done him in by the time we made it back. And then wouldn't you know it—there were two big old bull bison grazing right beside the car, and they were not about to move until they were ready. We knew bison gored people, so all we could do was hide behind a tree and shiver pathetically. We decided that as cold and hungry as we were, it'd still be wisest to wait them out. At least an hour passed as we shivered in the dusk behind a tree. Just when I thought Woody was never going to stop whimpering, the bison moved on.

"It was almost midnight before we showed back at the barracks. We looked every bit as though we had survived a forced march through a hundred swamps. And, there still wasn't any way to get anything to eat, for everybody was in bed, the shops were closed, and there weren't any vending machines in the park then. We were a lot emptier than when we'd left to go feast on all those trout that were supposedly up there."

"Supposedly?"

I cleared my throat. "Well . . . I don't know how to say this, except that it turned out that the lake the ranger said was a pretty good bet for catching fish was a barren one. There hadn't been a fish in it in years."

"What? A lake with no fish?"

"That's right. You see, I was to learn later, the wilderness you read about in magazines and books is not always quite what it's like in real life. The fact of the matter is that many of the lakes and creeks in Yellowstone didn't have fish when the first explorers happened along."

Cameron's jaw was halfway to the fire.

"Why? Well think about it," I said. "There just wasn't any way for the fish to get to them in the first place. It wasn't until the Park Service and others started stocking a lot of those virgin mountain lakes that they ever saw their first fish."

"But wasn't the lake you and Woody fished in ever stocked?"

"Might have been at one time. But that doesn't always work: Sometimes there's not enough natural food in the lake, or it's too shallow and freezes solid over the winter, or there's no creek coming into it where the fish can go to spawn and repopulate."

"So you mean to say that you and Woody went through all that, and almost got eaten by a grizzly, and then drowned, to fish in a lake that was empty?"

"Well, you *might* say that."

He was still laughing when I went to bed. But I liked that a lot.

Sometime in the night or early morning I thought I heard a twig snap just outside the tent on Cameron's side. I figured half drowsily that it was Cameron going outside to pee. And that was that.

At daybreak I crawled out of the tent to do likewise. And when I stepped around to the back of the tent, I stopped dead.

There, just ten feet from the tent, was the largest pile of grizzly bear scat I had ever seen. It was at least ten inches in diameter and five inches high. It had to have been left by the biggest grizzly in the park.

And it was still steaming.

9

*E*arth First! was what they called themselves. Purportedly they were a new breed of radical environmentalists who were not above using violence to get their points across. And on this crisp July morning they were in Yellowstone for the second time in a month to protest on behalf of the park's grizzly bears.

Fifty or so Earth First!ers had filtered into the park in groups of twos and threes over the past couple of days from all across the Rocky Mountain region. Dressed in L.L. Bean vests, Patagonia sweaters, and Jansport day packs, they weren't out of the protest mold of the 1960s and early 1970s. Still, some wore long bushy beards and drove around in old Volvos and Volkswagen Beetles that earlier generations of "antiestablishment" protagonists could have related to.

They had protested earlier in the year at Fishing Bridge and the Lake Hotel. Then, there had been quite a bit of snow on the ground and a bone-chilling crispness to the air. Understandably few journalists had bothered to leave their warm offices to follow Earth First!'s demonstration against the intrusion of man's developments on what was known to be prime grizzly habitat. And, few visitors had been in the park then because it was so early in the season.

So the Earth First!ers had asked for another permit to protest—this time at the highly controversial Grant Village, also built in a prime grizzly habitat area, and again at Fishing Bridge.

The Fishing Bridge complex had been built in the early 1920s. It consisted of the usual stores, gas station, and campgrounds for automobile and RV travelers. It was one of the park's most popular and scenic spots. But of late the park's own scientists considered it a tragic "ecological mistake" that should never have been constructed.

The complex had been located at the northwest corner of Yellowstone Lake, right at its outlet, smack in the middle of what over the years had become recognized as a major ecological crossroads for the grizzlies. There at the outlet and at nearby Pelican Creek each June and July were large trout spawning runs on which the bears loved to feed. And the campground and its campers interfered with the grizzlies' routes to those streams. So much so that over the last half century many of the endangered and rare creatures had had to be relocated or destroyed because of encounters with humans.

Large bold stenciled phrases such as SAVE THE YELLOWSTONE GRIZZLY, U.S. PARK SERVICE—GRIZZLY KILLERS, and GIVE OUR HABITAT BACK fluttered in the light breezes on the protesters' bright yellow and green banners, which stretched across the empty parking lot assigned to them at the Fishing Bridge visitor center. They waved back and forth their flag: a green one about four feet wide with a large circle on it around a raised fist. Though I couldn't see much of them from where I was sitting on my horse atop a small hill near the actual Fishing Bridge, the voices of my rangers on my walkie-talkie informed me that the Earth First!ers were stirring up more yawns than scrambles from the attendant media pool. And virtually none of the park's visitors were paying any attention.

Some of the Earth First!ers were said to be handing out publicity pamphlets to passersby. Others were pounding on bongo drums and shouting an occasional Indian-style whoop. Two or three were said to be in bear costumes and acting like bad imitations of Yogi Bear and Boo Boo.

The songs of the protesters that drifted over to me from the woods had an almost primitive pagan tone, one that hinted more of sacrifices than politics.

I had no intention of any confrontation with the protesters. As long as they followed the rules on their permit to demonstrate, the day should be fairly uneventful.

But some of them had forewarned us that they didn't mean to leave the park this time without making a stronger statement and getting more media coverage for their cause. They were going to blockade the bridge and close down the public facilities at Grant and Fishing Bridge at some point today, they had solemnly promised.

One of their leaders, a former farrier named Dave Foreman, had dressed himself in a bear outfit and chained himself to the main restaurant's door at Grant Village earlier in the day. He was arrested, as he had evidently wanted.

Earth First! had bragged that they would bring up to two hundred protesters to Yellowstone with the intent of being disruptive and shutting things down. As much as I supported individuals or groups exercising their First Amendment rights, I supported equally the rights of other citizens to have full use of their park.

A nice July day could see forty thousand people enter the park. It wouldn't take much to interfere with the traffic flow, or to prevent services being provided to the visitors. If the Fishing Bridge was shut down, it could prevent our responding to serious accidents or fires. The hospital in Cody, Wyoming, eighty miles east of the bridge, was our closest major medical facility. Closure of the bridge would tie up traffic for miles to the east entrance, north to Canyon, and south to the Lake area. In other words, the entire middle eastern part of the park. And there were no alternative routes. Earth First! was probably very much aware of how a handful of people could paralyze much of the park.

We did not know what exactly their plans were, or even how many of them had come into the park. They could be just trying for the publicity at the Lake/Fishing Bridge and Grant areas, or they could be planning to shut down several of the developed areas at once. With as many people as they claimed they were going to have, they could shut down places throughout the park's 370-mile-long road network.

I had organized the park staff into an incident command system structure with myself as the incident commander. Snake River district ranger Jerry Mernin was set up as the operations chief for

Grant Village, Lake district ranger John Lounsbury was assigned as the chief for the Lake/Fishing Bridge area, and Gary Brown was designated to oversee all the other park operations during the protests.

A few weeks before I had put fifty of our 120 law enforcement rangers through some extensive refresher training on crowd control and mass-arrest techniques. The training included the use of horses, water cannons, and tear gas. The last thing the superintendent and I wanted was the national media reporting that Yellowstone rangers were hitting demonstrators over the heads with batons. I was confident we could avoid any such action.

With a group as unpredictable as this one, however, there was no telling what might happen. They had been around since 1980, and among their beliefs was that sabotage of anything harmful to the environment was not terrorism or vandalism but a form of worship of the earth. Viewing themselves as "true patriots taking care of the land," they had been born out of the environmentalist movement's dissatisfaction with the Reagan administration's pro-industry, antiwilderness attitudes. Now it was up to me to make sure they didn't harm the wilderness they were out to protect.

So I had brought in most of the available rangers and dispersed them nearby so as to be visible (but not too visible). Now we were settled in to see if the Earth First!ers would be true to their threats.

After what seemed a very long time, a couple dozen of the protesters, including Yogi and Boo Boo, broke away from the parking lot and strode toward the long bridge and its log railings. They marched onto the middle of the busy bridge, locked arms, and sat down in the road. As predicted, every vehicle in both directions had to stop.

I raised my walkie-talkie to my lips to tell the other mounted and vehicle patrol rangers to assist the traffic in both directions. Within minutes it was a mile long both ways.

Ranger Lounsbury was already in place on the bridge. I watched him give the protesters our prearranged message about disbanding. They were warned they would be arrested otherwise. They refused to leave. I could see Lounsbury raising his walkie-talkie to his mouth.

My radio squawked back to life: "Protesters have been read all necessary statements . . . Arrest teams in place . . . Advise."

"Initiate the arrest plan," I said calmly.

It was an easy enough decision to make, since they were clearly breaking the law and the stipulations of their permit. But there was still more than a little irony to the scene unfolding below. The reason for the protest was a perfectly honorable one. Indeed, I suspected every one of us rangers would have loved to see a lot of the tacky Fishing Bridge complex removed. We had removed many of the facilities in the area and were still continuing to do so. But to Earth First! what we were doing wasn't enough and we were going too slowly. Though Yellowstone's rangers and Earth First! had a lot of philosophies in common, how they were practiced was where we parted company.

Fishing Bridge was a perfect example of the complexities the Yellowstone administration faced every day in trying to adhere to the congressional dicta that Yellowstone was "for the benefit and enjoyment of the people" *and* that its wildlife was to be enjoyed by those same people "in such a manner and by such means as will leave them unimpaired for the enjoyment of future generations."

Such an exercise in contradictions guaranteed controversy. No one could ever be totally happy. And it would never get easier, for the more people who came to the park each year seeking enjoyment and needing services, the harder it was to preserve the natural state of the ecology. But it was what we had to work with. We tried our best, and we made mistakes along the way.

Just as the bears wanted the Fishing Bridge spot, so too did the people. Yet how could one win without the other losing? Or, in the case of the grizzly, maybe even becoming lost entirely to the Yellowstone ecosystem? What the animals needed and what the people wanted were usually as different as the moon and the sun. National parks like Yellowstone were never meant to be like any other kinds of parks. Yellowstone's natural setting was supposedly just as important as the visitors' enjoyments. Yellowstone, in other words, was an ongoing experiment.

* * *

The spot at which the Fishing Bridge crossed the Yellowstone Lake outlet had always been one of the more poetic spots in the park. It was where the grand blue expanse of Yellowstone Lake gently emptied its glass-clear waters into the meandering channel of riffles and rapids of the Yellowstone River. Back in 1871, Ferdinand Hayden, leader of the government-sponsored expedition that led to the founding of Yellowstone Park, had written in his log: "On the 28th of July we arrived at the lake, and pitched our camp on the northwest shore, in a beautiful grassy meadow or opening among the dense pines. The lake lay before us, a vast sheet of quiet water, of a most delicate ultramarine hue, one of the most beautiful scenes I have ever beheld. . . . Such a vision is worth a lifetime, and only one of such marvelous beauty will ever greet human eyes. From whatever point of view one may behold it, it presents a unique picture."

People were as naturally attracted to the area as were the bears, and sometimes for the same reason—fish. From the time Fishing Bridge was built in 1902, it was a highly popular place from which to dangle a line. The thousands of large cutthroat trout that swam below in the glassy current must have looked like the greatest assemblage of trophies imaginable to a fisherman. Stories still abounded of the daily hordes of kids and moms and dads crowding the water below the bridge with enough hooks and lines to tie down an ocean liner.

Where people congregated, so too would things like gas stations and stores and, of course, the campground—all under the supervision and planning of the park's administration. Up to the middle of the 1960s the development grew, including the building of the park's only campground with hookups for campers. And all along the way the tragic bear-human confrontations continued. From World War II to 1960, nearly half of the fifty grizzlies killed in the park were at or near the Fishing Bridge campground. And the scenario would get worse, as almost three fourths of the visitors injured by grizzlies since 1968 were attacked in the same area.

Something desperately needed to be done. Each destruction of a troublesome grizzly brought that endangered species closer to

97

extinction. Each mauling of a visitor only garnered the frustrated administration more criticism of its preservation and management styles.

It was the bears who sort of won the upper hand at first, when it was decided to close the campground once the Grant Village complex was constructed twenty five miles to the south at the southwestern corner of the lake's West Thumb. But then came yet another reminder that no decision in Yellowstone was isolated from outside criticism and influence.

That decision five years ago to close Fishing Bridge was drowned in howls of protest by numerous special interest groups, such as those representing RV owners and the tourist businesses in Cody. Fishing Bridge was the nearest development in Yellowstone to Cody. To close the campground, argued those in Cody, would only encourage many of the park's visitors to enter and exit the park at its other four gates. Which would in turn leave Cody— never an easy place to get to—ever more isolated from the traveling vacationers and their purses.

In time the battle became more about politics and economics than about bears, while the grizzlies' population in the park continued to decline at an alarming rate. Those outside the park who had selfish reasons for keeping Fishing Bridge alive kept yelling the loudest and getting the most attention. What was "right" and what was "wrong" ceased to be a factor, even though the final decision could affect the survival or demise of an entire species within the region.

As had become a trademark of problem-solving in the park, a compromise had to be worked out—as much to appease the powerful Wyoming politicians, who could wreak havoc with the park's budget back in Washington, as for Cody and the other special interest groups.

Even with overwhelming evidence of how much harm was being done to the area's delicate ecology by the campground, the park administration relented and agreed to prepare an Environmental Impact Statement concerning the closing of the campground. What that study concluded was that only the regular campground should be closed. The RV park, the visitor center, and the store could remain.

The end result was, in effect, not the total closure the park's biologists had recommended. But then it was probably enough to cut down drastically on the bear-human conflicts. Or was it?

Would the grizzlies start roaming even more through the RV campsites? An RV camp might not have the food lying around that a regular tent site in other campgrounds might, but there was still the very huge problem of the odors. Grizzlies have a nose and a determination for edibles that is nothing less than amazing. They have been known, more than once, to rip apart the walls of a cabin or an RV to get at food they smelled inside. So were we just delaying the inevitable deaths and injuries of yet more bears, and visitors?

And of course, should the tragedies be repeated in the area, I knew full well who would be blamed: the rangers and administrators in Yellowstone.

Perhaps the most glaring lesson I had learned thus far as the chief ranger of Yellowstone was that no answer to the park's problems would ever be without controversy. An awful lot of outsiders, I was seeing, seemed to think that they were experts on the running of the park, and that the Park Service, which had kept Yellowstone intact over the past seventy years, was just an amateur club. And so we could expect some retired college philosophy professor, or a Sierra Club member, or a senator, a housewife in Detroit, or even a religious fanatic to call up and say how little we in the ranger corps understood of the way nature worked. Even those who never intended to visit Yellowstone's collection of mountains and plains and valleys were quick to jump to its defense if they perceived a threat.

I suppose that under such a barrage of advice and criticism from the public I should have been angry or frustrated. Yet I was actually, as strange as it sounded, quite proud and thrilled to see such an eagerness on the part of the public to participate in our affairs. It meant those people *cared*. Even if most of their criticism was misdirected or unwise, at least it showed Yellowstone was still a powerful entity in our society. Yellowstone might lose a battle here and there, but as long as each of those battles involved the participation of many, many parts of America, the park's survival was assured. It was when something like Yellowstone was left to the control of just one person or agency that it was most likely to die. Indeed, some of our harshest critics were former Yellowstone rangers.

I sympathized with the Earth First! members' frustration at the continued existence of Fishing Bridge. After all, the very same sense of idealism and love of wilderness that drove them existed in any true ranger's heart. Though not always so blindly.

How nice it would have been to have looked down from this hill and have seen only what Hayden beheld in 1871. To have only the wildlife and the terrain in this panorama as my chief concerns. Or, even better, to know that the park was like an island, with borders impenetrable to all the bickering, and politics, and pollution, and physical impacts that came from outside.

But Yellowstone is not, and never has been, a place completely independent and unto itself. Yellowstone is connected to the rest of the world, and the rest of the world is connected to it, in ways that scientists, ecologists, politicians, and even rangers do not understand completely. The winds that sweep over faraway Salt Lake City sweep over Yellowstone, too—sometimes cursing it with the city's smog particles—just as Yellowstone's winds may bless cities to the east with the pollen of wildflowers. As the park's waters have no choice but to tumble and meander their way eventually to the murky seas, so the droplets from those oceans cannot help but someday splatter onto Yellowstone's pristine peaks and pine boughs. Any attempt to keep the rest of the world out of Yellowstone is doomed to fail.

To manage Yellowstone was, I could see, a matter of knowing where to draw the line and where to compromise. Compromising has never been one of my favorite activities; where my job responsibilities are concerned, I can be as stubborn as a granite boulder. But I knew already that given the tremendous overlapping of regional and national politics, agencies, and special-interest groups with the interests of the park, we were going to have to swallow our pride from time to time—and be very patient—to get some things done.

The park's policies are almost always reflective of society's at large: When the emphasis throughout the country is on materialism, the building of facilities inside the park is up; and when conservation is once more the dominant theme everywhere, so it is in the park.

The day when the campground at Fishing Bridge would be done away with entirely might very well arrive yet. There was no way to know what the future would hold for Yellowstone, especially with the world's population increasing and the need for more places for outdoor recreation ever greater. I just hoped that the principle of loving the outdoors, which had been the guiding light of the rangers, didn't disappear.

Over half of the two dozen or so protesters on the bridge had been arrested and taken off the bridge by the time I rode down on my horse. Everything seemed to be going smoothly, though a few were passively resisting arrest by lying or sitting down, and had to be carried off.

I rode the horse back to the small command post we had set up about a mile to the south near the grand yellow colonial palace that was the Lake Hotel. The afternoon was nearly half over. Except for a light lapping along the shore, the lake's water seemed to be basking lazily in the sun's glow. I have always thought that a sunny summer day in the high Rockies is about as close to paradise as anything ever gets in this world. I would have loved to continue my ride around the entire shoreline of the lake, feasting my senses on the grand blending of sky, forest, peaks, and water.

Off on the horizons to the east and south were shores that I knew saw very few people in a year's time. In those places, I thought with a smile, a grizzly could still fish in peace.

At the stables I traded in my horse for my Chrysler Fury and then drove back to Fishing Bridge. The last of the protesters was being fingerprinted when I pulled up. As soon as his wrists were shackled to his waist as the others' had been, he was loaded into the big yellow bus that was to bring the arrested protesters to the magistrate in Mammoth. I got back in my car and drove on ahead.

A dozen miles up the Hayden Valley I had to slow my car to a complete stop. In front of me were twenty or thirty vehicles that had been left abandoned and idling in the road's two lanes and a nearby parking spot. The drivers and their friends and families were milling about, excitedly pointing their fingers and cameras at something across the Yellowstone River.

I added my car to the jam and strolled over to see what was causing the commotion. The valley was famous for its large bison herds, which oftentimes grazed right beside the road. But I knew it wasn't the bison this time that had the people murmuring: There was just too much awe in their voices for something as ordinary as a bison herd.

My adrenaline rose too, for just a couple hundred yards away, in the yellow-flowered meadows just on the other side of the Yellowstone River, was a large cinnamon-and-tan grizzly sow. She was walking on all fours and feasting on the succulent plant growth. At the same time she was trying to ignore the playful pawing of a little cub that looked every bit as huggable and cute as a toy-store teddy bear.

For most, if not all, of those around me, this was the first time they'd seen a grizzly in Yellowstone. Watching those bears playing and carrying on as if there weren't a human anywhere within a million miles, as if danger and fear were not things of this world, I thought how there had to be a lesson there for each of us.

"Isn't life special?" they seemed to be saying.

The groans of the air brakes on the bus with the protesters told me I needed to start clearing the traffic jam. I glanced at the bus and saw that everyone in it—protesters and rangers alike—was crowded against the windows facing the bears. Their wide eyes and open mouths hinted even from so far away that most of them were seeing a wild grizzly for the first time too.

I had to laugh a little: Maybe some of the protesters would view the bear sighting as a sign from the gods or some omnipotent "Allness" that theirs was a holy mission indeed. If so, then that was probably not all that bad, I thought. At least that might guarantee there'd still be others out there for a while longer who realized it wasn't just enough to have the bears, that the wildness also was needed.

I stayed at the spot until another ranger came to replace me. Then I continued on to Mammoth, to what I knew would be a lengthy and tedious processing of the ecology movement's latest "POWs." There before the magistrate each was found guilty of disorderly conduct and interfering with agency functions, fined fifty dollars, and sentenced to eighteen months probation. As long as they didn't commit the same crimes or something similar in the United States during the probation period, they would be fine. Otherwise, it would be back to the park for further sentencing.

10

I leaned forward in my saddle and savored the ending of a perfect July afternoon.

An occasional sunbeam trickled through the spaces in the trees on a ridge and fell on Shibida's black mane.

We were going to a very secluded place. Few people who visited the park ever heard of it. Few of the park's rangers ever visited it. It was on the sloping bank of a glacial canyon that loomed straight ahead of me now, high upon that forested canyon's south side in the ragged deadfall of what centuries ago was a stand of Douglas firs.

The horse traversed the steep shoulder of the canyon's side as if half his ancestors had been in the goat family. I watched the dark-bottomed stream grow narrower and the needles on the pines flicker in the updrafts as the horse's hooves crushed the brittle volcanic soil.

The perfume of wildflowers wafted up from the bog of a small spring. Their white-petaled faces peeked at me from the grass. Dismounting, I guided the horse around the bog to firmer ground. The bleached vertebrae of an elk stretched across my path.

The grasses grew taller and drier and hissed against my legs. A gray jay hopped from tree limb to tree limb, cocking her head at me. I glanced past her dark eyes to a grayer jumble of deadfall and standing snags. There, almost invisible in the midst of the dead trees, were thin ancient poles standing upright, their tops crossing, tepee-fashion. They were the skeleton of a *wickiup*, one of the crudest of Indian shelters, and my secret place for being alone with my thoughts.

I tied the horse to a dead tree and dug through a saddlebag for something to eat. I found my package of cookies and withdrew them eagerly. As usual I sat at the fat end of an old fir trunk. And instantly was no longer alone: a tiny, tawny streak of brown stripes and jittery nerves watched me from a nearby rock.

I addressed my chipmunk buddy.

"What sorts of crumbs did the Indians scatter around for your great-great-great grandpas?"

He gave his teeny blackish ears a quick rub between both paws, as if trying to think back that far. I laughed and he stood to attention, as if the sound had been that of a robber jay clamoring for my—*his*—cookie.

There were, of course, no Indians living in Yellowstone Park anymore. It had been well over a century since they had last passed among these trees. They were gone from the Yellowstone Plateau as completely as they were from most everywhere else they had called home in America.

But as so often is the case where man has trod, they had left behind traces of their enterprise. On the high narrow ridges and peaks around the park many of their arrowheads had been found. And inside the park itself some of their abandoned shelters, such as this wickiup, had weathered all the winds of the past century's skies and politics.

The wickiups were a study in simplicity: long skinny sticks forming a cone upon which blankets, hides, or even boughs could be spread. The wickiups had been meant as temporary shelters: used mainly overnight or on short hunting trips. And they had been designed as much for hiding the glow of their occupants' campfires from other Indians as for shelter.

It was possible the wickiup I was seated beside had been built by a roving band of Crow or Bannock Indians. Just below it, but out of sight, was the remnant of an Indian trail that those tribes had used when they crossed the Yellowstone Plateau to their bison hunting grounds. But it was more likely that it had been another of the elusive hideouts of the mysterious Sheepeater Indians, the area's only native humans then.

There was something about the wickiup domain that always pricked at my imagination. Not many afternoons ago, I had tried thinking as an Indian might have, and I had sought on foot and alone all the reasons why they might like such a spot to dwell in. Rather than being sentimental about the scenery, I tried to be practical; I wondered what the land immediately around the wickiup might offer in terms of comfort and survival. I tried to become a creature of the forest.

The first thing I noted was that I was within sight of a favorite range of the bighorn sheep, which had been one of the Sheepeaters' main staples. Then I thought of the spring nearby and of the canyon's fish-filled creek.

But it was only when I walked in broadening circles around the site that I could fully appreciate its value to those Indians. Only then did I *feel* how softly and quietly the ground met my soles, how the firs the wickiup had been sheltered beneath blocked the breezes of the north, and then further on how treacherous the scree cliff behind the wickiup site would have been to any surprise attackers.

I was certain that to the casual passerby the wickiup was nothing more than a pile of old deadfall. It had no etchings on its sides; only grasses and a faint trace of carbon black on the underside of its poles.

And yet to me its very fragility spoke strongly of the poverty and hardship of its occupants—much more so than did the wax figures of Indians in tourist or museum displays.

While most Indian tribes had settled into the more hospitable and bison-laden valleys around the park's plateaus, there were a hardy few who had dwelt among the park's peaks. Known as the *Tukudikas,* or "Sheepeaters," they had been considered, as I have said, the lowliest of the low in the Shoshone Indian tribes. Lacking either the will or the courage to compete in a world upset by the introduction of the horse and gun, they had sought to eke out an existence in the then mostly undesired rugged country between the Continental Divide and the Wind River Mountains of what would later be Wyoming.

Even when they lived, the Sheepeaters were largely unknown. They stayed mostly to themselves, were timid, small in stature, and traveled everywhere on foot in small family-sized groups, usually with large dogs trailing behind as their beasts of burden. They lived on berries, herbs, small animals, and the bighorn sheep from which they derived their name. In written accounts they were described either with sympathy or contempt by outsiders: The French trappers described them as worthy of pity: "Wretched beasts who run from the sight of a white man, or from any other tribe of Indians," scoffed Lt. Gustav Doane, commander of one of the earliest military escorts into the region.

Dirty, destitute, primitive . . . the Sheepeaters were anything but fodder for the Indian romancer.

The first residents of the Yellowstone Plateau since the last great ice age of ten thousand years before, the Sheepeaters were not even recognized by their white conquerors as having any valid claim to the area. Their wickiups were considered as worthless a stake as the bones of their fathers and mothers beneath the region's soil. They were made to leave, forced to become as fleeting in the pages of history as they had been in life. It was to the Wind River Reservation in the Wyoming Territory that they went. And died out as a race.

I had learned of the wickiups on a summer night in 1963. My foreman on the blister rust crew was telling several of us around a campfire stories of Indians and mountain men, when he mentioned coming across one of those shelters during his back-country excursions.

I had resolved then to seek one out someday—to experience history in its original state.

Growing up with horses and cowboys in the harsh wilderness of a place like Big Bend had forever whetted my appetite for such seemingly intrepid characters. They were my heroes: the lone man versus the huge and unforgiving—always potentially dangerous—elements of the unsettled wilderness. They dealt with life in its rawest, in buckskins or loincloths and with blood under their nails and an eye always in the back of their head.

I realized I could never be as they, for the wildernesses that had been their setting were mostly gone. But I used to imagine what it had been like for them as I hiked alone down the park's old trails while doing my blister rust chores. Would I have been able to survive for as long in such untamed wildness? Would I have had the tenacity to get through a pass covered in ten feet of snow? Or been wily enough to close in on a wild animal and hit it with an arrow or a musket ball?

To the passive spectator of nature, there is a tendency to take everything seen for granted—not to probe very deeply into its real significance. How could a person looking from the seat of a vehicle at this wickiup appreciate the hardship behind it? Where for such a modern-day "explorer" is the sweat, the fear, the uncertainty of a true adventure?

As chief ranger, I had to ask myself what should be done with something like the wickiup: Should we let the public know about it, so they might come and view it and have still one more photograph and pamphlet to stick in a drawer at home? Should we simply let the humble dwelling and its ghosts fade away completely, with their dignity still intact?

I didn't know what the right answer was. One side of me said the public should be invited to see firsthand this rare aspect of the park. Another side of me cautioned that it was the very seclusion and peace of the place that was its beauty. To accommodate the public would mean building a foot path, then signs, then parking spaces, then toilets, then . . .

In our endeavor to make it a *sight* we would quickly enough kill the very solitude in which it belonged. Behemoths like the mountains and Yellowstone Lake could be visited by hundreds of thousands a year and still retain their magic. But certainly not this little shelter.

I left my chipmunk and the log and walked back to Shibida. Leather creaked once more as I mounted the horse. Surely not everything in Yellowstone had to be publicized, I told myself. Those who wanted to find it could do so on their own or by asking for directions. The park could stand to have a few secrets alongside its many wonders.

I spurred Shibida lightly. Somehow he knew automatically that I wanted to go home.

A phrase from Henry David Thoreau passed through my head: "You cannot perceive beauty but with a serene mind."

He was so right. We can never really hear what nature and history have to tell us when we are busily cluttering up our minds with noises and random thoughts.

A time for silence—true natural silence—to me is critical in a world where the clamor seems to be growing each year, where there are so few places left that encourage the soul, rather than the mouth, to speak.

Not long after I had arrived in Yellowstone, I learned that people could continue to make all the noise they wanted from sunrise to ten o'clock at night. How, I wondered incredulously, did those who came to Yellowstone looking for peace and quiet ever find it? On some days in the developed campgrounds there were RV generators and radios going from the moment campers woke to when they crawled into their sleeping bags. Surely there was no way any of the sounds of the surrounding wilderness, except the most dramatic like thunder, could have reached those campers' ears. Somehow, all those people seeing the park without hearing it had seemed ludicrous to me.

So I had pushed for new restrictions against loud noises, ones that would ban the use of portable generators until after eight A.M. and require them to be off by eight P.M. To my surprise, I was initially criticized by many, including some in the Park Service, for such a proposal. How, for goodness sake, could those who wanted to watch their televisions or start their electric coffee pots do so?

Apparently some had forgotten already that Yellowstone was supposed to be a nature experience.

11

"Is this Mr. Dan Sholly, the chief ranger of Yellowstone National Park?" boomed a big, friendly, southern-sounding man's voice over the kitchen telephone.

"It is," I said, wondering who was calling me so late in the evening and in the middle of a *Monday Night Football* game.

I waved at Brooke to turn down the volume of the TV in the living room.

"And what can I do for you, sir?" I asked.

"Dan, you don't know me. But me and the missus live down here near San Antonio, Texas. You ever been here?"

"Well, it's been a while," I replied.

"Hey, you gotta get down this way sometime again. We'll treat you just fine. And talking about treating people fine, that's the reason I had to make this call."

"Oh?"

"Yes, sir. Me and the wife we've been up to that great park of yours for the last, er—Honey, how many years was that?—eight or ten years. My wife and me just love that park! You guys really take good care of us when we come up there."

"We try our best." I switched the phone to my other ear and fidgeted.

"Dan, I've just been reading here in the paper how you're trying to take care of your people, and you don't have any money for TV satellite dishes," he continued.

So that was it. Apparently the Texan had read the news story that I had authorized the purchase of about $25,000 worth of hot

110

tubs and exercise equipment for employees who are snowbound in Yellowstone's interior during the winter. The story had been played around the country as a controversial news feature, noting that the employees had requested satellite dishes as well, but that the purchase of those were not authorized due to their high cost.

"Yes, sir, that's correct," I said with a touch of resignation. "I guess the rangers in the interior will just have to continue watching their football on the radio, so to speak."

"Hey, I don't think that's fair. After all, this is the twentieth century and everyone else has television."

Something told me he was about to make a sales pitch.

"It's nice to know there's still a few people out there who like a ranger," I kidded.

"Listen, Dan, I want to *give* you and your boys them TV dishes the paper says you can't afford. How's that strike you?"

I was struck, and highly skeptical. But what if he really was one of those philanthropists I read about every so often?

"You're talking a lot of money, sir. Roughly ninety thousand dollars to purchase and install the dishes at the park's seven interior employee housing areas."

"No problem. I have a big business. I'm into real estate." He laughed happily. "Big time, you might say."

I knew Texans sometimes liked to talk as big as their state.

"You sell houses?" I asked cautiously.

"Sure do!"

My hopes sank.

"And skyscrapers, too. And banks, and resorts, and—well, you name it!"

I sat on the edge of the kitchen table. I was starting to forget about the football game.

"Listen, Dan, I know how important it is to take care of your people. I think you are doing just the right thing there by getting those hot tubs and weights. Anyone but a darn fool can see them winters have to be about the worst thing a man could try to live through for months on end."

"It can get to you," I admitted, thinking how some employees in the interior posts—Madison Junction, Old Faithful, Canyon,

Lake, and Grant Village—had complained there was nothing to do in the winter after work but go home and drink beer. "I'm sure they would love to have some television to watch. But . . ." I was still harboring serious doubts about the stranger's sincerity. "How much will this cost us, all in all? I mean we've been cutting back on our budgets lately. I'm not sure we could find the money from the park's operations budget to truck your dishes up here and install them."

"Heck, Dan, I wasn't gonna give you just them dishes. I was including *everything*. I don't want you to spend a dime. You give me the word, and me and an engineer will get up there soon as we can in my helicopter."

"That's real interesting. We'd certainly be willing to look at something like that. Course you realize I'll have to consult with the superintendent. He has the final say on everything like this."

"You bet!"

"And even if we got permission tomorrow—which of course would never happen—I don't think we could beat the snows. In fact, the roads should be closing any day now."

"We'll make it!"

Hmmm . . . I was beginning to become a believer. Anyone that determined had to have something going for him. Maybe he really was the answer for all those rangers and spouses who had been praying for something to look at over the six-month-long winter other than each other.

"Dan? Dan, you still there?"

"Yes!"

"Just how many hookups will you need?"

There were about sixty rangers and maintenance employees who lived all winter in the park's interior. Most of the houses they lived in had been constructed for summer use only. There was little insulation and limited storage space or room for hobbies or other indoor activities during the winter.

"I'd say we have over sixty residences," I tossed out.

". . . Well, that's more than I thought. But, that shouldn't be a problem."

Could I believe him? If only he knew how much it would mean

to those people to be able to follow the news and sports and to watch movies.

"I tell you what, Dan, you get some dimensions, and I'll call you again tomorrow and get them from you. I'll start my engineers working on this thing right away so we can have the dishes to your people by Christmas. Sound okay?"

Sound okay! Christmas was less than a month and a half away. I wanted to pinch myself, but a part of me was sounding caution bells nonstop.

Early the next morning at Superintendent Barbee's weekly meeting with the park's division chiefs I mentioned the Texan's offer.

"I think this guy is just pulling my leg," I said across the table with a languid wave of my hand. Of course I was hoping otherwise.

Laughter welled up, and I knew then to let the matter drop, unless something more substantial happened. The last thing I needed was to stir anew the controversy my ordering the hot tubs and exercise equipment had started.

While most of the rangers realized the mental and physical benefits the tubs and exercise gear would provide over the winters, and while Superintendent Barbee supported me from the beginning, others in the Park Service bureaucracy and among the public were quick to brand me a frivolous manager. It had been a struggle of wits to gain from our bosses in Denver and Washington the approval I'd needed for the purchase of the hot tubs. Along the way I had undoubtedly made enemies. More than one middle- and top-level pencil-pusher had tried to stop the purchases. But each time I'd appealed to those above them who had worked in the field and knew the rigors the Yellowstone rangers and maintenance workers faced in the severe winters here.

For ten years now, I pointed out, Yellowstone had been open to the public in winter and had kept a large staff in the interior. Yet not one recreational item had been placed in the park's interior in all that time for the benefit of those employees!

I felt it was way past time to do something meaningful for those people's morale, health, and safety. Some of them put in twelve to fourteen hours a day in snow groomers that bounced and bucked the spine around mercilessly. Others put in two hundred miles a day on the even more tiring snowmobiles in wind chill temperatures close to 100 below zero. After being frozen, beaten, underpaid, and in various sorts of danger from dawn to dusk, they surely deserved something better than to spend their nights months on end in a cabin, trailer house, or shack that was virtually un-insulated, drafty, without television, and badly cramped. And since many of those rangers were law enforcement officers, I wanted them to be as physically fit as possible, for their own protection.

When I'd gone on the snowmobile ride with Assistant Chief Ranger Gary Brown that first time, I'd been appalled at the con-ditions I saw. Some employees lived in tiny trailers with only ten-gallon hot water tanks; they couldn't even take a long shower after having worked outside all day in subzero weather. Others were crammed with all their belongings and furniture and mountains of food supplies into dwellings that were little more than plyboard huts. There was, frankly, nothing to indicate that the personal needs of those workers had ever been seriously tackled by their prior bosses.

No one had even bothered to provide freezers for the workers' families. That meant having to take thirty- to fifty-mile snowmobile trips on their days off to West Yellowstone or Mammoth, then traveling another ninety miles by car to the nearest major grocery store to restock their supplies. It was shameful to think that after spending all week working in subzero weather, the rangers had to spend most of their free days snowmobiling to cars that were fifty miles away, buried under several feet of snow, and probably needing a jump start, just to keep supplied with groceries.

Yellowstone had a reputation as the most conservative of the national parks in the country. But to me that was no excuse for the almost total lack of social and domestic amenities for the winter interior employees. They were just as human as anyone else.

Having lived in deep snow for half the year in places like Crater Lake National Park, I knew full well how relaxing it was to soak in hot water at the end of hour upon hour of biting winds and stiff joints. Unfortunately there were still many who thought the rangers of today shouldn't be any different from those of a more simple era.

Back in my office, I read a letter from yet another newspaper reader upset at my purchases. In the first three paragraphs it was obvious how little outsiders really knew about the personal side of the modern ranger.

"What the devil is going on down there?" wrote the angered Montanan. "Few people in this country are so privileged as those fortunate enough to work and live in the backcountry of Yellowstone National Park. Surely, no one could lack for exercise or entertainment in such surroundings. Half an hour's outing on cross-country skis would keep a ranger fit. Even the smallest cabin can hold enough books for a winter's reading. Moreover, the wonders of the natural world should prove a constant source of fascination.

"There is no need for resort-style amenities in Yellowstone's backcountry. If the lack of such amenities is boring the hell out of your backcountry employees (and possibly causing them to get drunk and race around on snowmobiles), then you should correct the situation by hiring people who are capable of functioning in YNP's backcountry environment without the luxuries of a health spa."

I rose from my chair and paced the length of the room. Hot tubs set up in the back of an oily, dark maintenance garage, an old water chlorinator shed, and a former paint storage room hardly struck me as being health spas or resort-style amenities. Neither did cramming an exercise bike and weights into some already cramped ranger station. Yet that was the best those in the interior posts could expect when their items arrived. Space for indoor recreational and cultural activities had never been considered a necessity for those employees and their families. Obviously no one considered them human enough to want anything besides solitude and fresh air.

It was as if everyone—young and old, man and woman—was expected to be forever content playing in and staring at the same snow they had just spent half the day struggling through! Was it any wonder that the morale of the interior employees had been extremely low for years? No one liked to have to live the life of an ascetic for half a year every year of their career. Nor did anyone like to be ignored for so long.

Large corporations such as Xerox and IBM had recognized years ago how important the mental and physical well-being of their employees was to productivity. It was expensive to train employees to operate Yellowstone, yet how could they be expected to stay for long in such discouraging conditions? When would the government ever figure out that it was cheaper to take good care of its employees than to constantly hire replacements for those who left?

What we had for recreation at Mammoth was luxurious compared to other places in the park. When it was open, the hotel could be used for social functions, and it had its share of parties for holidays like New Year's. It also had hot tubs that could be rented on an hourly basis, and a small courtyard that was transformed into an outdoor skating rink. For those wanting to stay inside, there were radio and television, a tiny library of donated books in the basement of the old commissary building, a small gymnasium in back of the hotel, and soon, I hoped, a place to lift weights. I had learned that the old unused powerhouse for Mammoth had been vandalized, and so I'd gotten permission to sweep it out, replace its broken windowpanes, and to use a part of it for the exercise equipment.

At least in Mammoth we had access to the outside world. Whenever the urge struck, we could get into a car and drive to where there were shops, theaters, clubs, whatever. Granted, the nearest town of any size, Bozeman, was over ninety miles away and wasn't exactly overflowing with cultural events. But just the knowledge that it was there, and *accessible*, made it easier to forget that Mammoth was so far off the beaten path.

In the dead of winter, life could be particularly lonely for those snowbound rangers' wives whose husbands were gone for days at a time on patrol or rescues. Many of them had no children or were the only women in their area. They learned all too well how overwhelming the silence of a wintry Yellowstone forest can be.

And then there were couples in which both the husband and the wife were rangers and each was assigned to different parts of the park. One couple, Dick and Mona Divine, had lived that way for years. He was the assistant subdistrict ranger at Canyon, and she was the subdistrict ranger at Lake. In the winter the combination of short days and the fact that they had to stay near their posts even when not working in order to handle emergencies made it impossible for them to see each other most of the time. For half the year they saw each other only on their two days off each week—and then only if no unusually bad blizzard made snowmobile travel hazardous.

There were also instances in which the husband was assigned to the park's interior, but the wife had to rent a home in or near Mammoth or Gardiner so that their children could attend school. Except for the little elementary school in Mammoth, there simply wasn't any schooling for employees' children inside the park.

Anyone who applied for a permanent position in Yellowstone was told that living in the park entailed greater sacrifices than was true for most other national parks because of its remoteness from urban areas and its size. Still, few were deterred. Cyd Martin, the wife of a ranger at Old Faithful, had snowmobiled to West Yellowstone every week the past winter with her daughter and her infant twin sons so the girl could attend kindergarten. I wondered how many other mothers would have threaded their way on a rattling snowmobile through sixty miles of country rife with avalanches, bison, and 30-below-zero blizzards just to get a child to and from kindergarten!

So life in Mammoth wasn't all the splendor of its setting. It involved complexities that most outsiders would never have to face. First of all, Mammoth was an artificial village. It had, for example, no old people, no poor or rich, no unemployed, no vagrants or street people. Most of its permanent occupants were professionals, college educated, healthy, ambitious, and materially and financially comfortable. Because it was very close-knit and had a oneness of purpose, it was a community that strongly encouraged conformity. As Debby Iobst, a good friend of Tana's who had lived in Yellowstone for ten years, said: "The bad is that everyone knows every breath you take; the good is that because they do, when there is a hurt there is someone right there to help."

She thought the advantage of having a helping hand close by outweighed the lack of privacy. I tended to agree. All I had to do was think back to the week my family had moved here. A total stranger called and asked if our kids could come to her house to play with her children; it was just the welcome Tana and the children needed. That unexpected act of hospitality endeared Tana to Mammoth more than any amount of scenery could have.

Of course there were those who found they could not live with everyone aware that they (and/or their spouse) were all too human. Rumors flourish in such tight quarters. Every bit of odd behavior is magnified and made to seem eccentric. All of which only fuels more rumors.

When Debby, Tana's friend, was newly married, she told her husband she would go anywhere but Alaska or Yellowstone. She had worked in the Park Service regional office in Denver and had often talked on the telephone to people in Yellowstone, and heard horror stories of divorce, drinking, and rumormongering going on there. Now, after having lived at Yellowstone for all these years, she realized the tales were just that—tales—and she was happy with the social scene.

Part of the reason for her happiness was that there were those in Mammoth who tried their best to bring culture to the place despite limited resources. There was the superintendent's wife, Carol, who with other wives hosted teas and their "Great Book Club"; the minister and his wife and the choir; the school with its plays; and the Ladies' Skiing and Hiking Club with its "gourmet" lunch fests.

In the old days upper Mammoth was where the bosses lived and lower Mammoth was where the rest lived. But no more. Except for the superintendent, everyone had to take more or less whatever living quarters were available when they came. And when not at work, everyone was on an equal footing. But that didn't mean some didn't strive for a semblance of old-fashioned ways. One of the older ladies demonstrated her special flair at her tea parties. Dressed in a hat and flowered print dress, and serving her crumpets on china arranged ever so perfectly, she offered quite a contrast to her usually very earthy guests. The union of her fine tea cups with their grizzled beards was a sight to remember.

Criticism has dogged me all my years as a chief ranger. I have a reputation for trying solutions that other chief rangers wouldn't have dared to use. For example, I used helicopter-borne, commando-dressed assault teams against the marijuana growers in the Hawaii Volcanoes National Park. It was the war it looked to be, but for the first time those armed and arrogant drug "warlords" were sent scurrying with all their dangerous booby traps.

I was never satisfied if the park and its rangers were anything less than the best possible. Or if the men and women I was in charge of were treated with any less respect than they were due. I always considered myself closer to the people in the field than to my peers in the office. I didn't expect the men and women in the field to do anything I wouldn't; I spent every minute with them I could, even training with them and assisting on rescues and searches and law enforcement incidents.

As soon as I became the chief ranger of Yellowstone, I realized that the morale issue had to be tackled. The park would not get the high degree of protection and care it deserved if its rangers' hearts were not in their work.

This past spring a survey had been done of the interior workers' needs and concerns during the winter. The bulk of their comments on the survey sheets reinforced my feeling that the life of a winter season ranger or maintenance worker could be awfully lonely and boring at times.

"It is very hard to live inside the park during the winter when the only recreation is x-country skiing. The stress from being so isolated is enormous," one respondent wrote.

I knew that there were many days when the weather was far too nasty for recreational skiing. Temperatures of 30 to 40 below zero with the wind blowing were no fun even to the most diehard of outdoor enthusiasts.

"Nice to see some thought being given to field personnel. It gets a little frustrating to get the *Yellowstone News* with all the TV offerings and know that none are available to you," penned another hopefully.

"Have you ever lived at Grant? Spent 12–14 hrs per day grooming roads?" taunted one.

"I think it is essential for the government to provide both the ways and means for those of us who are in the field to obtain some sort of stress reduction from the isolation factors. . . .The interior park employees have been ignored too long . . ." lamented one more.

I agreed wholly that something needed to be done. That was why I had ordered those five hot tubs, at a cost of $3,050 each, for the most remote areas. The exercise equipment, which included fourteen weight sets, eleven benches, eleven canvas punching bags, eleven stationary bicycles, and eleven gym mats, was divided up among all the ranger stations. Also included were four freezers at a total of $1,276.

The $25,034 grand total was, I thought, one of the best investments made in the park in a long time. In a budget of millions of dollars the expenditure was merely pocket change. Yet its benefits would be incalculable both in the short and long haul. With an expected minimum service of twenty years per hot tub, their cost to the park budget would average $150 per year per unit. How, I wondered, could anyone make a bad deal of the project?

But I found out how many did.

It was incredible the animosity the hot tub purchases had brought out. It was as if I had committed some crime. I'd had to spend hours on the telephone trying to justify the purchases to my superiors and trying to reassure the staffs of the Wyoming and Montana representatives and senators that American tax money was not being frittered away on "luxuries." I had even had to refer to the tubs as "hydrotherapeutic baths," and to get a doctor to write a letter saying such things were indeed beneficial to a person's health and well-being.

Poor Barbee was probably beginning to rue the day I went to his office with my request for the tubs and exercise equipment. A lot of his time, too, had been spent on the Briefing, Justification, and Rejustification reports demanded by Park Service administrators in Denver and Washington. The whole project was turning into the kind of embarrassment Barbee certainly didn't need.

It was a perfect example of the nightmarish red tape and headaches any request or action out of the normal could produce in a governmental agency.

Fortunately, I had laid the groundwork for the purchase with the key operations staff all the way to the Washington office. And I had the personal support of Bill Horn, the assistant secretary of the interior. I had known Bill from when I was assigned in Washington, and he had since visited the park and been briefed on the need for the purchase.

Even after the tubs were installed, certain regional and Washington officials told us to remove them at once and send them back to the vendor, even if it meant a large loss to us. But Bill Horn ruled the day.

Most of those who would have denied the winter employees the purchases couldn't have lasted two days in the -30^0 to -60^0 temperatures and blowing and drifting snows the rangers knew as their daily workplace.

Someone, I thought sadly, needed to tell the broadbutts in those offices far from Yellowstone that the twenty-first century was just around the bend.

With all the flap that had accompanied my orders for the hot tubs and exercise gear, I wasn't so sure the sky wouldn't fall in if the Texan actually did provide the TV satellite dishes. To the sizable segment of the public who thought rangers should be the quintessential woodsmen, the chatter of TV filling those rangers' homes on snowy evenings would probably have been sacrilegious. So I was not too disappointed when I realized the realtor in San Antonio had not called me back by the time I headed home from the office.

But just after dinner the phone in the kitchen sprang to life. And there was that same big friendly voice of the previous night.

"Dan, did you get that information I needed?"

"Not yet."

"No?"

"It isn't all that simple," I explained, though my voice struck me as sounding guilty. "I'm going to need several days to get all the proper measurements and whatever done. Is that okay?"

"Sure, I understand," he replied kindly. "How about if I call again next Monday? Think that will be enough time?"

"I'm sure it will be."

When he hung up, I was more confused than ever. Had I been wrong not to believe in him? Or was this still some kind of perverse joke?

Better to go through with his request than take the chance of blowing such a tremendous offer, I decided.

The next day I went to Tim Hudson, chief of maintenance, and to Jerry Townsend, the park's telecommunications supervisor, and asked them to come up with how many thousand feet of wiring would be needed to connect the dishes to the winter residences, as well as how much concrete would be needed to support all the dishes.

Sure enough, the Texan called back on Monday.

I gave him the figures, but in the end he decided the project was turning out to be too complicated to deal with during the winter. There was no way to get supplies in except by snowmobile or helicopter.

"Dan, I'll tell you, we just aren't going to be able to do anything this year, since it's nearly over. But I will be there first thing in the spring."

The Texan called every so often during the winter and continued to fuel my hopes. And, sure enough, in the spring he showed up, along with his wife. He had just paid $400,000 for a home in Jackson. He was still going to get the TV dishes in. Only now we'd have to wait till summer.

But when the summer came, he called to say he had come onto hard times financially. The oil bust was evidently catching up with him.

"I don't think I can pull it off this year, Dan," he said apologetically. "But I got some donations coming in and got lots of boys interested in this thing. We'll get it done for you, but we just ain't going to be able to do it anytime soon."

In the years that followed he would call and claim he was collecting hundreds of thousands of dollars.

But as for the hot tubs: They made it into the fabric of Yellowstone by that Christmas, my second in the park. And as I had predicted, many of the winter employees' spirits soared. There seemed to be fewer injuries and sick leaves. For the first time ever the families in the interior had a *warm* public place in which to socialize. It wasn't really all that much, but it was a start.

The true measure of the hot tubs' benefits was simply one of those things that—like dignity—couldn't be easily compartmentalized.

And, it was not to go unnoticed by me that many of the early critics ended up in those same hot tubs, whenever they came to visit in the winter.

12

I shut my car door quietly and followed the ranger to a small rolling sage meadow on the northwest side of the Hayden Valley. As we climbed the hill and neared the roped-off area, my heart beat a little harder. Earlier on that clear and chilly October morning I had been briefed about what was ahead.

John Lounsbury, the Lake District ranger, and the rest of the investigating rangers greeted me with drawn faces. I eyed the stake and the limp red flagging that marked the scene of the grizzly attack. I made for it with little hesitation. A mangled corpse was unfortunately nothing new to me. I had been the coroner on over 150 deaths during my career thus far.

At the stake I bent over a pair of human legs and a jumble of bloody, dirt-encrusted muscles bulging from hips no longer attached to a torso. I'd seen my share of gore, but this was one of the worst cases. It was almost too gruesome to be real.

How could it have happened?

Staring back at me from the victim's wide leather belt, still somehow intact in the loops of his jeans, was the name BILL. Each letter was hand-tooled and in bold relief—the kind cowboys have on their saddles or truck drivers on their wallets. Though the belt was crusted with blood and dirt from where the bear had dragged the victim across the field, the man's name jumped out at me like a desperate cry for help. I stood and looked away. I hoped to God the end had been swift.

Not four steps away I looked down at the lifeless form of the dark brown female bear that the search party had shot when they found her feeding on the man's remains. She was lying on her left side, her broad head and muzzle snuggled into the short dried grass. Except for a slight bullet wound above her right shoulder, she looked as if she could have been sleeping. What had provoked this beautiful animal to do such carnage to a human body?

Whatever it was, one thing was definite: Once the bear charged, the man hadn't stood a chance. Only a few steps from the legs were the camera and tripod he had probably been stalking the bear with. One leg of the metal Vivitar tripod was bent and slightly twisted about the midpoint. Bear hair was on the tripod leg. A plastic foot from one of the other tripod legs was detached and lying by itself. And the camera, a Pentax 35mm with a zoom lens, was covered with dried blood and smeared with dirt and grass. Something powerful had pushed the camera into the ground. Even more telling was the metal shutter release cable: The threads where it screwed into the camera were stripped out. There was a drag trail starting uphill from the camera, crossing it and the tripod, and continuing downhill to an upper burial mound, where the bear had stored some of the man's body to eat later.

By the time I left to return to Mammoth, I had a very good idea of what had happened back in that meadow. But it would be another several days before all the reports and investigations were completed. And when they were, it was obvious that this was another classic case of someone not respecting the fact that in a wild setting nature, not man, was the master.

William Tesinsky, the man killed by the bear, had been born thirty-eight years before and raised in the Little Belt Mountains in central Montana. He was said to be an expert woodsman, a hunter who seldom came back empty-handed. In excellent physical shape, he was described as able to keep up a pace in his frequent outdoor roamings that would wear out anyone else. Indeed, he hardly ever took anyone with him when he went on his hunts, because he felt most people could not keep up. He was cocky, confident, and used to getting what he wanted. And, tragically, the one thing the

125

recently divorced auto mechanic and father of three children had desired more than almost anything else was to be a professional wildlife photographer.

At the time of his death many of his amateur wildlife photographs hung in galleries around Great Falls, Montana. But he had not yet captured in his lens the mightiest and most elusive of all wild creatures in North America, the grizzly.

Sometime on a cold afternoon three days before his remains were discovered, the beast of his dreams had appeared as if by magic in a meadow Tesinsky happened to be driving by in his 1963 blue Chevrolet Impala. And so Tesinsky left his car in a pullout and began stalking the distant brown furry form—on foot, alone, camera and tripod in hand, his whereabouts unknown to anyone.

Tesinsky had been determined to get the closest picture possible. He probably crept from one low rise in the meadow to another, to another, to yet another, his camera at the ready.

The bear—known as Bear 59 to the rangers who frequently homed in on her radio collar—may have known nothing about the approaching man. But maybe she did: Bear 59 was known to move along whenever approached by people. She may have seen him and kept moving steadily away trying to avoid a confrontation. That we will never know.

Very likely, though, Tesinsky had used the winds to his advantage when he approached her. He had been raised among hunters; he knew the tricks. Bear 59, meanwhile, would have been driven to the meadows by the tremendous hunger in her huge stomach and her natural urge to eat before the winter came for good. The yampah that grew thickly underfoot was her favorite, the peanut-sized roots with their nutty, carrotlike taste.

But then . . . somewhere in the darkest part of her mind there must have come a sudden jolt. Somehow she decided that something near her didn't belong in her field—something that was her enemy.

She probably turned with a quickness and agility that made Tesinsky gasp. And before he could even press the shutter release on the cable to capture the grizzly whose dark eyes he was suddenly seeing *too* close, he was in the grasp of a set of jaws whose teeth were nearly as long and thick as the upper halves of his fingers.

No one will ever know if he had time to cry out. Or if he tried to curl into the fetal position and play dead, as is recommended when a bear attacks. It was likely that he struggled. But not for long; to a grizzly that could break the neck of a moose with one swat of its massive paws, or wrestle down an elk, Tesinsky would have been but a toy.

From the large amount of blood around the collars of the camouflaged jacket and woolen shirt found at the scene, it was evident Bear 59 had gone for Tesinsky's neck from the very first. In the blink of an eye he had been torn apart—his most cherished dream turned by his own foolishness into a deadly nightmare.

Bear 59 was one of an estimated two hundred grizzly bears that lived in the Yellowstone Park area. Her untimely death offered the tragic lesson that while man and the wilderness could survive along-side each other, there were very definite limits to how much they could mix.

The family history and origin of the bear were unknown. She did not become known to the park's rangers until she was first captured by accident in 1980 in the Canyon area. She was then two years old.

As was the policy with any grizzly caught in an area where it might become "habituated" to humans, the sow was relocated in a very wild and rugged northwestern part of the park rarely visited by people. In her case she was taken nearly thirty-two miles to a peaceful and fish-filled lake in the Gallatin Mountains known as High Lake. But, as happens with so many relocated bears, she turned her back on what had seemed the perfect setting for a bear and somehow found her way directly back to her old haunt.

The very next summer she was again prowling and rummaging through the Canyon residential area. Once more she was trapped, this time on purpose, and relocated. Her new home was twenty-five miles away to the east, an even more isolated and rugged place called Saddle Mountain. Yet within five days she had somehow traversed dozens of natural barriers and arrived back at Canyon.

By the summer of her attack on Tesinsky she was frequenting the Canyon area. In June she was photographed preying on elk calves with two cubs she had borne over the winter. In July she was reported feeding on a bison carcass nearby. In August she was often seen grazing in the softball field and walking near the campground. The visitors to the area crowded around her daily. But she never displayed aggression and seldom acknowledged the people, other than to move away from the more pesky ones.

When in late August the bear was caught trying to get into an electric freezer left outside an employee's trailer, as well as trying to get into garbage cans at a nearby picnic area, it was decided to move her once more to avoid a potential conflict. That time she and both cubs were captured and moved twenty-two miles. But in only two weeks she was back, having abandoned her cubs in the meantime—something a mother grizzly usually didn't do until after their second summer.

Despite her more than seven years' experience around people and her attempts to get at human food, there was no evidence that she had ever become dependent upon any human food source. And until Tesinsky, she was not known to have even approached a human in an aggressive manner. As were most bears, she was tolerant yet wary of humans and seemed highly unlikely to kill one.

But Bear 59 was a wild animal, and that meant she was unpredictable. And Tesinsky had approached way too closely while she was feeding in an area where she was not used to seeing a human. The would-be wildlife photographer had crossed over that fine line between being just another pesky photographer and being a potential threat or a food source competitor.

Normally, any wild animal will flee when approached by people. However, with repeated exposure not followed by negative consequences, an animal will eventually not flee as readily. Or, as rangers and biologists term it, it will become habituated. In the case of a bear, the animal will likely retain most of its normal characteristics, but reduce its usual "flight distance."

The bison and elk that graze in the meadows near roads and developed areas are two excellent examples of large wild animals that have become habituated to humans over the years. They rarely flee in the presence of people.

But even while allowing people to approach closely, bears and

Steamboat Geyser, Norris Geyser Basin
(Michael Pflaum)

Upper Falls, Yellowstone River
(Michael Pflaum)

Cow moose with newborn calf *(Steven Fuller)*

Grand Canyon of the Yellowstone River, looking toward Lower Falls
(*Steven Fuller*)

Cow elk with calf of year in thermal are
(*Steven Fuller*)

Mud pots, Grand Canyon area (*Steven Fuller*)

Great gray owl *(Michael Pflaum)*

Trumpeter swans on Yellowstone River
(Steven Fuller)

Steam from Norris Geyser Basin grows icicles on a tree *(Michael Pflaum)*

Mammoth Hot Springs *(Michael Pflaum)*

Heart Lake patrol cabin *(Michael Pflaum)*

Dan Sholly on Electric Pea
(Michael Pflau

Ranger Steve Frye with bison skull, south of
Hayden Valley *(Dan Sholly)*

Ranger ski patrol, Heart Lake *(Michael Pflau*

zly with cubs (*Marilynn G. French,*
owstone Grizzly Foundation)

Grizzly at sign warning of grizzlies, Fishing
Bridge (*Marilynn G. French, Yellowstone
Grizzly Foundation*)

olitary grizzly (*Marilynn G. French,*
ellowstone Grizzly Foundation)

Grizzly fishing (*Marilynn G. French,*
Yellowstone Grizzly Foundation)

Bulldozer fire line near Northeast
(National Park Service)

River otters in Norris area *(Michael H. Francis)*

Coyotes on a carcass, Pelican Valley *(Steven Fuller)*

Bighorn sheep, Lamar (*Michael H. Francis*)

son in winter, Lamar (*Michael H. Francis*)

Bull elk during rut in autumn (*Steven Fuller*)

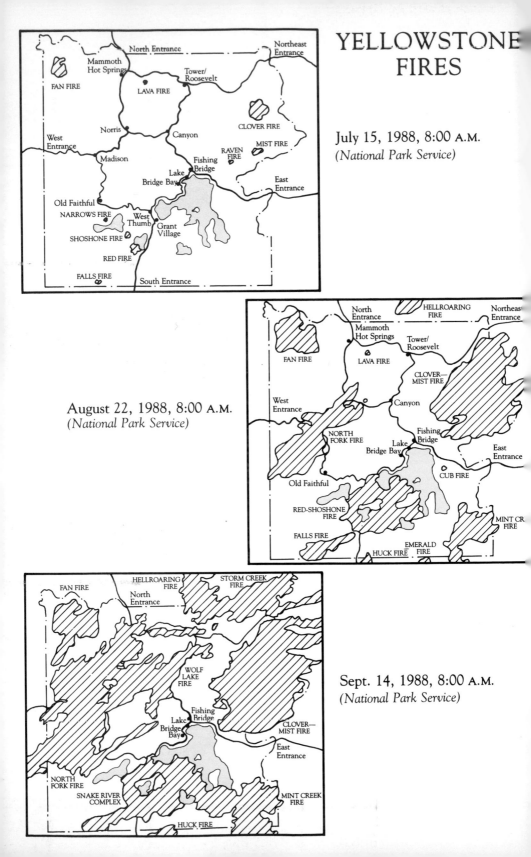

YELLOWSTONE FIRES

July 15, 1988, 8:00 A.M.
(National Park Service)

August 22, 1988, 8:00 A.M.
(National Park Service)

Sept. 14, 1988, 8:00 A.M.
(National Park Service)

other wild animals still have a point at which approach will no longer be tolerated. Once that "critical" or "individual" distance is breached, attack may occur. All the same it was still highly unusual for a grizzly to kill a person. Since the turn of the century only four other persons were known to have been killed by grizzlies inside the park: The first was a man who in 1907 poked a female's cub with an umbrella; the second was a driver in 1916 who tried to chase a grizzly away from a food supply wagon; the third was in 1972 when a man who was illegally camped near Old Faithful came across a bear feeding on food he'd left outside his tent; and the fourth was a Swiss hiker who was pulled from her tent in 1984 while she was sleeping in the backcountry.

Whenever I think of the fact that only five out of the seventy million people who have visited Yellowstone in this century died from bear attacks, I know the reputation the grizzly has among much of the public as a bloodthirsty man-eater is not at all accurate. Yet I also know that whenever a grizzly does fatally maul someone, it is bound to be a major story. A grizzly attack, after all, sweeps the imagination back to times when white men still dressed in buckskins and the natives wore loincloths.

It was sad for me to think that most Americans' knowledge of the Yellowstone grizzly might be based on their reading about an occasional attack against a hiker or camper. How was the public to know that grizzlies are usually not human predators when it read about them only when there was a mauling? Tesinky's especially gruesome ending would only fuel the strong abhorrence some had of allowing such a creature to be free in a national park visited by millions each year, especially since the photographer's demise had come so soon after the seemingly senseless maulings in 1984 of a Swiss woman and in 1983 of a male camper just outside the western boundary of the park.

In the 1983 attack in the Gallatin National Forest a grizzly had awakened two men, Ted Moore and Roger May, at around 2:30 in the morning by shaking their tent and then pulling May right through the tent wall. Moore charged through the same hole with a tent pole and managed to get the bear to drop his companion, but the minute Moore turned his back to rush to the tent for his eyeglasses and a flashlight, the bear came back to reclaim the still conscious, coherent May. There was one more scream, then silence. When the unlucky man's body was found by a search party an hour later, the bear had already consumed nearly seventy pounds of May's flesh and insides.

Even more played up by the media, especially the international media, was what happened to Brigitta Fredenhagen of Basel on a stormy July night in 1984 at White Lake, at the north end of the Pelican Valley. Despite warnings from rangers about the dangers of hiking alone in the backcountry, she had gone confidently into that grizzly domain. And though she had done everything necessary to "bearproof" her campsite—such as caching her food in trees far from her camp—she was still, for some mysterious reason, pulled from her tent during the night by a grizzly and eaten.

When her lonely camp was found two days later, it was eerily tidy and clean, except for a tear in the tent. But six feet away from the tent was her sleeping bag. And next to it, a piece of lip and scalp.

Still, as horrible as any grizzly mauling is, the public when polled has always been overwhelmingly in favor of keeping the grizzly a part of the national park scene. Even the majority of those who never or rarely ever visit the parks feel it is wrong to destroy en masse such a rare animal. They are wise enough to realize that the grizzly does not actually "murder" anyone, and that in those confrontations where someone is killed or injured, it is usually because the person has done something to provoke the bear.

Fortunately most people do not support eliminating the grizzly for doing something that is only natural behavior. Many realize, as we in Yellowstone do, that to destroy the grizzly would make the park's wilderness but a false shadow of what it was created to be.

Because it is so uncommon now to see a bear in Yellowstone—unlike in the period prior to the late 1960s when, as I said, dozens of black bears begged along the roadsides—many visitors to Yellowstone are concerned that something has happened to the bears.

The truth is, Yellowstone still has lots of bears, but they are no longer seen very often, if at all, because the Park Service and most wildlife biologists realized that the practice of allowing bears to consume human food and garbage was both unhealthy and unnatural for the bears—as well as increasingly dangerous for the visitors. As the bears became more dependent upon the visitors' handouts and the park's garbage dumps for their nourishment, they became less able to survive in the wild and more likely to confront people and raid camps for their food.

The decision by the park's administration to close forever all sources of human food to the bears and to try to get them to use the park's backcountry was highly unpopular initially both with the public and with some bear researchers. They said the bears would just turn to the campsites for their food, resulting in an increase in the number of human-bear conflicts. A hungry grizzly, after all, is something like an eight-hundred-pound gorilla: It can go anywhere it wants.

However, it was done, and by the fall of 1970, when the last open garbage dump was closed, the park's grizzlies and black bears were on their own again. And a controversy began that had yet to subside entirely by the time I came on as chief ranger.

When the population of the grizzlies began to decline after the new park policies, there were plenty of critics ready to put the blame squarely on the park's rangers. Couldn't they see, those critics cried, that Yellowstone did not have enough *natural* food to support a healthy grizzly population? The three fourths of the park covered by lodgepole pine forests was a sort of biological desert because of the lack of sun and nutrients in a soil always covered by thick pine needles and shade. Little ground vegetation grew there, especially anything edible to bears.

And how, those same critics wondered, could the rangers shoot such a rare animal for returning to the park's developed areas to scavenge for the food they had long associated with such places? Tempers flared frequently between the Park Service and those who accused it of trying to diminish, if not wipe out, the park's grizzly population.

Perhaps forgotten in all the accusations and nastiness was the incredible tenacity and resilience of nature. Though it is true that more bears than normal were killed in the first few years after the relocation of the beggar bears and the dump closures, that figure quickly dropped to below what it had been before the dumps. In the backcountry new generations of both black and grizzly bears were discovering that the rivers and mountainsides and meadows of Yellowstone were bountiful with forage and prey. The grizzlies became leaner and faster—and hunters of elk calves and spawning trout.

In the process, Yellowstone's biotic communities became more natural, more healthy, and more likely to survive man's pressures.

Assistant Chief Ranger Gary Brown perhaps said it best when he stated that bear management was "truly ninety-nine percent people management." People needed to realize that the best bear was a wild bear, that to live at peace with such a creature people must learn to respect its rights too.

"In bears I see so many humanlike traits," he said. "They are intriguing, and mischievous, and playful and fun-loving at times. There is nothing to match seeing one that is wild. I feel that the wilderness is a better place because we have the grizzly bear. I like risks, knowing that there is something more powerful than me out there."

He felt just *knowing* the grizzly was out there around him was enough to make the wilderness more alive. It was not so easy to take it for granted when there was something out there more powerful than he. Besides, in his many years as one of the park's bear experts he had encountered enough bears to become hopelessly enchanted.

"I came upon a little female one time that had come to a small stream where the fish were spawning. At first she wasn't any good at snaring the darting fish with her paws—she would slap and bite, and always miss. But then when she did get a fish, she didn't know what to do with it and dropped it as soon as another fish scurried past. She would chase fish after fish, occasionally catching one and even eating it. But the chase became the most important thing to her, and as soon as a fish swam past she was off and after it. The fish wasn't just fish, you see, but a game."

GUARDIANS OF YELLOWSTONE

*　*　*

The phones back at the administration building were kept busy for days by reporters from the national and local media calling to get still more details, not only of the bear attack on Tesinsky, but also of the park's bear management policies. After all, thanks to the old Yogi Bear cartoons and tales of the roadside beggar bears that used to be, Yellowstone was still equated with bears in the public's mind. When Yellowstone's bears got themselves into trouble, so did the park's rangers. In fact it seemed a lot of people were always looking to blame the Park Service for any bear-human confrontations. Yet actually it was almost always the fault of the victim.

If people would only use common sense and take a minute to read the bear precautions in the pamphlets handed out at the entrance stations, so much tragedy could be avoided. Too many would-be woodsmen think they know everything there is about surviving in grizzly country, when in reality there are many safety precautions that most people would never guess in a hundred years. Probably most campers have heard or read that food should be stored away from the campsite. But how many know that the same should be done with the *clothes* one has had on while cooking? Or that the odors of such things as perfume, cologne, suntan oil, menstrual fluid, and even sex can very possibly invite a bear mauling?

The Tesinsky mauling was, of course, unfortunate, but he had brought on the fatal attack and ultimately the death of Bear 59 by disregarding common sense.

The world's grizzly population is not so large that there are many to spare. At the time of the first European settlement in the New World, there were an estimated one hundred thousand grizzlies in what is now the contiguous United States. Today that figure is down to less than one thousand bears and still declining, according to many biologists. To have had to kill a grizzly—our nation's most spectacular wild animal—because of an overeager photographer was indeed unfortunate.

Anytime we lost a bear, it was serious. While the Greater Yellowstone ecosystem's grizzly population was thought to be on the rebound, the death of even one reproductive female was threatening.

It was estimated by the scientists involved that losing only seven of the bears or even just two of the females in any one year to human-related causes could halt the grizzly's climb back from the brink of extinction.

But even if the public were kept out of Yellowstone completely, the grizzlies wouldn't be immune from man's foolishness and dead-liness. The average grizzly needs hundreds of square miles of territory for range. That means many will inevitably cross the park's bound-aries to parts where they are not as well protected. The struggle to ensure the continuation of the grizzly is not, as so many in the public assume, just the job of the ranger. It is everyone's. Yellow-stone is a beacon of hope, but not the entire answer. It will take the cooperation of those agencies inside and outside the park's boundary to save the Yellowstone grizzlies. Unless something is done in the near future to slow down and eventually halt those developments and activities that destroy the bears' habitats, the bear may be doomed.

Fortunately the necessary cooperation and compromises are beginning to happen. The various government agencies that man-age the federal and state lands around Yellowstone Park joined with the Park Service in the late 1970s, to study and formulate a general overall grizzly policy for the entire Yellowstone ecosystem. Those places that were deemed grizzly habitat and seen as important to the bears' survival would be less likely to be subject to oil and mineral exploration until their importance to the entire bear eco-system was evaluated. Such major threats to grizzlies as clear-cut timber harvesting, livestock grazing, oil and gas exploration, min-ing, and road building—all of which are forbidden in Yellowstone but permitted to various degrees in the adjoining national, state, and private lands—would be reviewed for their short- and long-term effects on the area's grizzlies.

That dark period during the 1970s, when the hundreds of bears that had become habituated to man had to readjust to the wild or be killed, was hopefully behind us for good. Just last year the last two of the grizzlies known to have fed in the open dumps of the 1960s had had to be killed. When their number was added to the more than one hundred others killed in the name of control before them, and to the more than two hundred other grizzlies that died in the Yellowstone area from other causes—such as hunting and poaching—during the same time frame, it seemed a miracle the grizzly was still hanging on to its home and even its existence.

It would be ideal if all the grizzlies that had to be killed could be given to a good zoo, and that was usually our first choice for getting rid of a troublesome bear. But unfortunately it seemed that zoos had all the grizzlies they needed.

I remembered the first time I saw grizzlies in Yellowstone. It had been back in one of those blister rust summers, at the huge open Trout Creek dump. I had been awed tremendously—no matter that they were up to their noses in garbage. Sometimes more than thirty had come to feed there, and I had marveled at the sight.

But now I was much more cognizant of how insulting that dump had been to the very ideals Yellowstone stood for. A grizzly belonged in the wild—*deserved* to be truly wild—as much as the peaks and the winds. To kill the wildness in a grizzly by letting it grovel in garbage was to kill the true grizzly.

And each time that happened, a little of Yellowstone itself was killed—something I as a ranger had vowed to prevent.

13

There are few places you can go in Yellowstone's developed areas, or "front country," without encountering a rustic-looking wooden sign of some kind: from the large redwood ones at the entrances warning about feeding the animals to the little pine ones used to identify each thermal feature. And all the buildings except one have signs at their entrances identifying their purposes.

Ironically, the one building that doesn't have any sign on it is the very one in which all the park's signs are designed and made.

That little white shed, stuck onto the rear of the carpentry building, is so unobtrusive that unless you have a reason to go there you may never notice it. It is compact but a bit bent and worn from many years of long workdays. As was its sole occupant.

Virgil Hall, the park's signmaker, had been working in his corner of Mammoth since 1968. That was when the signmaker before him, a feisty old Yugoslavian named Charlie, had asked his help in painting some signs. Before then Virgil had drifted from odd job to odd job in the park, doing everything from flagging on the road crews to counting garbage bags at the old incinerator. But by the end of that first day with Charlie and the sweet resiny smells and warm polished woods in the shop, Virgil knew that at last he'd found what he wanted to spend the rest of his life doing.

More often than not, Virgil and I hardly saw each other. He was not only in another division, maintenance, but he was also quite removed physically from the general hubbub of the administration building. When we did happen to meet it was usually either by accident or because I needed some high-priority sign work done.

He was one of Yellowstone's "invisible" workers whose talents and energies were unknown to the general public, even though the park could never have worked as well, or been as charming, without his contributions.

Contrary to what the public seems to think, rangers alone do not make Yellowstone work. While we are in the spotlight an even larger work force that ranges from garbagemen to scientists is constantly at work behind the scenes. They are a part of the much-overlooked human resource of Yellowstone which, in its own way, is as much a part of the park as the geysers and bears.

Like the rangers, the other workers also feel much pride in being contributors to something as unique and historic as Yellowstone. While they work for the most part under conditions that are cramped and not half as modern as those of their peers in the private sector, they still bring to their tasks a sense of pride that most bosses can only dream of getting out of their employees.

Whenever I walked into Virgil's sunlit shop, its many little panes of glass sparkling clean, I couldn't help noticing how orderly and uncluttered he kept it. Even though he worked alone and his job called for long hours of sanding, sawing, drilling, painting, and lacquering, he somehow managed to keep the long worn workbenches and the slightly warped floorboards clean and scrubbed.

Sometimes on chilly fall and winter evenings when I rode my mountain bicycle on the back road linking upper and lower Mammoth, I'd see Virgil's short figure inside his lighted shop long after everyone else had gone home. With his carpenter's apron still hanging from his middle-aged waist, he might be tracing some stencils onto a board that was to be a future sign. Or he might just be sweeping up another day's pile of sawdust. It didn't seem to matter to him that his day in the shop was longer than his paycheck would indicate.

Perhaps he sensed that in a place like Yellowstone he was not just another worker, and his shop not just another workplace; that he and his creations were intrinsic to Yellowstone. Maybe he felt his workplace was as much his home as the simple government tract house he and his wife, Madeline, had been renting for many years in lower Mammoth. So powerful was the park's aura that— given time—caring for it was no longer a job, but a mission. It was an infectious feeling that no man or woman who stayed in Yellowstone long enough could escape.

Perhaps that partly explained why so many seasonals wanted to return year after year. Why so many others applied for the few permanent jobs that opened in the park's ranks each year.

But of course a love for the park wasn't necessarily there at first. Some applicants looked at the park as just another place to pick up a few bucks and bide time until fate pushed them along to something else. Virgil had been such a person, he once admitted. When he arrived in Yellowstone, it was mostly because he had had nothing better to do. He and his two favorite drinking buddies had heard the park's transport company was hiring bus drivers. They thought they'd pick up a little extra spending money. Since leaving school in Great Falls, Montana, he'd mostly played it footloose and easy. He'd bartended for his uncle in Missoula for a while, and even washed dishes in Las Vegas. The last thing he wanted to do was settle down.

It turned out there were no bus driver openings. But there were some elk corral fences needing to be torn down in the Lamar Valley near Tower Junction. They were vestiges of the period from 1961 to 1967 when the Park Service sought to reduce the park's elk overcrowding problems by gathering them in the corrals and shooting them by the thousands at point-blank range. But that had horrified too many of the public, to say nothing of those rangers who had been sworn to *protect* the park's wildlife. So thankfully that policy's days were ended.

Virgil was smitten with Yellowstone by the time the snows chased him and his buddies away. He returned, but landed nothing better than the garbage and road tasks. His home was a lumpy bunk bed in a row of thirty others in the workers' dorm that eventually became my office. Still, he fell ever more in love, especially when near the end of that second season he met Charlie and his shop.

Virgil asked the usually taciturn Charlie, who had a reputation for being short-tempered, if he would teach him how to be a sign-maker. Charlie did so only begrudgingly, and with a warning that his student either learn the first time around or be quickly on his way out the door.

Virgil did learn—so much so that Charlie began sneaking him into the shop after hours to let him run the table saws. That was not allowed a mere seasonal laborer in those days. Over the years Virgil became Charlie's assistant; the two even started to dress alike, in cowboy boots, dark-rimmed eyeglasses, and bib coveralls.

"He could be mean," remembered Virgil one day while waiting for the paint on a metal road sign to bake dry. "If he didn't like someone and they put in a work order, he would put it at the bottom of the pile. But for all his cantankerousness, he was a hell of a teacher. I learned a lot from him."

Charlie evidently saw a lot of promise in his seasonal student. Virgil tried not to let the older man down as the years passed, especially when Charlie's pains and deafness from all those years of bending, lifting, and using power tools began to take over. In some ways, they became like a father and a son, and Charlie told Virgil stories of the park's history. He told the usual ones of the bears and the pranks of the seasonal workers, even some about presidents and Indians and fires. But the one that tickled Virgil the most—but still embarrassed Charlie—was the one about the Old Faithful "geeser." Somehow Charlie had misspelled the park's most famous attraction on one of the largest directional signs to its parking lot. OLD FAITHFUL GEYSER PARKING had become OLD FAITHFUL GEESER PARKING.

Incredibly, it hung there for many years before it was fixed.

It would be almost eleven years before Charlie would retire and Virgil, who had remained a seasonal worker all that time, could finally apply for the one job he wanted. He was unquestionably the best qualified and most deserving. Still, even with all the experience he had as Charlie's assistant, he was forced to compete with other applicants—all, as it turned out, outsiders with higher rankings in the civil service ladder because of having served in the military.

In a classic example of how insensitive a bureaucracy as huge and removed as the federal government could be, an applicant from

New Jersey was selected, based on his greater ranking. The New Jersey man hadn't even been to Yellowstone Park.

Disenchanted, Virgil packed his bags to move on with his young wife and their little son. But at the last moment there came a telephone call: The New Jersey man had been unable to find a home to rent near the park and so had backed out. The job was Virgil's after all.

"There are days I wouldn't give you this job for any other in the world. I love it," he said once. "When I go home, I'm thinking all the time about some new sign I have to design and make for the park. I even dream about how I should do the lettering or shape."

Even when he reminisced about the hardships of his job, he did so with a thinly disguised pride.

"If everybody would stop stealing the signs for two years, I'd be out of work," he liked to say with a kind of mock frustration.

His problem was all those who stole his signs from the trails and geyser areas—even from the rest room doors!—for souvenirs to take home. Some signs, like WHISKEY FLATS, were so difficult to keep in place that he finally had to stop making them.

"Before Charlie left here, we made eighteen sets of WHISKEY FLATS, and it wasn't a year and a half before they were all gone."

Living in the park had been anything but easy for him at times. Like so many of us he had put up with more than one visitor peering in his house windows or snitching his firewood. And then there was a period where it had seemed his border collie, Chrissy, could hardly go an hour tied up in the yard without being gored, or kicked, or stomped on by one of the elk and bison that passed her each day. Still, he was happy the park had been his home and career the past two decades. And he expected to be around for many years to come. He wasn't even fifty yet.

As for his favorite memento? It was a letter from a park visitor who had popped in on Virgil one afternoon, been impressed by his work and friendliness, and then written to the superintendent: "Thanks for spending our tax money so well."

In a place that was first and foremost the property of every

140

American, that letter was the highest compliment anyone could have given one of Yellowstone's workers.

While there were those who, like Virgil, largely worked with their hands, there were others who might have been called the park's scholars. Paul Schullery was certainly one of those cerebral beings.

Paul wore many hats, but his craft was working with words. He was the author of books on wildlife, conservation, national parks, and even fly-fishing; he was a former teacher, editor, and columnist; an accomplished lecturer; and the park's technical writer and historian. When a report needed polishing, or an informational newsletter or booklet was wanted, he was the man to see. He had a master of arts degree from Ohio University, down the road from his boyhood home in Lancaster.

What he and Virgil had in common was their feeling that Yellowstone was one of the very best places a person's heart could call home.

"It is my favorite place," he reflected one evening in his little office in the basement of the old wooden building that had been the enlisted men's barracks. "Every time I leave, I know I am going to come back. This time I am here for as long as I can be."

Paul's first relationship with the park was as a seasonal naturalist, a part of the circuit that cooled its heels in Yellowstone National Park over the summer and then warmed them back up in Everglades National Park over the winter. Like virtually everyone, he had had to put in his years before he became a full-timer. And when he did, he was a very happy person—low pay, politics, and all!

Raised by a Lutheran minister, he had learned a lot of the self-discipline which in later years served him well in his studies, writing, and, his most fulfilling calling of all, fly-fishing.

Paul, like Virgil, had had a cantankerous and demanding mentor. His, however, was not a human, but the same dark, fast-flowing Gardner River that sang to me every time I rode a horse through the valley below Mammoth to my secret wickiup.

As Paul said: "My first summer, in 1972, I got a job as a seasonal naturalist and came out here with a fly-fishing rod and reel my brother had given me. After a few practice casts I headed to the Gardner River below here, but somehow got my instructions mixed up and had to climb down a steep cliff to get to the water. Once there, I tied on a fly and tried my best to get it out in the current, not knowing really what the heck I was doing. It was a mess, and the river, the rocks, and the shrubs only made me pay more dearly for each mistake I made.

"But then"—he sat up straighter, and his big hands waved idly through the air—"after a while I got the fly out there a little ways. And as I was trying to gather in some of all the loose line around my ankles a fish grabbed my fly! And I landed it! I took it home right away, as though it might melt if I did otherwise."

He was to return to the neighborhood river every chance he could.

"I found that literally I was never fishing the same river twice. The whole action of fishing was so much more animated a process than in the Ohio ponds, where everything was forever there in one spot. I was forced to think a lot more, to try to 'outsmart' the land and the water and, of course, those trout. It wasn't just a simple act anymore, but an *experience*."

Yellowstone has some of the best, if not *the* best, fly-fishing in all the world. But to tap into it best requires the fisherman to study closely the motion of the water to see where there might be backwash, and underwater boulders, and sunken logs behind which fish would be lurking. And also to study closely what insects are flying or darting or skimming in that part of the world, so one can best match one's fly with the locals' appetites.

Thus Paul, whose formal schooling had been almost entirely in American history, found that on his almost daily jousts with the Gardner River he was slowly becoming something of an expert on biology, geology, hydrology, and entomology. A scientist by degree he was not, of course. But he was getting there.

He grew to love the sense of life and community that was Yellowstone Park. And he reached the point of wondering why in a national park where the hunting of game animals, the picking of flowers, and the collecting of antlers and rocks or anything from the setting was deemed incompatible with the ideals of preservation and against the law, fish were allowed to be caught and killed. Weren't fish wildlife, too?

"I don't think I have killed a fish from the park in years. Probably the last time I killed one was in 1977. I don't even have any of the big ones I've caught mounted, for it is the stalking and that first tug on the line that are the best 'trophies' I could have.

"I would not want to see local businesses hurt by any banning of fishing in Yellowstone. But I think that it would be a good lesson for everyone if all the fishing in the park were catch-and-release only. It would show people that it's not just a fish they're catching, but a very important part of the food chain in the park's ecology. It would make them think just how rich all of this really is."

Lest his listener think his love of the park was centered around water and fish, he offered: "I think the whole experience of living here is a spiritual one. I don't think of myself as being here because I am a fisherman. Actually my favorite season is winter, when the fishing season is closed. I realized years ago that I would still want to be here even if I couldn't fish. There . . . there is drama here. Peace."

He shut down his word processor, heaved his giant feet upon his desk, and put his hands behind his head—the epitome of relaxation. What makes living and working in Yellowstone so much more special than any other job he ever had, he said, was knowing there would always be new discoveries to be made.

All he had to do was get a little smarter.

14

Electric Peak had intrigued me from the very first day I arrived at the north entrance to the park and saw that lofty cloud-shrouded mountain. I was caught too by its wonderfully frightening name, which summoned thoughts of its eleven-thousand-foot summit attracting the lightning bolts that coursed through singed clouds. It is said that one of the men in an 1872 survey team descended from its summit with his hair standing on end, the air snapping and crackling about him.

So what better way to celebrate the beginning of a new year, I thought, than to go to the top of that glaciated horn—the highest peak in the northern half of the park—to revel in the spectacular view it surely had to offer?

Cross-country skiing with me to the mountain's summit on this gorgeously clear January morning were four others, each of them as excited as I. There was Terry McEneaney, bird specialist and biologist; Mike Pflaum, a park ranger at Mammoth; Colette Daigle-Berg, a park ranger at Grant Village; and her husband, Bill Berg, a former ranger who was now assistant manager of the Yellowstone Park Service Stations. I wished that Tana could have come along, but she didn't feel she was in shape for so physically demanding, as well as possibly very risky, a trek.

It wasn't even five A.M. yet, and as cold and dark as a deep freeze, but that dampened none of our enthusiasm. Terry, Mike, and I had wakened around three A.M. to get prepared for the ski trip, and had pulled away from Mammoth just after four in a four-wheel-drive truck, with the moon resting on the western horizon.

We all knew we had to be a little crazy to be out in below-zero temperatures, let alone to be making a cross-country ski trip up such an imposing mountain. But we were experienced cross-country skiers and in excellent physical shape. And after all, the constant arm-swinging and leg-striding that such skiing entailed would burn away the coldest drafts.

The weather forecast had called for clear sky and light winds. Otherwise, we would never have tried something so risky. Each of us had been on our share of winter rescues over the years; we knew how easily a ski outing could become a tragedy in bad weather. To us a mountain as huge and powerful as Electric Peak spoke more of snow, rocks, cliffs, ice, and wind than of poetry. There could be no understating its dangers for those as fragile as we. But we knew, too, an almost indescribable high would be waiting for us on the pinnacle.

All of us except Terry had packed a small ton of supplies in our backpacks. Most of us including Colette had around forty to fifty pounds of clothing, food, and emergency survival and medical gear.

"Terry, you must feel pretty confident," kidded Bill.

"I think he overslept. Bet he's just got his pajamas and a box of cereal he grabbed off the kitchen table," I added.

The wiry park biologist's face turned redder. "I was just smart enough to know all of you would take care of me."

We pushed off into the still dark morning, chattering as though we were heading for a festival. Terry and his twenty pounds of gear bore the brunt of our joking, but secretly the rest of us were soon wondering why we hadn't been at least half as judicious with our packing. The going was steep and highly challenging almost from the start. There were twelve to eighteen inches of fresh snow on our route, and every few minutes the lead person breaking the trail had to be changed. Traversing back and forth across the ridge sloping toward the peak was extremely cumbersome; we did a lot more shuffling than gliding.

Our voices rang through the dry crystalline air with the clarity of chimes. The snow clung to my knee-high gaiters and my woolen pants.

Snow had been a rarity in my childhood. Unlike a lot of people I now looked forward to it each winter. Neither the sharp *slishhhh* sounds my long skinny skis made as they sliced through the powder nor the thundering of my heart in my ears meant exertion to me. No, they were music.

Our path up the mountain started just above where the park's northwestern boundary touched the shoulders of the valley in which Gardiner sat. The gradual trail paralleled the Mol Heron Creek drainage on the mountain's north side, while rising toward a corner of the park that was explored by hardly any visitors in the summer—almost none in the winter. On a map we were about eight air miles northwest of Mammoth and not much closer to Gardiner, which was due east. But to look around at the large snow-coated pine tree boughs was to feel we were a million miles from any civilization.

Before too long the mountain began to exert its mastery over us. As the sky grew lighter and the earth more phosphorescent, my breath stretched longer and my thoughts shorter. The words offered every so often by others came to my ears from far ahead or far behind, like the sounds a rock made tumbling off one of the huge cliffs to my far left.

A raven flapped overhead as we continued on our way. I was surprised to see one up so high so late in the winter. It made no attempt to acknowledge our presence, but simply flapped onward to the valley as if in a hurry to get out of the way of the rising sun.

My body seemed at last to have adjusted to the pull of the mountain. From all my years of running I knew that I had gained my "second wind." I could take more notice now of my surroundings. What I saw made me feel all the warmer.

The dawn was a soft red glow that seemed to come from everywhere and everything. It was as if the mountain were enshrined in a halo. The air was stirring restlessly. There seemed to be whispers in the trees that my ears were unable to decipher.

We emerged now from a forest of trees into a forest of rocks and clustered together on the lip of a massive rocky glacier-carved bowl that dropped precipitously to our left and rose again into dizzying cliffs on the other side. The gnarled pinnacle of the mountain rose high above us. It was another world . . . another time. One that was cold. Hard. Unforgiving.

Daylight came quickly after that. The miles did not. For the ridge became steeper with each minute.

At two in the afternoon we were still over a mile from the summit when winter's winds lowered upon our heads. They had to be blowing at least twenty-five to thirty-five miles per hour. The sweat that I had worked up now became a curse and helped the wind chill my bones. Ice formed on my lips and chin from my breath.

We had to hurry. The razorblades in the wind would get sharper with each dip of the sun toward the early dusk. Carefully, we crept further along on our skis, stretched out along the ridge's thinning edge.

Surrounded by so much openness, I felt more in tune with the sky overhead than with the snow-splotched barrenness around. It was easy to see why Montana was called the Big Sky Country. So clear was the air that there seemed no limit to my vision.

Further along the ridgeline, the old volcano became too wind-blown and rocky for skiing. About one mile from the summit, we unstrapped our skis from our boots, tossed our packs beside our upright poles, and began scrambling up a chute to the apex. The first few hundred feet were not difficult: My soles bit firmly into the wind-packed snow.

But the last few hundred feet were almost straight up, and very windy and cold. The snow and rocks we dislodged tumbled hundreds of feet to either side.

Around 3:30 we reached the very top—and a view that justified every complaining tendon and labored breath. I revolved slowly, almost on the verge of dizziness. Such a pantheon of light and color!

Stretching forever to the south was the silent mountainous park. The tops of its peaks were hazy in the light of the sinking sun. They were so majestic, each and every one. We remained as long as we thought our bodies could stand the $-30°$ wind chill. Very, very few people had ever been to the summit of Electric Peak in January. There was no telling if we would ever be able to do it again. We stayed lost in the spell of the experience for at least an hour.

It was hard to believe that the Himalayan-like jumble of ranges and valleys to our south had ever been disturbed by human hands.

Behind us, just outside the park's north border, however, it was a totally different scene: In the darkening dusk of the valley blue and orange neon signs blinked amid the streetlamps and traffic in Gardiner; clusters of spotlights and headlights of ore movers scarred the peace of the mountain bearing the gold mine of Jardine. And long rows of electric glows defined the new trailer courts of that abomination misnamed the Royal Teton Ranch.

CUT was the acronym for a very unusual California transplant known as the Church Universal and Triumphant. The wealthy New Age religious cult had purchased in 1981 the former twelve-thousand-acre Forbes Ranch and renamed it the Royal Teton Ranch. CUT's newest world headquarters shared five miles of border with the park. It was a classic example of the new and the old not mixing well.

For many of the six hundred Gardiner residents, life was basically hunting, fishing, and working for the park or the three concessionaires. Peace and quiet was what most people in Gardiner and the Paradise Valley liked waking up to more than anything. For the six hundred CUT disciples, however, who lived year-round on the Royal Teton Ranch, life was strangely regimented: very long days spent in the Aquarian Age commune's farm, prefab offices, construction crews, and food processing plant, followed by hours of chanting at night.

Their leader, Elizabeth Clare Prophet, or "Guru Ma," as her disciples fondly called her, was a middle-aged brunette woman who claimed in her writings and in interviews to be the messenger for so-called "ascended masters" who included Jesus, Moses, Buddha, the Virgin Mary, Confucius, and even Hercules and Athena. She herself had supposedly been in earlier lives the repentant prostitute Mary Magdalene and the magician Merlin, among others. I had seen her on television, wearing her hugely gemmed rings, sheathed in angelically white flowing dresses, sitting in her high-backed chair

148

before her rapt audience, her heavily made-up eyelids shut, her open palm extended toward her faithful, while she let the ascended masters speak their dire prophecies and warnings through her lips. Her followers—of every age and usually well educated—struck me as believing deeply everything she ever said, even as her words struck the rest of us as outlandishly pessimistic.

The CUT members had chosen one of the most magnificent settings in the world as the place to preach their message of doom. Even now they were busily constructing enormous bomb shelters in the shadow of Electric Peak. They believed that nuclear war with Russia was very likely soon, and they were preparing to be the survivors of the new world that would result. Something had told them the Paradise Valley was the Promised Land; that when the missiles did come, the valley would become the new world's bread-basket. But how could that happen when they were raping the valley with their bulldozers and scrapers?

To the locals—who were convinced the CUT people were brainwashed and satanic—it was as if Jim Jones and his poisoned cultists had been resurrected on their doorsteps. A Hollywood scriptwriter couldn't have put two more opposite types of people side by side in such a remote and spectacular setting.

The accusations that flew back and forth would have made a tabloid reporter dizzy. And while the life-styles of the cult members made for a lot of interesting talk around the dinner tables in the park rangers' homes—members were said to follow a macrobiotic diet and to have sex with their spouses no more than twice a week, with lots of chanting before and after—it was the cult commune's damage to the ecology that concerned us in the park's administration.

In the seven years since CUT had sold its 218-acre "Camelot" in the Santa Monica Mountains near Malibu and moved to its predestined "Place of Great Encounters" in the Paradise Valley, cult members had constructed a community of trailers and roads that was threatening to rival Gardiner in population and impact.

Dirt was flying where before only deer and hunters had trod. The addition of hundreds of people filled with the building impulses of ants was changing the valley with a speed that was heartbreaking.

In only four years what had been empty ranchland, easily crossed by the herds of elk and antelope that migrated out of the park each winter, had become unsightly trailer courts, miles of gravel roads, constant exhaust smoke, the dust of busy earthmovers and cement trucks, a deepening gravel quarry, and a new food processing plant that handled almost 200,000 pounds of carrots alone each summer from the also expanding acreage of the irrigated truck farm. And that was just the beginning.

In CUT's master plans for the future were retirement housing projects, a bigger university, more offices, and heaven knew what else.

Almost a year and a half ago CUT had drilled into an aquifer that fed the La Duke Hot Spring on their property. Though they were perfectly within their rights to do so, since they had acquired the one-hundred-year-old rights to the spring when they purchased the ranch, the Yellowstone administration had complained loudly for fear that the plans to draw the water from the aquifer to possibly heat a spa and several buildings would destroy the thermal plumbing that made Yellowstone's geysers and hot pools so special.

There was too much unknown about the geothermal systems of the Yellowstone area to risk the chance that the La Duke Spring was connected to the park's own thermal features. It may have seemed an overreaction to think that CUT's tampering with the La Duke aquifer could harm Mammoth Hot Springs or Old Faithful, but the history of geothermal development in other parts of the world gave cause for concern.

The natural "plumbing" of hydrothermal systems everywhere has proven to be very susceptible to the tinkering of man and his drilling rigs. Even the most seemingly insignificant of leaks by drill holes has proven again and again to destroy once lively geyser fields. From New Zealand to Europe to Nevada—which was once the second-largest thermal area in North America—drilling has destroyed the largest geyser basins. The danger for Yellowstone was too great to be ignored.

The demise of Old Faithful and the ten thousand other geothermal delights spitting and sputtering and bubbling away each day inside the park was unthinkable. Fortunately, CUT had agreed to cap its well and allow the U.S. Geological Survey to determine if there was any relationship between its hot spring and those in the park.

I looked down from Electric Peak on the blue glows of the recently installed security lights and streetlamps at the CUT headquarters and at their trailer courts and felt sure that those artificial lights would be multiplied many times over. If history was any lesson, they would eventually, inevitably, blanket most of the valley.

Already CUT had purchased two other ranches in the valley—only twelve and fourteen miles north of the old Forbes property. They were to be Camelot's newest suburbs, Guru Ma's latest gift to the world whose end she kept prophesying. Divided into 171 parcels of twenty acres or more, and sold to outside investors (who then further subdivided the land) for prices ranging from $13,000 to $50,000, the mostly open, sage-covered ranchland and the planned four-thousand-acre community of Glastonbury—"everybody's favorite neighborhood just waiting to happen"—had for the past five years been the scene of a lot of construction activity. Work crews and landowners had installed roads, bridges, power lines, homes, septic tanks, water wells, and all the other basic services that came with instant suburbias.

Also in the works was "another Glastonbury lifestyle" called the Golden Age Village, a huge mobile home park for retirees—"for students of the Ascended Masters, it's a place to have a crack at really making those things they've only dreamed about happen."

Along with all the housing and agricultural developments, CUT had other projects that affected the park directly: Along half of the five-mile-long border they shared with the park they had constructed a fence that hindered the migration of the elk to their wintering ranges in the valley. And in the gorgeous Mol Heron Creek drainage, a prime grizzly area, each summer they held an outdoor conference that attracted thousands of their disciples from around the world.

The CUT frenzy of activity was in preparation for the financial market collapses, wars, and famines that their guru warned were approaching. Enormous and very elaborate bomb shelters were being dug, and tons of vegetables were being dehydrated for long storage.

151

CUT was but one of many outside threats to the integrity and health of the park. Threats like oil exploration, logging, road building, vacation home construction, and four-wheeling in the lands that adjoined the park; the ever larger, more powerful, and noisier motor homes crowding the park's own roads; the creeping boundaries and commercialism of the nearby tourist communities of Jackson, West Yellowstone, Gardiner, Silver Gate, Cooke City, and Cody; geothermal energy exploration near the Idaho border; a new gold mine opening near Gardiner and one planned for Cooke City; pressures from special interest groups representing hunters, kayakers, snowmobilers, mountain bicyclists, hang glider users, and four-wheel-drive vehicle enthusiasts to let their people ply their skills in the park's wilderness; and such silent dangers as acid rain, the effects of which were still largely unresearched in the West's mountain areas.

Because of the growing affluence of the world's other nations and the accessibility of jet transportation, there was the very real possibility that the present 2.5 million visitors a year would be small in comparison to future crowds. How were a possible ten million visitors going to be housed, fed, and serviced?

Firmer and more encompassing long-range plans were needed—quickly. The local and national governments, the public, the national forest and Yellowstone administrators, the environmentalists, the chambers of commerce, the scientists, and the game and fish agencies needed to begin cooperating more if Yellowstone was to stay intact.

An area that—as the CUT literature described it—was "a living cathedral with walls of uncut rock, spires of lofty pines, grassy floor softer than carpet, and unlimited vaulted ceiling of the sky" was almost certainly doomed to become part of civilization's noises and scars. Would Yellowstone be next?

At the base of Electric Peak's summit, we snapped ourselves back into our ski bindings, then wasted little time in getting down the mountain. It was dark, and the temperature had taken a sharp drop into numbers we didn't even want to guess at. And we knew that it would be getting a lot colder before we reached the truck, which was at least a couple of hours away.

As we zigzagged down to the valley, the coldness stinging my cheeks imbued me with energy.

A fat yellow moon rose in the east. I could see my breath in the moonlight. As the stars filled the sky, I knew why people believed in miracles.

15

The first time I saw a wolf in the wild I was in the arctic region of Alaska, fording the rugged Koyukuk River.

I stood very still, as if the freezing water rushing around my ankles had iced the blood in my veins.

At first I thought it had detected me, for it was moving away across a large open area on the other side of the river. But then as I watched more I realized that it was busily hunting, and that in all likelihood it had not heard me above the noise of the river, nor smelled me, since I was downwind.

I watched entranced as it trotted tirelessly over the spongy ground of that high plateau. There were in its weavings through the grassy tussocks the thoroughness of a hunter and the joy of a child at play.

At times it seemed intent upon finding something to eat. But then it would surprise me by dashing at a grass stalk and giving it playful light nips and swats.

Finally, it topped a slight ridge and dropped from sight.

I had been very lucky to see a wolf running free. Since the end of the last century wolves have become one of nature's rarer creatures in North America, for which man has to take a lot of the blame.

In 1927, the superintendent of Yellowstone wrote in his report for February: "Wolf signs have been rarely seen in the Park this winter and we have every reason to consider there are only a very few in the entire park area."

In the very next year he wrote: "There have been no wolf signs reported this year."

Apparently the trapping by the park rangers of two wolf pups in October 1926 had brought to a close one of the saddest chapters in Yellowstone's history—the extermination of the entire wolf population in the name of "predator control." Since 1914, the year Congress passed an act to exterminate wolves on all public lands (including national parks), the park's administration had worked with relentless thoroughness for the demise of every wolf inside the park's boundaries. Using traps, strychnine-laced baits, guns, and even clubs, government-paid "wolfers" had wiped out the beautiful creature, which up to that point had survived for probably ten thousand years in the park's rugged paradise.

Nor were wolves the only victims of such madness. So too were such predator "vermin" as the wolverine, mountain lion, coyote, bobcat, and lynx. Over 1,300 of the park's coyotes died alongside the wolves, as did many of the cats. By the advent of the Great Depression, there weren't many such "bad" animals left in the park.

Predator control had been sweeping the West since the first stockmen showed up on the prairie. Wool growers and cattlemen had demanded the extermination of those animals that might attack their livestock. For the frontier of America to be tamed enough for raising livestock, the wolf had to go.

Thus from a range that had once covered most of North America, the wolf was to be driven into hiding in just a few isolated spots in Montana, northern Minnesota, and Yellowstone Park— less than 1 percent of the territory the animal had originally occupied when America was settled.

And Yellowstone was to prove no refuge either. The park's administration, at the prodding of other departments in the federal government, eventually declared war too on its population of *Canis lupus*.

No one will ever know just how many wolves died in the whole of the lower forty-eight states during the wolf killings, but it had to have been a staggering number. From 1885 to around 1913, for example, there were an estimated eighty-one thousand wolves killed in Montana alone.

The campaign to kill the wolf was carried out with such emotion and relentlessness that at times it would seem to have been the work of madmen. Very often the wolves were not just killed but actually tortured: There tormentors hanged them, ripped out their jaws, burned them alive, and even cut the tendons in their legs and then set packs of dogs loose to tear them apart alive. There is even a famous Frederic Remington painting in the Buffalo Bill Historical Center in Cody that depicts cowboys on horseback lassoing a wolf around the neck and pulling it in opposite directions.

In modern times came the airplane and the snowmobile, and killings on a huge scale, with such popular outdoor publications as *Field and Stream* glorifying those who hunted the animals from the air. From an airplane, it was possible to shoot hundreds of wolves in a month. Many did.

Caught in the scale of the hatred shown the wolf by society were millions of other animals, such as foxes and ground squirrels and even pets, that were accidentally poisoned or shot.

In Yellowstone the government-sanctioned killings lasted from 1914 until there were no more wolves to be killed. Or, in other words, until those two last pups were trapped near Soda Butte in October 1926. Over 136 wolves were known to have been eliminated within the park's boundary. Six out of ten were pups, including some buried alive in the dens in which they were born.

The cattlemen and sheep ranchers had brought to the edge of extinction part of America's wildlife heritage. If not for the classification of the wolf as an endangered species in 1973, and the resultant federal protection, the entire species would have probably disappeared from everywhere in North America except Alaska and Canada, where cattle-raising had never become a dominant industry.

With the coming of my fourth year in Yellowstone, the cry of the wolf was still missing from the park.

But there was a glimmer of hope. Many were talking of reintroducing the wolf into Yellowstone. Indeed there was more than just talk: There was a very concerted effort being waged, with optimistic timetables calling for the wolf to be back as early as 1992.

The Endangered Species Act of 1973 had mandated that the northern Rocky Mountain wolf be restored to parts of the West in a manner that would bring it back from the brink of extinction. As a result a plan was developed by a team of federal and state agencies to maintain for three consecutive years a minimum of ten breeding pairs of wolves in each of three "recovery areas"—central Idaho, northwestern Montana, and the Yellowstone area.

As expected, the cry against the reintroduction of the wolf into its traditional habitat in Yellowstone Park was vociferous from the animal's traditional enemies. The stockmen and wool growers of Idaho, Montana, and Wyoming had been—and still were—understandably worried that the wolves would eventually move outside the Greater Yellowstone area and once again attack their stock.

So loud was their opposition that Wyoming's senators managed in 1987 to thwart a Department of the Interior plan to do an Environmental Impact Statement for wolf introductions into the park.

But much of the distrust toward the wolf that had existed in the public for centuries was disappearing. Few, if any, still thought it was some kind of glinting-eyed devil incarnate out to destroy man and his children. And while some still thought wolves attacked people, more were waking up to the fact that in all of modern history there was not a single verified attack on a human by any wild healthy wolf in North America. The wolf of "Little Red Riding Hood" was plainly no longer so believable.

The surviving wolves in Canada, Minnesota, and Alaska had been scientifically studied and restudied to the point that many of the old arguments against wolves no longer had any validity. While, for example, it was true that wolves did attack livestock, it was now known that they did so with nothing like the frequency the purveyors of antiwolf hysteria had led society to believe.

One of those convinced of the importance of bringing the wolf back to Yellowstone was a wiry naturalist named Norm Bishop.

"I am enthusiastic about having wolves back, because I am enthusiastic about seeing the park become once more a complete ecological system," he explained. "There is only one major piece of the puzzle still missing from Yellowstone, and that is the wolf."

Though he himself had never been lucky enough to see a wolf in the wild, he talked fondly of the time he heard one in Canada's Prince Albert National Park.

"It was a quiet clear night, about the end of August, and I was in a mixed hardwood forest. I was with the park's chief naturalist. We were very quiet and he started to mimic a wolf's howl. He did it very low at first, and when there was no response he howled a second time more loudly. This time from not very far away there came a reply.

"It was a very low howl, not the high pitch of coyotes. I was tickled just to hear that sound the one time, and when he howled again and once more the wolf answered I was really excited."

Norm's was an enthusiasm that he thought the majority of Americans shared. He told of a public opinion poll conducted in Yellowstone in 1985 that had revealed that visitors—by a ratio of six to one—thought the presence of wolves would improve the Yellowstone experience. And he had in the hundreds of other wolf papers and articles in his office in the administration building the results of other scientific polls showing that even in those states bordering the park—Wyoming, Idaho, and Montana—the majority of residents wanted to see the wolf returned.

Clearly the wolf belonged in Yellowstone as much as any other animal in the North American wilderness. But would it stay in that wilderness, or end up leaving to feast on the outside livestock? Nearly every expert believed a place as huge and rich in large animals as Yellowstone and its adjacent wilderness areas are should be more than adequate to satisfy its wolves. Yet no one was foolish enough to think wolves wouldn't leave the park. Wolves love to roam, and as the population grew, so would their need for more territory. Wolf packs, according to Norm, established and maintained territories, but the young wolves would disperse. From a recovered population of 100–150 wolves, fifteen to twenty-five might disperse annually, but would be vulnerable to hunting or trapping. In Minnesota, it had been found that about one in thirty of their 1,200 wild wolves had to be removed annually. So, if Yellowstone had 120 wolves, that would mean four per year might get into trouble with livestock.

Plans were already being formulated to compensate financially those stockmen who suffered losses. Such compensation funds had been available for many years in Canada and Minnesota, set aside out of provincial and state funds. For the Greater Yellowstone area, the environmentalist group called Defenders of Wildlife was building a private compensation fund.

In the Wolf Recovery Plan for Yellowstone there would be three zones for the management of the animals. The wolves used would be translocated from western Canada and put into a core recovery area, called Zone I, where their welfare would take high priority. Around that area would be Zone II, where human activities such as hunting were common and grazing was sometimes permitted. And then at the outermost, where stock grazing was long established, would be Zone III, where any wolves would be subject to control by authorized persons.

But all was still not settled. It seemed that no sooner was one controversy ended than another began. Even as some stockmen were softening their antiwolf stand as a result of the compensation guarantees, other groups like the big game hunters and outfitters were raising their voices. The 120 to 150 wolves that Yellowstone would probably eventually be home to would kill too many of the park's elk and bighorn mountain sheep, they claimed. There wouldn't be as many of those game animals left to migrate to neighboring lands, where they could be hunted each fall.

So it began to seem as if the wolf would be the park's greatest ongoing controversy. And that the only way to solve the matter was to go ahead and proceed with the next step in the great experiment called Yellowstone Park. There was a growing consensus that mankind owed nature something for all the taking we had done from it.

"I think people all over the country are extremely interested

159

in wolf recovery, because there is a natural concern that we are losing wild species at too alarming a rate worldwide," Norm had remarked.

The natural laws of the wilderness work toward diversity. Each part, we realize more every day, has a reason for being, and that reason is important to the survival of many other animals and plants.

It just isn't sensible or possible to have only a predatorless wilderness. To do so would upset too greatly the dynamics built into nature. In the long run it would result in something far more problematic than at present. The land is as one organism, and the parts of it that compete against one another are as useful and needed as those that cooperate. Both predators and prey got along quite fine before man started seeing "problems." If the wolf was actually going to kill off all the mountain sheep or deer or elk, why hadn't it done so in those tens of thousands of years before the wolfers came along?

Everyone—environmentalists, government workers, stock-men, politicians, the public—needs to realize that we can have the wolf as well as everything else. But, first, everyone has to look at the whole picture and not just at their own needs or desires. No one answer is the perfect one in today's world. Compromises on everyone's part are in order. Perhaps the world would be safer for livestock without the wolf's presence, but would it be authentic?

"Wilderness without wild creatures is just not complete," Norm observed.

No, of course not. And the more I thought about it, the more I wanted to leave to my children a truthful picture of nature.

But the debate over the wolf's fate continues.

16

The dark low form might have been mistaken for a mallard or a cormorant as it drifted out of the shadowy reeds of the marsh just past sunrise. But its haunting yodellike call rolled across the bay and prodded me to reach for my binoculars.

I focused my lens on the white-checkered black body that made the loon so unique.

The loon was an uncommon sight in Yellowstone in August; only fifteen pairs were thought to be nesting in the park at the time. I had heard their lonesome cries several times before over the summer, but this was the first one I'd seen.

I had been lazing beside the tiller of my newest love, the *Makoa Brooke*, when the loon appeared. The twenty-three-foot-long sailing sloop had been mine since June, and I'd anchored it overnight in this quiet hidden bay.

From the open cabin door still came some faint odors of a pan-fried trout I had had for breakfast. The fish had struck at the first lure I'd cast over the starboard side.

A morning like this was the sort that tempted a man to forsake forever his ambitions. It wasn't often that I got to be off on my own for more than a day. When I'd set sail yesterday morning from the lake's marina sixteen miles to the northwest, the water had been sparkling, the distant mountains purple and majestic, and I hadn't been able to get enough of the cold spray that splashed onto me from the sloop's sleek white fiberglass hull. Even the mainsail's straining sounds had had me singing along. Everything about the trip had been so pure, so peaceful, so *perfect*! But for the glint of

a couple of canoes along the forest wall of the lake's western shoreline, I might have thought I was the only person lucky enough to
be out on the lake.

Now that I had a sailboat I put it to use when at all possible.
Normally I took along Tana and the children. But not this time.
This time I wanted no distractions. At such a high altitude—over
7,700 feet—the summers of the lake were fleeting ones, and I
wanted this one more chance to soak in the lake's charms fully.

I had decided not even to go ashore on this trip. Thus I had
stowed aboard lots of reading material, some cassettes of guitar and
flute music, my classical guitar which I never seemed to get around
to playing, and plenty of hunter's sausage and cheese. I was out to
clear my head and recharge my spirit.

I stretched like a lazy cat and put aside the binoculars. Here
and there shafts of sunlight were breaking through the trees on The
Promontory at my back, crowning the ripples in the bay. The forest
was resplendent with animal sounds, the air filled with pine perfume. Everything promised another glowing day.

But today I had to return to the "real" world to meet with
some visiting dignitaries this afternoon. And if I was to get back
to the marina on time, I would have to leave within the hour. At
least, I had a five-hour sail ahead of me.

I scrambled barefoot over the cool smooth gunwale to the bow's
point. There I stood, poised to take a dive, when a large trout just
below caused me to bend down for a closer look. So perfectly clear
was the water that even though it was probably fifty feet to the
bottom I could see the fish's dark spots and large fins plainly. It
was as though between us was a magnifying glass of incredible
proportions.

Once on an earlier sailing trip I had donned a snorkel and
tried exploring that part of the Yellowstone wilderness. But it had
been so cold down there I hadn't dared stay for more than a few
minutes.

The world of the fish is as much a part of the park as that of
the elk, or the moose, or the bear, but because it is not as visible
or as accessible as that of the mammals, it is a world virtually
unknown to those park visitors who aren't avid fishermen. The

same is undoubtedly true for the worlds of the birds and the insects. Few visitors to Yellowstone ever ask, for example, where they might go to see the rare Yellowstone checkerspot, a dark orange checkered butterfly that occurs in small isolated colonies in some of the moister meadows.

The birds, fish, and insects are as good as invisible to most visitors, though their wilderness is thousands of times larger and more diverse than that of the mammals. A lot of people know Yellowstone is home to seven native species of hoofed animals, two kinds of bears, ten rodent species, badgers, mountain lions, and coyotes. But I wonder if anyone other than the scientists and a few birdwatchers and fishermen know that in the park there are over 225 bird species and there were once eleven kinds of native fish. Or that there are insects other than the mosquito?

It is a good assumption that *everyone* knows the mosquito. But how about the fact that there are forty different kinds of that one insect alone inside the park's ecosystem? Or that there are also eighty types of bees, two hundred kinds of butterflies, two thousand moth species, and just as many kinds of beetles? Why, even the lowly cranefly comes in sixty different forms.

The larger mammal species have dominated everyone's attention since the beginning of the park. They, the grand scenery, and the geysers are what attracts most visitors. And, of course, the more visitors who come each year, the more money the park is likely to be able to get out of Washington. So it is natural that the larger animals like the moose and the elk should become the stars in the great Yellowstone "show." And that everything is done to keep them visible and in the minds of the visitors.

The region's invertebrates and smaller vertebrates have been largely unknown and grossly neglected. But the present emphasis on allowing nature to take its own course without our purposefully propagating one species over another is allowing us to see just how every species in the park's animal world is crucial to the park's overall health—that there is no good or bad animal there.

For instance, it is now recognized that the pine beetles, which were once considered undesirable and an enemy of the forest because they killed the pines and made the forests "ugly," are actually vitally important. By destroying trees they allow more sunlight and water to reach the forest floor, which in turn allows a far lusher undergrowth, which in turn attracts and supports more deer and elk, which in turn means more calves and does being born, which in turn means more prey and carrion for the bears and coyotes, which in turn increases the numbers of those animals, which in turn provides even more thrills for the visitors.

It seems incredible that something as lowly as the pine beetle can actually be important to the gigantic grizzly. But then to nature it is just, well, natural.

Over the decades many had been critical of Yellowstone's policies regarding its large mammals: If the bison and the elk and the bears weren't too numerous then they were probably about to disappear. But overlooked in all the bickering about the celebrities of the park were the tremendous success stories of the smaller animals. The cutthroat trout beneath my gaze was one of the best examples of how healthy and vibrant Yellowstone really is overall.

Yellowstone Lake, because of its huge size—87,450 acres and an average of 139 feet deep—was used extensively for over half a century starting in 1899 as the primary cutthroat fish hatchery for the nation. More than 818 million cutthroat eggs and 48 million adult trout were harvested from the lake by the hatchery operations and commercial and sport fishing in that time. Such pressure was put on the lake's historically rich fish population that by 1968 the number of fish being caught by sport fishermen reached a record low, even though there had been a daily limit of three per fisherman since around 1960.

But then starting in 1969 the trout were recognized as wildlife too: The fish trapping and shipments were stopped; the trout were left to reproduce as they wished and only in natural settings; and though fishing was still allowed, only those cutthroat under thirteen inches could be kept. As a result the larger and stronger fish were at last able to survive in decent numbers and so reproduce more than ever.

Now the lake has the largest inland cutthroat trout population in the world, and the fishing in the lake is nearly back to the fabulous levels of the previous century. The whole park's ecosystem is benefiting from the comeback of the trout: birds like the eagle, pelican, osprey, ouzel, and kingfisher that feed upon the fish, as well as the bears, otters, and fishermen. It is estimated the birds are taking over 200,000 pounds of cutthroat from the lake each year, with the fishermen harvesting an additional fifty tons and the bears not far behind. (Some grizzlies have been seen taking an average of one hundred trout a day for ten straight days at some of the spawning runs.)

I didn't get to spend nearly as much time with the small animals of the park as I would have liked. In fact very few of the rangers did, because of their heavy workloads. A handful, however, were lucky enough to have that part of the Yellowstone world as their work. One in particular was a forty-year-old wiry New Englander of Irish descent named Terry McEneaney. His job description was "resource management biologist," but it would have been more appropriate to have called him the "Bird Man." He loved to study birds. He always had. As a boy in New Hampshire he had watched birds while his classmates played their games and sports. He never grew tired of their color and song. In time he would believe there was a unique harmony that existed between people and birds.

While other rangers' offices were filled with paperwork and family photos, McEneaney's resembled a bird museum. He had once salvaged over eight hundred stuffed birds from an old estate in Maine, and those he had hauled along to Yellowstone gave his workplace the air of a medicine man's spell room.

"There is so much discovery to a bird," he once said. "No matter what bird you study, you always discover something new. I look for all the aspects of their lives—habitat, food, roosting places—not just one particular thing. And I would say that there is still so much to learn about birds that we haven't even seen the whole tip of the iceberg."

He worked on his bird studies for many years in remote parts of the American West, as well as in Greenland and Mexico. When the chance to work with Yellowstone birds came along a couple years back he had eagerly taken it, because it was still a relatively undiscovered region as far as birds were concerned.

Wrote McEneaney in a recent book titled *Birds of Yellowstone:*

"There are certainly other places on earth where birds are more abundant and concentrated, or where a greater diversity of birds can be observed. But where else can you watch an Osprey carrying a fish in its talons fly past a spectacular waterfall, or a Common Raven feeding on a bison carcass as a geyser erupts? Or where can you hear the simultaneous bugling of an elk, hooting of a Great Horned Owl, howling of a coyote, calling of a flock of Sandhill Cranes, and trumpeting of Trumpeter Swans in a dissonant but unforgettable wilderness concerto? Watching birds in Yellowstone is like going to a multi-media show."

Yellowstone might well be the greatest playground left in the lower forty-eight states for wildlife. They—the animals of every size and kind—can be themselves completely, unhindered by man or his buildings. And we—the people—are only the richer for observing them as McEneaney did: seeing an eagle plunge into the rapid water, grab on to a huge trout beneath the surface, then float away down the river to a sandbar with the fish because it was too heavy to fly away with. Now *that* is birdwatching.

I stood back up and looked around me. It was a good thing we had finally come to our senses and realized that attempts to make the park "better" usually did anything but that. Maybe some changes—such as the introduction of trout into "barren" lakes—were indeed better for the visitors, but what did that do to the delicate balance of the park's ecology? Nature had done quite well before man came along. Anytime we sought to alter it we needed to be extremely careful that we weren't sacrificing life-forms that had every right to be there.

Every year hundreds of the world's smaller animal species vanish through man's meddling. It is estimated that every week an average of twenty plant and animal species disappear forever. Many of the insect and fish species in other parts of the world had gone so quickly that they hadn't even been named and classified.

In Yellowstone it had been found that animal life existed virtually everywhere—from the pikas in their burrows on top of the coldest peaks to the flies, larvae, and spiders at the edges of the hottest thermal pools. There actually was no such thing as a barren spot inside the park.

It was heartening to know that the eagle, the bison, the grizzly, the trumpeter swan, and the peregrine falcon—once all but gone —were now holding steady or even coming back strongly in the park. But there still was no room for gloating, because for every one of those larger species that were saved there were smaller ones that became history due to ignorance or the opinion that they didn't matter as much.

We *had* to realize that the park was not in existence merely to provide for the needs of man, but that even more important it was there for the needs of nature. Someday it might be the last hope for many of this country's wild creatures. If a species of plant or animal couldn't survive in Yellowstone, then chances were good it couldn't out there in man's world either—at least not free and wild.

Yet several of the animal and plant species that had been abundant in the park in 1872 were no longer here or were not as abundant: among them the wolf, the white-tailed deer, the beaver, the lynx, the cougar, and the Montana grayling.

What was important now was to offer Yellowstone the chance to recover more of its vitality. And that would mean admitting the park needed lots of firm protection.

I couldn't figure out how some people and organizations could be so blind to the true value of the park as to try to turn it into a playground. The tranquility and wildness of this bay would have been destroyed forever, for example, if boat owners and those who represented the motorboating industry had had their way several years ago.

It was not enough that boat motors large enough to propel a house and spewing all sorts of noise, fuel, and fumes had been allowed on one of the world's most beautiful and fragile high-altitude lakes. No, then they had demanded that those incredibly destructive machines be allowed to go anywhere their owners wanted. The fact that such intrusions into the lake's wilder areas were visibly polluting the waters, wrecking any semblance of peace, chasing the birds away from their habitats, and leaving behind ugly trails of litter seemed not at all important. Fortunately the Park Service was able to have the extreme lower parts of the lake's three arms declared off-limits to motors. It was admittedly a small victory to the rangers, but an incalculable one to the wildlife and to those who wanted to experience a water wilderness.

Those who would have the park opened completely to such blatant destroyers of the environment as snowmobiles, trail bikes, motorboats, and four-wheel vehicles have to be made to realize that the animals and plants already in place have rights, too.

How utterly arrogant of some not to think that other creatures are just as important as they; or not to realize that just as they want to zip about through the park there are others who simply want to be at peace with the environment and experience it on the animals' level.

The pressures by special interest groups to have the park's backcountry opened to their activities will likely continue to be one of Yellowstone's biggest battles for a long, long time. And not all of those activities—especially kayaking, mountain bicycling, and hang gliding—seem at first glance to be very harmful. But they are. All bring more stress to the animals and affect their environments. All bring still larger numbers of people into conflicts with animals that would not otherwise occur.

For every kayaker who would be quiet and would limit his or her physical impact to where they put in and then exit from the river, there are simply too many others who would stop to tramp through previously safe and incalculably valuable wildlife nesting spots, to camp illegally, and to scramble with much ensuing damage over beautiful thermal areas. It is, quite simply, too great a risk even to consider.

Yet more and more there are those who are willing to put their hunger for thrills above the interests of the park's ecology. Kayakers make dashes down the rivers despite the threat of fines and jail. Perhaps the greatest irony of all is that when asked *why* they have chosen to disregard the rules of the park, they usually state that the rivers of Yellowstone had called to them because they were the last ones left in America that *weren't* crowded and littered and tamed.

Could anyone truly believe that the heaven that was the Hayden Valley would not be ruined by the sight of pink- and purple- and yellow-garbed kayakers and rafters suddenly cutting through the valley's peaceful bottom, their appearance sending the Yellowstone River's waterfowl and moose scattering in terror? It seems to me that our allowing all manner of boats on Yellowstone's lakes for the past century was compromise enough for the boat enthusiasts.

We have a long way to go to understand exactly how this park—and world—work, I thought, as I sat back down beside the tiller and watched the sail slowly fill. A lot more of the little animals and maybe even a few of the bigger ones will disappear before we get it right, but at least we have to keep trying our best. We need places like Yellowstone so much right now. And those in the future will be needing them even more.

And I wasn't about to be the one to deny them the chance to see just how wonderfully beautiful this old world of ours had once been.

17

I slid shut the side door of the van and turned to find Trevor and Brooke already slipping into their little backpacks. Before I could get my own heavy pack onto my back, they were off and away down the trail to the old backcountry ranger cabin where we were going to spend the weekend—our last family camping trip before the season turned cold. Tana and I nearly had to run to catch up with them.

The Saturday afternoon was filled with sunshine, and the fall wildflowers were at their most splendid. The crazily angled rocks seemed alive with all sorts of furry and feathered small wildlife searching for food. They seemed to know that in only a matter of weeks this same sunny ground would be covered with snow.

At a sharp bend on the side of a hill, we came upon some very short, finely stemmed herbs.

"Trevor, Brooke! Come with me," Tana said.

They followed their mother closely as she led them off the trail and into the small clearing with the yampahs. They watched intently as she knelt beside a plant barely as high as the middle of her calf.

"See these?" she asked, holding the plant aloft so that its three tubular-shaped roots were clearly visible.

"What are those?" Trevor wondered.

"Candy!" she answered with a straight face.

Both Trevor and Brooke shot me looks that said Mom had lost her senses.

"Well, maybe they're not candy to us," I offered. "But they

are to the grizzly bears. They'll spend all day digging up a field like this to get at those little roots. How about a taste?"

To my surprise they wanted to very much. I took out my pocketknife and lightly scraped away the wrinkled brown skin from one of the roots. When all that was showing was their white meat, they bore a resemblance to a miniature parsnip. I handed one root to Brooke. She crunched down on it and her eyes lit up.

"Well, what do you think?" Tana wondered.

"I think it tastes like a carrot!"

I gave Trevor another of the roots. His eyes grew even larger as he ate away, partly because it was good tasting but mostly, I was sure, to outdo his sister's theatrics.

The area was excellent moose country, and I hoped we might see one. Sometimes when I was hiking if I saw one and sat or stood perfectly clear they would pass close by. It was not at all unusual for the younger ones to graze around me almost as if I had changed into a tree. Their innocence was so much like that of human children.

But I was always very careful about approaching the wildlife, to remember that I was in *their* home, and needed to respect their rights to privacy and space. In Yellowstone it was illegal to approach wildlife any closer than twenty-five yards—one hundred yards in the case of bears. I had instructed the rangers to enforce strictly the rule about approaching wildlife, but I knew it was broken many times each day by visitors where there was no ranger around to enforce it.

It was understandable that people would want to get a close look at the animals. There is, after all, something mysterious about these creatures. But too many people forget that the animals *are* wild, and potentially very dangerous. A bison, for example, can weigh a ton and yet sprint at thirty miles per hour—three times as fast as a human can run. If spooked, bison often charge blindly forward, simply knocking aside anything, including humans, in their path. Each year we had our share of visitors gored or trampled by the bison, despite the warnings we handed out that bison were wild, unpredictable, and dangerous.

If we had continued to the end of the trail, some several hours away, it would have led us to the park's border, near the extreme northeast corner. Most of its dozen or so miles passed through a broad, lush valley. The high and sweeping grassy plateau to the west of the valley was an excellent area for spotting many of the park's larger game animals, and in the bottom of the valley the deep, dark, and wide Slough Creek was reputed to be one of America's blue-ribbon trout streams.

The cabin we were going to was some two miles from where we had parked the van, and it sat on the thickly forested east slope of the valley, looking out over the beautiful plateau's wide rolling shoulder and the deep green of the valley bottom.

The late summer wildflowers were still at their height. Acres upon acres of intense colors bordered the creek's path.

Yellowstone was a wildflower paradise. To hike upward toward the sky with such flowered carpets at one's feet was to approach heaven. To me, a wildflower was quite simply nature at its finest.

It was in the spring and early summer when the wildflowers burst forth to herald the land's rebirth that the park was at its most beautiful, a universe of wildflower tapestries.

Most people came to the park to see its peaks and geysers and animals: Too few bothered to leave their vehicles to search out the colorfully named and colorfully petaled prairie smokes, shooting stars, fringed gentian, columbine, kinnikinick, lady's-tresses, elephantheads, fairyslippers, mountain lovers, steersheads, and bleeding hearts.

Yellowstone has one of the greatest concentrations of mountain wildflowers in the world. Yet if I asked most visitors if they'd seen any purple-cloaked monkshoods in the canyons, or red skyrocket gilias in the sage fields, or yellow monkeyflowers along the stream banks, they might think I was making fun of them.

Because of rapid land development, many of these same wildflowers were being obliterated elsewhere in America. Some, like the tiny mountain orchids, were so fragile that it was likely they would be gone before many more decades passed. And parks like Yellowstone might not only be the last wild home for many of the animals, but also for many of the flowers.

172

* * *

At the cabin there was work to be done: the thick shutters on the windows to be unlocked and opened, the bunk beds to be made, the cookstove to be stuffed with wood, and pails to be filled from a small spring in the woods behind the cabin. As Brooke and Tana handled the water chores, Trevor and I made a quick inspection of the entire cabin to see just what shape it was in. These back-country cabins were homes for the rangers on summer horse and foot patrols and winter ski patrols. There were forty-one of them in the park, spread out along 1,200 miles of trails and over three hundred miles of boundary.

I was happy to see that the last occupant of our cabin had left four kitchen matches on the flat black top of the potbellied stove and inside it a pile of dry kindling and crumpled wax paper. It upset me to go into a cabin and find the previous user had left it messy or—worse—with no matches and kindling around the stove.

"Every second is precious when you are freezing," I explained somberly to Trevor. "With no way to see in the dark, it is essential—a matter of life and death—that a person be able to feel for the matches and start a fire quickly."

I walked across the rough pine plank floor past the white-painted table and its old wooden chairs to a tall gray metal cabinet. It was unlocked, and on its deep shelves were rows of canned food and boxes of instant potatoes and pancake mix. Along with wool blankets for the beds and split wood for the stoves, every cabin was stocked with lots of nonperishable foods for possible emergencies. There had to be a goodly amount of food in the cabinet: A ranger could be snowbound for weeks.

I had noticed fresh scratches and gouges in the thick shutters on the cabin's windows and on the front door. From their height above the ground they had obviously been made by some very frustrated bears that hadn't made it into the cabin—yet.

I wasn't sure how it was that bears knew there were goodies inside a cabin when everything was in cans or boxes and closed up tighter than money in a bank vault, but they did. I had seen the inside of more than one secured backcountry cabin after a bear had somehow forced its way inside, and the sight had been anything but pretty. There was rarely a single thing left intact. Fortunately, however, they seldom did make it inside a cabin.

On one of the food pantry's shelves was a small hardcover notebook, the cabin's log book. I took it over to the table to read while Trevor sat in my lap. On the lined pages were the thoughts and observations of the rangers who had recently visited or stayed at the cabin. Some notations were funny, some philosophical, some filled with the thrill of being amid so much natural beauty.

The voices of Tana and Brooke made me look up. Trevor jumped down and ran off to greet his mother and sister, who set their pails of water down beside the huge cast-iron-and-ceramic Monarch cookstove.

"What's up?" I asked.

"Frogs!" Brooke shouted excitedly.

"Frogs?"

"They're everywhere in the water—can we get some?" she pleaded.

Trevor for once was completely in agreement with his sister. He squeezed my hand as hard as he could. I looked at Tana and saw from the expression in her eyes that she had tried to explain to Brooke that none of the animals, even the frogs, should be taken from their homes.

"Don't you think they would be happier if we left them with their friends?" I asked.

The little ones' faces dropped, and I felt my heart melt.

I surrendered to their wish but not before striking a compromise that I thought would satisfy all, including the frogs. I would catch a frog or two for them and let them hold them, but they would have to set the frogs free after a few minutes.

I followed them across a small clearing of wild strawberry plants into the lodgepoles, then over a faint path that hugged a tiny steep trickle thick with moss.

After a few minutes we came to a small pool scarcely larger than the seat of a chair. It was from the lilliputian waterfall that dropped from it to an even smaller pool that they had filled their pails. Sure enough, there in the two pools were some light brown frogs barely an inch long. They seemed not the least bit concerned about the sudden appearance of our giant figures and sat about the pool like webbed lords.

Trevor and Brooke watched with hushed anticipation as I crept on hands and knees toward what I thought would be a quick capture. With a speed that I imagined was that of a lightning bolt I snatched at the frog.

It eluded my grasp as easily as if my fingers had been made of concrete. So did the next one and the next one. In seconds that bunch of half-asleep frogs was swimming hither and thither with all the speed of world-class swimmers. And behind me was an awful lot of laughing.

At last I managed to pin one against the side of the pool. Both Trevor and Brooke took turns cupping the frog in their hands, marveling at the smoothness of its flesh and the way its yellowish sides rapidly expanded and contracted from its breathing. Watching them I felt a tug of envy. Why couldn't that same sense of almost innocent wonderment stay alive in us all of our lives?

We released the frog back to the pool and returned to the cabin. From there Brooke and Trevor ran off to play on a high bald rock hill that poked above the valley's meadow floor. Brooke liked to call it one of her "thinking rocks."

"I think I'll go along and keep an eye on them," Tana said.

"That isn't a bad idea. Brooke likes to get a little too close for my comfort to the edge of some of the cliffs."

I watched the children and Tana descend into the valley. Their small bodies parted the waist-high grasses as if they were wading through surf. In the lemon-yellow afternoon light the children's blond heads reminded me of wildflowers.

Tana would not only watch them, I knew, but would also be their teacher. She is the family expert when it comes to wildflowers and plant identification. Her experience as a biologist and park naturalist in Crater Lake and at Great Falls Park near Washington, D.C., and as an environmental education instructor in Yosemite, made her the perfect teacher. She was a naturalist during the summer season at Yellowstone, and one of her favorite activities was to go on flower walks with the visitors. The visitors loved them, and from their excitement Tana grew more excited. She wanted to go back to school, perhaps to Montana State University in Bozeman, and get a teaching certificate. I wanted her to; I knew she would be a true blessing to any young student.

When my family became too small to see anymore, I went inside to get a pair of binoculars. They were hanging from a nail on the back wall, right above a large metal trash can with a note on it that said: *Mountain Lion Study winter supplies—Do not disturb.*

On the way back to the door I spotted the log book where I had left it on the tabletop. I picked it up and carried it out with me.

I made myself comfortable on a flat stone beneath a large old Douglas fir and held the binoculars to my eyes. Scanning the meadow below I saw that the children had been distracted by the creek. They seemed to be chasing grasshoppers and tossing them into the creek—probably much to the delight of the creek's finned residents.

Sweeping the view in the lens to the northeast I focused on a jagged row of purple peaks. They belonged to the Beartooth Mountains. The highest of the peaks did indeed resemble something that would be in the jaws of a monstrous grizzly.

I put the binoculars down and leaned backward against the fir tree's reddish brown trunk. The ridges of its thick, deeply furrowed bark dug into my spine. At times like this I felt very much in touch with God.

I reached for the log book and idled through its pages. Every so often a witty phrase or wry observation caught my attention. That handful of men and women who were the backcountry rangers and who got to call such scenery their "office" or "shop" had to be some of the luckiest people in this world. Certainly their job was to me one of the most romantic.

Yellowstone's history is rich with stories about its backcountry rangers and their run-ins with everything from bears to poachers. They have become over the years as much a part of the American romance as the cowboy and the mountain man. It was nice to know that in Yellowstone the horse-mounted backcountry ranger would have a useful place for a long time yet. The park is simply too large, too rugged, and has too few roads to allow for any other kind of effective patrol of its backcountry. Yes, roads could be built into the forests and up to the high-country meadows and ridges, and more use made of airplanes and helicopters, but that would destroy the wilderness that Yellowstone is all about.

I enjoyed immensely being in the company of the backcountry rangers. Some were loners and eccentric, some idealistic, some bullheaded. But none of them was without lots of good stories. How could they be, when the responsibilities that filled their days were oftentimes the stuff of an adventure book?

One of the backcountry rangers I liked very much, a young man named Mark Marschall, had once described Yellowstone as a "spiritual park." It was, he said, a place of "grand panoramas." When he was out on his patrols in the very mountainous areas to the east and southeast of Yellowstone Lake, which sometimes could last as long as ten days, he couldn't top a mountain ridge or a piece of high ground without looking down from his horse's saddle and seeing memories all around him. No part of the park, it seemed, had been without special lessons and experiences for him in his six years as a Lake District backcountry ranger.

"The more I travel around the country and to other places in the world," the darkly bearded and compactly muscled mountain climber had observed, "the more I can see how there are so few places left that we have kept our hands off. Yellowstone, however, is still a place that is relatively untouched in the backcountry. It is a great thing to know the wildlife are out there surviving on their own. They are either making it or not, and we can watch those processes exactly as nature intended them to happen.

"There is just a spiritual feeling about the wildness of this place. I like to think I'm out there not just protecting the people, but also the integrity of that wildness."

He talked about going from the bullfrogs around his native Ohio to the grizzlies of Yellowstone with the enthusiasm of a boy. I suspect he will have the same excitement in his voice when he turns one hundred.

Dinner was a family favorite—tacos. I had brought along the hamburger and cheese and vegetables. The meat I browned in the cabin's cast-iron skillet on the wood-burning range. As an added treat we nibbled on some yampah roots that Brooke had brought back from the meadows.

Afterward we moved to a clearing at the cabin's side and roasted marshmallows until even the owls had to be getting sleepy. By the time we retired into the cabin, the night air was chilly enough that I could see my breath. Trevor was fast asleep and I carried him in my arms, while Brooke stayed behind just long enough to help her mother douse the fire with a bucket of water.

In the pitch black of the cabin I laid Trevor onto a bottom bunk, then felt the space above my head for the cabin's Coleman gas lantern, which I had hung earlier on one of the roof beams.

I struck a match and lit the silky cocoon-shaped mantle. The fuel-soaked fibers flickered to life, hissed, and cast about me shadows of every shape and size. It was probably a good thing that Trevor was asleep: The dark forms that leaped and loomed with the lantern's unsteady glow could have triggered his imagination.

Gently I slipped Trevor into his pajamas, then tucked the rough wool army blanket around his shoulders. Brooke had already climbed onto the top bunk, and was but a whisper away from her own dreams when I kissed her on the forehead.

For the first time all day I felt tired. But before I went to bed I went to the doors and made sure they were locked. I didn't care to have a bear mistaking Tana and me in our sleeping bags for a sack of potatoes.

Just before I crawled into my bag, I turned the lantern off. There was still enough fuel in the lantern's lines, though, to keep it burning for several more minutes. By the time it went out, I was already asleep.

18

The slight glow of daybreak lit up the room just enough to allow me to see my breath. From the thick way that it hung above my face I knew the day was going to be especially cold.

I slid out of the sleeping bag, crawled quickly to the edge of the cabin's loft, and climbed down the ladder to the ground floor. The clothes I threw on felt as icy as the floorboards they'd been heaped upon all night.

Glancing out the window I saw nothing but white upon white. Our beautiful Indian summer was over.

"Hey! Start the fire down there," a voice yelled from the loft. "It's cold in here."

"Just wait'll you get out of the sleeping bag," I grumbled.

The voice belonged to Stu Coleman, Yellowstone's resource management specialist and newest ranger. Only two weeks before he'd transferred from the Great Smoky Mountains National Park in North Carolina.

"Hey, Sholly, where's that fire?" he prodded.

"Not this morning, Stu. We gotta get going."

His head popped over the edge of the loft.

"You aren't serious, are you? I'm shivering to pieces up here."

As I slipped into a long oiled-canvas coat that hung nearly to the floor—my "outback" coat—I explained: "It's not so much the building of the fire as the waiting for it to burn down and cool off, so that we can lay another."

He gave me a strange look.

Stu was not familiar yet with the Yellowstone backcountry

"etiquette." I doubted he and the other rangers in North Carolina had had to keep the word *survival* uppermost in their minds when they went into the woods there.

"In Yellowstone we lay fire-starting material in the patrol cabin stoves so that they can be started with one match. It's a long-standing tradition. And a requirement."

"Why's that?" he mumbled through the turtleneck he was pulling over his head.

"Because just look how far away we are in this cabin from any other help. And, if you think this is cold, come back in January or February. I have to know that should any of our rangers end up stumbling into here in the middle of a storm, injured or freezing, he or she can get a fire going with just one strike of a match. Believe me, it's a tradition that's saved more than one life over the years."

"I think I want to go back to where they have beaches."

I tossed him his boots. "I'll start some coffee on the gas stove. That'll take the chill off."

While I was breaking the ice on the water bucket, Stu shuffled up like Frankenstein in his rock-hard boots. His pinched look hinted he was wondering if the stinging in his toes would ever stop. I lit a fire on the propane camp stove and put a kettle of the spring water on it.

"I'm gonna get the horses," I said, leaving him to endure his thawing boots on his own.

The view from the door of the cabin froze my breath as much as the chill did. The Yellowstone River meadows were blanketed in a two-inch mantle of snow. They looked as pure and unspoiled as they might have hundreds of centuries before.

It was still snowing, but very lightly now. I grabbed two halters from a nail just inside the cabin door and also some alfalfa cubes, then walked about a quarter mile through the snow to the meadow where I'd picketed our horses.

Crisscrossing the snow were all sorts of animal tracks, from those of mice to that of a moose. Maybe the snow wasn't so bad, I decided. We would be able to see the tracks of any poachers.

I'd come on this hundred-mile-long ride with Stu partly to introduce him to Yellowstone's backcountry rangers, and partly to watch for any of the poachers who normally worked this section of the park's eastern boundary during hunting season.

There were some hunters out there who didn't think twice about sneaking into the park and making off with one of our many trophy-sized animals—including the bighorn sheep, elk, and ol' *Ursus arctos horribilis*, the grizzly bear.

I had as many rangers as possible patrolling the boundary on horseback at this time of the year, but there were never enough. With hundreds of miles of some of the most rugged territory in North America to cover, theirs was a tremendous task.

The snow-flecked horses were happy to see me. I was happy to see them, too. Though I had never heard of any horse in Yellowstone being attacked by a grizzly, there was still the inclination to worry, especially when the horses were tied in the open. I was confident of the horses' ability to defend themselves—they were so powerful and no doubt knew how to use their hooves. But I was even more thankful that grizzly bears learned early on to hunt other kinds of animals.

The horses knew some oat goodies were at hand. I led them to the cabin and along the way rewarded their nudges with some alfalfa cubes.

Back inside the cabin I expected to be greeted by the smell of steaming coffee. Instead, I found Stu trying to figure out how to make coffee. Being an office creature, he was used to electric drip coffee pots.

I went to work to make "ranger coffee." I tossed a handful of ground coffee beans into a pan of boiling water, then removed the pan from the heat, waited a couple of minutes, and added half a cup of cold water to settle the grounds to the pan's bottom.

"Here, drink this and tell me if it isn't the best coffee you've ever had," I said as I poured the black, unsweetened concoction into an ice-cold mug.

He sipped and half-smiled, half-grimaced.

Breakfast was the coffee, canned grapefruit juice, peaches from the cabin's pantry, and some hotcakes. Then we tidied up the cabin and went on our way. We headed south along the river, beneath low-hanging clouds that looked as if they were on fire with the rising sun's light. Except for the croaks of two sandhill cranes and the honking of a small V of Canada geese, it was a world of silence.

We spoke very little, letting the scenery do that for us. This was indeed how America had looked before the European explorers arrived. The wild was still very much in the wilderness in Yellowstone.

Along the eastern shore of Yellowstone Lake we weaved through a mosaic of forest and meadow. In the thick pine forests that went right down to the lake's edge, the branches of the trees along the trail were heavy with snow. It was difficult not to get a face full of it.

The cold settled into my toes, and I wriggled them often. I wondered for probably the one-millionth time if those battery-heated socks I often saw advertised in the back of outdoor magazines really worked. But what would that do for the image of a Yellowstone ranger—patrolling primitive wilderness in *electric* socks?

I halted my horse and waved my hand at Stu. I pointed to some large humanlike prints crossing the trail. They were at least six inches across near the toes.

"No doubt a griz," I said to his very big eyes.

"God, those are *big!*"

"Your first grizzly?"

"Are you kidding? Of course! You can bet we didn't have bear prints like these in North Carolina."

I leaned over further in the saddle to get a closer look at the prints. "The bear must have been through here not too long ago. I can still make out the claw marks on the five toes."

The horses became restless. They seemed to know that there was danger somewhere very near.

"We better move on," I said with a long look ahead.

I talked loudly to the horse and my partner for the next half mile. Then suddenly I was quiet again. There, right in the middle of the trail, was a large steaming pile of what could only have been bear scat. We had to be right behind the creature. I wondered if we should wait a while before going any further. I heard elk bugling ahead and spurred the horse. About a mile further I saw the bear tracks leaving the trail, heading up one of the creeks toward the east.

By the time we halted for lunch, the snow had mostly melted. We devoured the cheese, crackers, can of tuna fish, and the hot chocolate we took out of our saddle bags. We were traveling light. No packhorses. We were planning to stay in patrol cabins each night, and those had plenty of provisions.

Continuing south, we left the trail every so often to ride up onto knolls and ridges that afforded us a long view of the Two Ocean Plateau area south of Yellowstone Lake. Always we halted the horses just short of the hilltops and hid them out of sight while we scanned with our binoculars for poachers.

The Two Ocean Plateau was where many streams congregated, some flowing toward the Pacific and others toward the Atlantic. It was said that on a high water year, when the streams overflowed into each other, the fish had a choice of either ocean and could literally swim over the Continental Divide.

Evening found us pulling into the Thorofare ranger patrol cabin. We corralled the horses.

I'd expected to find the two rangers who patrolled the Thorofare area at the cabin, but they were evidently still in the field. Stu started a wood fire in the South Bend stove in the corner. I climbed down through a trap door into the root cellar where the food was stored so it wouldn't freeze. I decided on some cans of beef stew, some dried rice, and canned peas. Also some Bisquick biscuit mix.

Figuring that the other rangers would be along soon, I started making the biscuit dough.

It wasn't long before we heard horses outside. The first ranger who entered was Bob Jackson, one of the park's most experienced backcountry rangers. Bob knew the area better than just about anyone. He had made it his business to know all of the outfitters and hunters who hung around the boundary area, and he had been responsible for catching quite a few poachers.

Next through the door was Andy Mitchell. Few rangers worked harder than he, or were more into the backcountry patrol. He went after poachers like a dog after a bone.

Andy and Bob had covered a lot of miles on their horses, but found only one sign of poachers, a pile of guts from what must have been a very large bull elk. Unfortunately they had nothing to pinpoint who might have killed the animal.

I would have loved to get that poacher myself. Generally the biggest bulls were also the strongest animals in the herd. They played a very critical role in maintaining the gene pool and overall health and welfare of the herd.

I took the biscuits out of the oven, set them on the table, then gave the stew another stir. "Dinner's ready!" I announced.

I had heard from some of the other backcountry rangers about Andy's legendary appetite, but I was hardly prepared for how quickly the stew disappeared from the deep serving bowl he was using as his plate. He was quickly back at the stove for more food.

"Guess I burn more calories up out there than I realize," he mumbled as he took his place at the table.

While I got up to get another tray of biscuits out of the oven, Andy disappeared down into the root cellar. When he returned he was holding a box of chocolate cake mix.

"Chocolate cake would hit the spot just right," I agreed. "I think the oven's hot enough, too."

He grunted, ripped the box's top off, and mixed half the box's contents into the stew still in his bowl. He licked the bowl clean, then calmly stirred hot water into the rest of the cake mix in his dish and slurped that down, too.

"Dessert," he muttered when he lowered his spoon for the last time and caught us still staring.

The next morning, three of us saddled our horses after breakfast and bid a goodbye to Bob. We headed west. Soon we were fording the Yellowstone River and heading up Lynx Creek. There were about two inches of ice on the small creek, and the horses had to be very careful while crossing and recrossing it that they didn't slip.

Every so often they would break through, but the water came no higher than their knees.

Our plan was to go to the top of Two Ocean Plateau, where Andy would return to his solitary way along the southern boundary, while Stu and I traveled west on the plateau along and across the Continental Divide. By the end of the day we hoped to have reached the Fox Creek patrol cabin, directly south of the South Arm of Yellowstone Lake and less than a mile east of the Snake River.

On the Two Ocean Plateau we came across Andy's spike camp. It consisted of a small tent, a sleeping bag, and a small bottled-gas stove. It was from there that he started his patrols most mornings. It was his castle from which to survey his private "kingdom." It was also a perfect spot to hear any rifle shots; they would ring for miles through the high and dry air.

It was around five o'clock when we arrived at the Fox Creek cabin, but district ranger Jerry Mernin wasn't there.

Stu eased himself gingerly into a chair while I rode on across the southern boundary into the Bridger-Teton National Forest to see if I could contact any hunters.

The daylight was pretty dim when I saw Mernin riding on horseback across a wide meadow toward me. He was on his dark Morgan horse, Rosita, leading a packhorse. I galloped across the meadow to intercept him.

Mernin was the dean of district rangers in Yellowstone, if not in the entire National Park Service. There were few rangers who knew of him who didn't respect and admire him. Tall, slender, dark-haired, and with the air of a scholar about him, he was in many ways the last of the traditional-type ranger of old. His twenty-five years as a Yellowstone ranger had given him a historical perspective matched by few others in the park.

"Howdy. Welcome to Snake River," he said as I came into hearing range. "Have a good ride?"

Riding side by side to the cabin I told him that in the national forest I had run into some hunters from Cheyenne who were patiently waiting for one of the park's trophy bulls to cross the boundary. Several of their friends had already killed an elk and they seemed confident that their turns weren't far off.

Stu had the cabin warm when Jerry and I rode up and tied the horses. The steaks, some green beans, and the six-pack of beer that Mernin had packed in helped to make Stu forget his sore muscles.

After supper Jerry told of a time many years ago when he had been on a boundary ride to stock the patrol cabins with winter rations.

It was late October and the snows had been deep. Jerry had to push himself hard but had finally reached the Park Point patrol cabin on the east side of Yellowstone Lake as night was falling. Tired and wet, he settled down in the cabin and read through the log book. One entry that piqued his interest was by a couple of hikers who had reached the cabin a few days before in a storm. Their day had been especially difficult, and they had written their thanks to the rangers of Yellowstone for letting them use the cabin. They had ended their report: "Really enjoyed a body-warming sip of 'Calvert the smooth one,'" and signed it "Orville E. Bach, Jr./ 1st Lt. U.S.A.F."

Jerry remembered having given permission to a Mr. Bach to use the cabin. The young man had said he was doing some research for a trail book.

Jerry traveled further south into the wilderness to the Cabin Creek patrol cabin. The weather had worsened considerably, and he barely made it to shelter before dark. As before, he wound down before going to bed by reading the cabin's log book. To his surprise there was another of Lieutenant Bach's entries ending again, "And before we turned in we really enjoyed a few sips of 'Calvert the smooth one.'"

And so the saga continued the next two days: terrible storms, struggling to get to a patrol cabin by sunset, finding lengthy entries by Lieutenant Bach in the log books—each ending "Really enjoyed a sip of 'Calvert the smooth one.' I plan to leave some for the rangers, for their hospitality, at the last cabin I stay in." Until at last, Mernin found himself thinking of that bottle of Calvert's whiskey constantly as his horse plodded across the Two Ocean Plateau.

He bounded into the Fox Creek cabin to see if Lieutenant Bach and his bottle of Calvert had been there. Sure enough, there was the entry. And—hurray!—the dear, kind fellow had written that he'd left the remainder of his whiskey in that particular cabin's food pantry.

Mernin flung open the pantry door and—there it was! He grabbed the half-pint flat bottle and held it up to the light.

His heart dropped to his socks; there wasn't so much as a drop in it. If he could have, he would have strangled Lieutenant Bach right then and there.

But, as it turned out, the log entry made clear that Lieutenant Bach had been true to his word. For the final sentences in the book belonged not to Lieutenant Bach but to a young ranger Mernin had working under him. That ranger, it turned out, had ridden through the area only a day before Mernin and had just beat him to the whiskey bottle.

"Sat around the stove as the wind howled outside, but found tremendous pleasure in sipping 'Calvert the smooth one,'" he had written with undisguised pleasure.

Mernin closed the book and tried to sleep. But on that night sleep hadn't come as easily as usual.

The next morning we were up by daybreak. Stu, Mernin, and I cleaned the cabin, then rode on to the Snake River. Two days later we finally arrived at Jerry Mernin's wooden home where his gracious wife, Cindy, stuffed us with lasagna and Rainier ale.

"Well, Stu, what do you think?" I asked as we drove back to Mammoth the next day. "Still missing the East?"

He looked long and hard at the meadows and mountains. When he turned around he had a big smile on his face.

"You know, I think I just had a nice long taste of the 'smooth one,'" he said.

I laughed. He had a good point there. There weren't many things better for the spirit than a good stout drink of Yellowstone.

19

The telephone shrilled belligerently. I threw aside my blankets, swung my feet to the bedroom carpet, and glanced at the lighted clock face. It was almost five A.M.

"This is Dan."

It was the communications center dispatcher. She wasted no time getting to the point.

"Nine-one-one call from Old Faithful Snow Lodge . . . caller Jack McConnell skied all night from backcountry . . . member of his skiing party fell into a thermal pool near Shoshone Lake last night, around twenty-hundred hours . . . second- to third-degree burns over sixty to seventy percent of injured subject's body—"

"Where's the burned skier now?" I interrupted.

"In a tent at the lake. McConnell left him with two female campers who are caring for him. We have no way of communicating with them."

"What's been done so far to get the injured man out?"

She reported that another camper, Jill Fitterer, had tried to ski to Old Faithful with McConnell but had bivouacked along the trail so McConnell could get to assistance quicker. Old Faithful ranger Steve Sarles had had the dispatcher call the only other ranger at Old Faithful, Bruce Blair, to tell him to go to the lodge to assist and further question McConnell, while Sarles telephoned the West district ranger, Joe Evans, and the Snake River district ranger, Jerry Mernin. A search-and-rescue operation was being organized.

I advised her that Mernin would be the incident commander, since the accident was in his district.

But I knew Mernin was going to need all the backup help he could get. Over the years I'd been a part of many SAR operations, and I knew a backcountry rescue in the Rockies in the middle of February was filled with innumerable risks. Nothing could be taken for granted.

"What's the weather forecast?"

"Snow, heavy at times, especially in the mountains, gusty winds, twenty to thirty miles per hour, blowing and drifting."

"How much snow has the area gotten the past twenty-four hours?"

Old Faithful had had five inches just overnight. In addition nearly a foot had fallen between South Entrance and Grant Village. I groaned. Shoshone Lake was situated between the Old Faithful and South Entrance areas and was higher than either by several hundred feet. All around it were the peaks of the Continental Divide.

The camp with the stricken man was where the snow would be deepest—way too deep along the roads and trails for snowmobilers or skiers to travel over. It would be an extremely difficult and hazardous task to get to, and bring out, the victim.

"What other information do you have?" I asked.

A brief tirade of radio static, bleeps, and rustling papers grated my eardrum. The dispatcher was evidently scanning her radio log book. Inside me a gut tightened uncomfortably; I needed to get to the office. I felt helpless just standing there in my underwear.

"Injured party is TW Snow Lodge pub employee John M. Williams. Twenty-four years old. Last seen screaming and in tremendous pain. The two campers with him, Melanie Weeks and Andrea Paul, are also Snow Lodge employees. They have little first-aid training. Ranger Bonnie Gafney is on her day off, staying at Cove patrol cabin—"

"Anyone tried contacting her yet?"

The Cove patrol cabin was only a little over three miles from the geyser basin. If we could reach Gafney, we could possibly get aid to the burned man before the other rescue parties even had a chance to get going. There would have been medical supplies in the cabin, and Gafney, like every other ranger, was trained in medical aid.

"Have been trying to reach her by radio," the dispatcher went on. "No luck so far. She should be monitoring her radio around eight A.M. for the morning report, if not before."

The personnel at the Mammoth Clinic, reported the dispatcher, felt that the burned victim was going to need oxygen badly. Some would have to be brought in from Old Faithful by the rescue party. Those forming the rescue party were coming by snowmobile from various parts of the park to Old Faithful and Grant Village to join together there and go on either the regular snowmobiles, the more powerful doubletrack snowmobiles, or on skis.

Again I shook my head at the thought of anyone trying to get to the camp in snowmobiles. The ones the rangers used were more for speed than for off-track use. They often got stuck in deep, powdery snow. The best chance for the rescuers, I felt, was to bully their way through the snow with the doubletracks until they could go no further, then cross-country ski the rest of the way.

I suddenly remembered that at Tower Junction were ten field rangers on an overnight winter survival course. I knew they were all competent and strong cross-country skiers. It would take an hour to get them from Tower to Mammoth by auto over the Cooke City road, which was always plowed, then another couple of hours by snowmobiles to Old Faithful. They would be too late to use for the initial rescue thrust, but they would be able to quickly catch up with the others and help bring Williams out.

"Let Mernin know that we have snowmobiles here at Mammoth from the recent congressional trip. We can have a team heading his way within an hour."

I returned the receiver to its cradle, took a deep breath, and rubbed my eyes. I needed to get moving. Helpers, supplies, information—the logistics were tremendously complicated. With such a large area of operations and the extreme blizzard conditions, there was a lot of preparation needed. We had to get a team assembled at Mammoth as quickly as possible.

Breaking a path through all the snow to the Shoshone Geyser Basin was going to take hours of hard work. The rescuers would need everything from emergency shelters to radio batteries to extra fuel. Those going in and those supporting the operation would have to be kept in continual radio contact. I got on the phone to Terry Danforth, the emergency services coordinator, and advised him to meet me at the communications center. He knew where every piece of emergency gear was in the park's rescue caches.

As soon as I hung up, I rushed to get dressed. Fortunately I always put a fresh uniform and my boots on a chair each night before I went to sleep. Getting roused in the night by emergencies was a common part of a ranger's life. I figured the more quickly I could get dressed and get help on its way to the emergency, the more likely it was that someone's life might be saved.

The image I'd been fighting to keep out of my head—that of a horribly burned young man screaming and thrashing on the thin cold floor of some flimsy backpacker tent—took over as I slipped on my boots. I felt both frustrated and angered: frustrated that there was no quick way to get help to him; angered that such a horrible accident could have happened. The pain Williams was going through had to be similar to that I had felt when the mine had blown up beside me in Vietnam. The powder burns and the hundreds of metal slivers that buried themselves in my body had been so excruciating I'd wanted to claw myself to shreds. It was as if I were burning alive, as if a million red-hot needles were piercing every nerve.

If by some miracle the young man was still alive, then every minute was crucial. Nine hours had passed since he had fallen into that thermal pool. He had to be severely dehydrated and in deep shock by now.

The snowflakes were settling onto the ground around me as I strode quickly to the administration building.

I thought again and again of how those rescuers sixty miles south of my office might get around all the obstacles nature would be throwing in their paths. Rescue by helicopter seemed only a remote possibility with such winds and snowfall, but maybe there was some way. The idea of going across the lake on snowmobiles played through my head. I made a mental note to find out what the others thought of going over the ice.

* * *

My office telephone rang. I glanced at my watch. It was 6:30.

"Chief ranger's office, this is Dan," I said as I turned down the volume on the radio monitoring the park's emergency channel.

It was Mernin, the incident commander. He was not only the park's most experienced ranger but also its slowest talker. I fidgeted as he took a brief eternity to spell out his need for more rangers, snowmachines, and equipment.

I assured him there'd be help leaving Mammoth for Old Faithful within the hour. I'd been on the phone almost nonstop since arriving at the office, calling and waking everyone I thought could contribute in any way to the rescue effort. In addition to rescuers, Danforth and others were gathering all sorts of survival and medical gear.

"Dan, I called Pat Ozment a little while ago. He had to go into the same area some years ago in the winter on an evacuation under similar weather conditions."

"How far did he get?"

"He said he made it to Grants Pass on his machine."

I pictured the slender ranger trying to wrestle a snowmachine through snow up to his waist. Pat Ozment was a very experienced ranger. If he had been unable to force his machine any further than the pass then it was a good bet no one else could either.

I walked over to the large topographical map on the wall as Mernin went on to explain over the phone's speaker that he had called the Jackson Lake ranger station in Grand Teton National Park, and one of their rangers was on his way with another doubletrack snowmobile.

In the lower left quadrant of the map the slightly bow-tie-shaped Shoshone Lake was the second largest patch of blue. I bent to read the fine elevation squiggles crowded about its irregular shoreline. There was Grants Pass, to the northwest of the lake's westernmost edge, just to the east of the Firehole River and right smack on top of the Continental Divide. A hiking trail went through it. Eight miles to the north of the pass was the Old Faithful area. About three miles to the south was the geyser basin area with the injured man.

I had been on that hiking trail several times and knew that even under the best of conditions it was almost a half-day-long walk to the lake from the trailhead near Old Faithful. Continually rising and dipping through thick forest, it was the kind of trail that kept you guessing where it was heading next. Along the way were many small streams that might well be hidden by the thick snow and trip up anyone on a snowmobile or skis. Unquestionably, it would take a miracle to reach Williams before noon, even if the rangers took off right away and somehow got to the pass on their machines.

"Say, what's the latest you have about the possibility of air operations?"

"I've been told that's probably out. Still too much wind and snowfall."

"Then we're left only with the trails?"

"Unfortunately so."

"Tell me again how the teams are going in," I requested, as I located the road connecting Grant Village and Old Faithful.

"The primary thrust will be from the Lone Star Geyser trailhead, and a backup effort will be attempted from the DeLacy Creek trailhead."

The first trail was the one that went through Grants Pass; the second, DeLacy, dropped down from the road near the lake's northeastern end. It was about three miles from the DeLacy trailhead to the lake, then at least seven more miles to the camp in the west by shoreline. Every bit of that trail, too, was uneven, full of deadfall and low pine branches, and crisscrossed with inlet streams. Another snowmobiler's and skier's nightmare.

At first glance the DeLacy route seemed a good choice. It offered the shortest distance from a packed road surface to the lake, as well as a possible route for the snowmobiles over the ice to the geyser basin at the lake's other end. Still, the trailhead was almost on top of the Continental Divide and had extremely deep snow all about it. And there was no guarantee the lake's ice was thick enough to support snowmobiles. If anyone fell through, there would be no saving them. The lake was over ninety feet deep in more than half of its area, with the deepest spot over 205 feet.

"I'll continue searching out some more doubletracks for you, and see what the medical people at the burn center in Salt Lake City suggest we do about first aid," I assured Mernin.

The minutes ticked away and the morning wound along. Always in the background on my radio was the squawking of the rangers' voices as they communicated with each other, the communications center, and myself. Mostly they were describing their locations, plans, and expected times of arrival at the rendezvous points at Old Faithful and Grant Village.

By 8:30 we had rangers and doubletracks coming from the south, the north, and the west toward the staging points. Others were waiting and poised to leave from the Lake complex.

Sarles and Blair, the two rangers at Old Faithful, had been advancing on snowmobiles along the main trail to the lake for an hour. With them were two concessionaire workers from the Snow Lodge who were strong skiers. They had covered nearly five miles and were slowly rising toward Grants Pass, but the going was getting more treacherous by the minute. Their faint, static-filled reports of stubborn six-foot-deep drifts, howling winds, poor visibility, and uncooperative machines made it sound as if they were arctic explorers battling their way across an ice cap.

Each mile Sarles and Blair advanced was a victory. But each mile also meant they were that much further from help themselves, should they run into trouble or become trapped by the blizzard. The rescuers themselves were increasingly vulnerable.

Having no communication with those in the camp at the geyser basin, we had no way of knowing if the weather on their side of the pass was better or worse. Sarles and Blair and the other two men would be exhausted by the time they crested the pass, and to have them then ski miles into ferocious winds and blinding snow would be dangerous.

Most important, lack of communication meant we didn't even know whether Williams was still alive. If he wasn't, then everyone could slow down and use more caution. And what about the three women? Were Weeks and Paul and Fitterer still at their respective camps? No one could have blamed them for thinking by now that

McConnell had not made it to Old Faithful, that they were stranded with no help coming. I could see one of them striking out wildly into the drifts to end up lost in a white hell. It would take only one wrong turn or one stumble to disappear forever.

It was essential that those on the rescue teams got to the camps directly and quickly. The longer they spent fighting the wind and the snow, the less energy they would have for the return trip. I was confident they would bivouac if they became too tired, but what if they were trapped for days by one of the monstrous blizzards that the Rocky Mountains were famous for? It was not inconceivable that they might have four or five feet of new snow fall on their heads in the next twenty-four hours.

What we needed desperately were some "eyes" in that area. So it was with a great sense of relief that at 8:38 we heard the voice of Bonnie Gafney crackle over the radio.

She reported that it was snowing and blowing at the cabin and that she would be on her way in just a few minutes. She left the cabin around 8:45, on skis and loaded down with oxygen, first aid supplies, water, food, and extra clothing. She headed to the geyser basin by going through the unbroken snow along the lake-shore. As we feared, there were spots of open water in the ice. Also hampering her was the ongoing blizzard, which she was skiing directly into.

With rescuers now closing in on the camp from two directions, the radio channels crackled and hissed and squawked nonstop. It was expected that Gafney would be at the camp within an hour at best, and a ranger was sent to Old Faithful to get from McConnell a more detailed description of where Williams's tent was located. There was some concern that he and the others had not camped in the site specified on their backcountry permit. Unless we could relay to the rescuers the physical description of where the tent was located, they might ski past it in the blizzard. Beneath several feet of new snow, a tent would look like just another buried bush or mound.

At 10:03 Gafney radioed that she was at the geyser basin and needed specific directions to the campsite. Sarles replied with the information he had.

At 10:37 Gafney reported she was at the thermal pool she presumed was the scene of the accident. Scattered around the pool were a plastic water bottle, some red nylon ski pants, a blue nylon ski jacket, a wool cap, and two wool mittens. Where, she asked, was the campsite from the pool? All Sarles could tell her was the number of the campsite the Williams party was supposed to be at. It was in Shoshone Meadows, he kept saying.

Between 11:08 and 11:19 Gafney radioed several times to say she could not find the camp. They hadn't camped at the site for which they had been issued a permit. The blowing snow was blinding, and she could see nothing even resembling a camp. Our fears were being realized.

Just then the ranger who had gone to question McConnell at Old Faithful broke in.

"Four-thirteen, this is four-eleven Moses. Do you copy?"

"Ten-four. I am copying you."

"I've just talked with McConnell. He says the camp is near the thermal pool, one hundred to one hundred and fifty yards due east, just north of a stand of trees on the peninsula."

"Four-thirteen copy."

Then, finally, at 11:26: "Seven-hundred, this is four-thirteen. I have found the camp. Will get back with assessment in a few minutes."

All down the line of command, every team leader acknowledged to the communication center that they had copied Gafney's good news. Now at last we would have the answer to our main question: Was Williams still alive?

At 11:28 Gafney reported she was performing CPR on Williams. Approximately one hour before, he had stopped breathing, according to the women who had been tending him.

At 11:54 Gafney reported to Dr. Hudgings at the Mammoth Clinic that she was getting no pulse or respiration, the pupils were fixed and dilated, the skin blistered over 70 percent of the body, some lividity, a slight rigor in the arms, and no rectal temperature attained.

At 12:25 Dr. Hudgings gave the order to cease CPR.

* * *

Despite all our efforts, we had missed reaching Williams alive by just one hour. He had sat straight up in his sleeping bag at 10:25 A.M., cried aloud to the women that he was fighting, that he was trying, then looked at one of them with his eyes wide open, slowly reclined with his throat gurgling, and died.

When Gafney arrived at the camp, Melanie and Andrea were outside the camp's two tents crying. "Bonnie, it's too late, nothing can help him now," they sobbed.

Just about then, Sarles arrived too.

For many of the rangers the rescue operation on that forsaken day would end with the news that Williams was dead, and that all three women had been found and led out to the trailhead and safety. Others were to continue on into the site to assist in the evacuation of the women and the recovery of the body. Because of the blizzardlike conditions and the fading daylight, it was not until the next day that the body was brought out. Two of the rangers on the recovery teams, Steve Frye and Terry McEneaney, spent the night with the body in the camp, while sixteen others crowded into the little patrol cabin on the lakeshore.

For myself, however, the Williams case would not end quite so soon. I had to pass the bad news on to his parents in Alabama, make sure that a thorough investigation was done into the circumstances leading to the death, critique the rangers' performances, and then review the autopsy and the rangers' reports.

Though I had not known Williams before his tragedy, after the dozens of reports I read, I came to feel I knew him as well as some of those I worked with. According to his camping friends, with whom he had worked at Old Faithful, the pub tender had been the sort of person nearly everyone would have enjoyed being around. He was described as in outstanding physical shape, intelligent, a great lover of the outdoors, a strong skier and rock climber, very sensitive to the beauty of nature, and one who loved to be around people. In short, a very happy and active person who loved life dearly.

I was struck by the disparity between the joyful person that

John Williams was and the cruel manner in which his life had ended.

For over half an hour that last night of his life, Williams had tried to get the four others at the camp to go exploring with him in the Shoshone Geyser Basin. He had explored it on earlier trips and talked excitedly to the others about its beautiful clear pools. Apparently he was too eager to see how the snow had transformed the scenery around the pools to stay cooped inside a tent. Perhaps, too, he wanted to do some "hotpotting"—soaking in the cooler of the thermal pools—for we later learned that he enjoyed doing this in the Old Faithful and Shoshone Lake areas, even though it was extremely dangerous and against the law.

McConnell and the three women, all experienced winter campers, had declined to accompany him. It was well after dark and very cold. So Williams had gone off on his own into the heavy snowfall, the gusty winds, and the steam from the thermal features.

Melanie and Andrea started to worry about Williams when he failed to return after an hour, and went out to look for him. Melanie had a dim flashlight and Andrea a headlamp. The wind was blowing snow everywhere, and the night was so dark their lights pierced no further than five feet ahead. At one point Melanie almost walked into a pool of water, but Andrea warned her just in time. The snow was drifting so much that they were unable to find the route they had taken to the camp only a few hours before. Their cries for Williams were answered only by the wind's eerie howls. After only fifteen minutes they became disoriented and returned to their tent. The only sign they had seen of other humans in the gloomy setting was some footprints near the pool Melanie had almost stepped into.

Forty-five minutes later, around eight P.M., Melanie and Andrea were in their tent in sleeping bags playing cards when they heard Williams screaming from the distance, then an eerie silence, then more screaming punctuated by: "Help me! Help me!" As the women in their tent and McConnell in his scrambled to get out of their bags, Williams's screaming grew even louder. What they saw in the swirling snow as they crawled from their tents was Williams limping the last few feet to them, his hands held up.

"My hands, my hands!" he cried out between screams. "I hurt so bad!"

They'd led him into one of the tents, stripped all of his soaking wet clothes off, and eased him into a sleeping bag—while he screamed nonstop. His body had been burned from his feet to his chest. Already the skin had begun peeling off the entire area.

While McConnell, the strongest skier among them, and Fitterer went for help, Melanie and Andrea tried desperately to keep Williams alive. Every three minutes they gave him a cup of either the fruit juice or water they had in their own packs. When that ran out, they tried to melt snow in a pan, but neither of their camp stoves worked: One would not light, the other would not stay lit. The fuel bottle on the second sounded like there was slush in it. They ended up melting snow in their mouths and spitting it into cups.

Although Williams screamed constantly throughout the night, he never lost consciousness from the searing pain, and even remained coherent. At times he sat up to hold out his arms and look at them. He continually thanked the two women for their efforts and stated more than once that he was afraid and so tired. He knew from the whistling of the wind and the snow pelting the tent's dark, sinking sides that there would be no quick help, that a helicopter couldn't possibly make it.

"God, let me rest. Take away the pain, take away the hurt," he cried. "Please, let me die. . . ."

Williams had a reputation for pushing things in the backcountry. Perhaps he believed his luck could never run out. Maybe he thought that he was too experienced outdoors to get into serious trouble. Whatever, one thing was certain: That night at Shoshone Lake he hadn't respected the fact that he was in a wild setting amid all kinds of dangers.

The park had known tragic death before. Accidents happen when there are over two and one-half million people visiting two million acres of cliffs, grizzly bears, avalanches, raging rivers, waterfalls, and boiling thermal pools year in and year out. Before

Williams, there had been ten deaths in thermal pools since the turn of the century. While a few had been simple foolishness—in one case a young man donned a scuba diving suit to explore a pool and was instantly scalded to death, while another time a man jumped in after his dog—seven of them were children who had somehow fallen into the water.

In the case of the children, the parents had not always acted responsibly enough. Many of the other deaths, however, were the result of the victims' having shown an utter disregard for the risks inherent in a wilderness setting. Tesinsky chasing the grizzly bear was a perfect example. So was Williams wandering off into a geyser basin in a blinding snowstorm at night. He, more than anyone at that camp, should have been aware of the dangers he was facing in such a wild setting: He had been the roommate of a young man who had died from a fall off one of the park's mountains, and he had been on a climb in the park during which a girl was lost long enough to necessitate a search party. Still he had acted so foolishly. Why?

That was a question all of us rangers asked ourselves dozens of times each year, as we watched visitor after visitor suffer death or injury amid the park's wonders.

Eleven-year-old David became one of those victims on a February day.

David couldn't resist racing ahead of his family and their friends down the trail through the unpacked powder snow. His father and the other father had gone off to Fishing Bridge to get some gasoline for their snowmobiles, and the others in the party were soon far behind him.

The way was rutted, uneven, slippery, and filled with holes where people had stepped through the snow before. Still, David kept going. In no time his mother and the others could no longer see him.

Only the summer before David had been down the same trail to the viewing area at the end. He and his parents had stood just a few feet above where the Yellowstone River plummets into the awesome Grand Canyon's misty chasm.

Scrambling around the last curve in the trail, David had a clear view of the observation area just ahead and below. Exposed to the bright sunlight, it stuck out from the canyon's side, its upper and lower decks buried beneath ice that shone brightly in contrast to the snow on the forest's shadowed floor. The ice covered much of the railing where the lower deck overhung the falls. Soon David was right above the gigantic icicles hanging from the 308-foot waterfall's brink.

In seconds he was at the top deck, where suddenly his feet slipped out from underneath him. He hurtled feet-first over the ice bank joining the two decks and into the canyon.

He landed two hundred feet down, on the side of a massive ice cone sticking up into the partly frozen falls.

It was another boy in the group who notified the rangers after hiking back to Canyon Village.

A helicopter was sent out, and ranger Andy Fisher, trained as a park medic, rappeled down a line from the aircraft into the canyon. There, as his boots were slipping on the ice cone's steep side and the river's waters were rushing by only yards away, Fisher loaded the dead boy's body onto a litter.

David was the second child to fall to his death in the canyon in the time I'd been the chief ranger of Yellowstone. The first one had been only a year and a half before, just a few hundred feet from where David had fallen.

In that incident, a seven-year-old boy from Indiana had fallen over 130 feet from a suspended walkway along the canyon's lip known as Uncle Tom's Trail. Dennis and his parents had stopped at a rest platform halfway up the metal walkway's steps, but his older brother had gone on ahead. Dennis had stood up on a bench to try to get his brother's attention. Though his parents were nearby—the father ahead and the mother behind—they made the mistake of looking also to the older son and not holding the younger one. As with David, tragedy came in the blink of an eye. Somehow Dennis slipped through the middle and top horizontal bars of the railing. He plummeted, then bounced, into a small gully directly below on the canyon's side.

201

While other visitors clambered up the series of grated metal steps bolted to the canyon's side to get help, the father rushed back down to the viewing platform for the Lower Falls of the Yellowstone River. There he was able to step out onto the steep, crumbly rhyolite rock slope. Somehow, he clawed his way up through the dangerously loose scree to where his son's body lay. The father took off his shirt and wrapped it around the boy's badly bleeding head.

Though rangers with first-aid equipment arrived soon afterward and were able to reach the boy quickly by going the way the father had, the one thing they needed most, a helicopter, couldn't get to the boy for nearly an hour because the winds in the canyon were too gusty. When the winds finally died down enough, the park's helicopter lifted off the parking lot near the trailhead, hooked onto the boy's litter, and carried the child to the parking lot. There he was transferred to a helicopter ambulance from the East Idaho Medical Center in Idaho Falls.

Dennis never regained consciousness. He died the next evening in a hospital far away from the lovely maple- and oak-covered hills of his southeastern Indiana.

Once more Yellowstone had reminded us that it was not a playground, but a place where even a momentary lapse of respect for its wildness could bring instant tragedy.

Kids are always rushing to look at something new and exciting. The thrill of the discovery often takes priority over caution. Unless an adult is there to supervise and properly discipline their enthusiasm, it can be too late. A perfect example was the hot pools, seven of whose victims had been children—ages three, four, four and a half, five, six and a half, nine, and fifteen.

As a father I know it is impossible always to watch or hold on to a child. But too many parents do not grasp the fact that they are not in some artificially controlled environment.

Perhaps because there are so many people around and signs of civilization, many have a false sense of security: Nothing bad is happening to all the other people, so why would anything happen to them? And a lot just plain don't care to be told what they should or shouldn't do.

For as long as anyone can remember Yellowstone has been

passing out warning handouts to every vehicle that enters the park: warnings against such things as feeding the animals, swimming in thermal areas, and approaching the bison. Still, over the years the injuries and the deaths continued to mount.

Few people, it turned out, bothered to read the handouts. And of those who did, many didn't believe the warnings.

So not long after I arrived, I decided it was time to get tougher with the warnings. I had lots of bold red ink used to highlight the warnings on the flyers. WATCH YOUR CHILDREN reads one warning: Your hand and your voice may be too far away once your child leaves your side. And, most disturbing of all to some of my peers who were worried about the park's "family fun" image, I had graphics included on the warning flyers: a geyser erupting in the face of someone who'd strayed off the boardwalk, and large animals such as a bison, a moose, and a furious mother bear charging pesky photographers.

It was a shame that comic book tactics had to be used to tell adults what would seem only common sense. But still that was far more desirable than having to keep the people out altogether, or having to put still more controls on their movements inside the park's wild areas.

It was understandable that many visitors had no concept of how dangerous the outdoors could be. To those raised all their lives in urban settings, a park meant little more than shade trees, swings, grassy fields, and animals about as ferocious as garter snakes and robins. To them a park was a place to play in—safe and cheerful. They expected to have their bird songs and inspirations without all the mess of danger and risk.

And for 99.9 percent of the over seventy million who had been to Yellowstone in this century that was just what they got. But there were the occasional exceptions. Exceptions which—unfortunately—usually received enormous press coverage. Which in turn led to more calls to "tame" and "civilize" the last remnant of wildness in the lower forty-eight states. Too many wanted their bears and peaks, but without the wild parts.

The question of just how far we could go to make the park

"safe" without compromising its wilderness character was never ending. As the number of visitors to the park grew each year, so would the probability of a tragedy. And with an American public looking more and more to the federal government to take over responsibilities once thought to be the domain of the individual, there would be increasing demands for more warning signs, more fences, more railings, more roads, and God only knew what else. Until, perhaps, some day the whole park would be little more than a sophisticated playground.

In 1970, a nine-year-old boy became the first to stumble and plunge into a thermal pool from a boardwalk. The little boy's ghostly white body rose out of the water for a second, his right arm raised above his head, then disappeared under the surface, never to be seen again. As the public read about the child's tragic death, there was a natural reaction of horror and rage. One congressman went so far as to ask the House and Senate for an investigation into the "safety hazards of our national parks."

So far the Park Service had avoided turning Yellowstone into an eyesore of "safety features." But even if it had, there was just no way a net could be placed under every mountain climber who scaled cliffs he had no business being on, or a life vest thrown to every boater who capsized while trying to cross Yellowstone Lake in the middle of a storm. No amount of compromising of the wilderness scene would ever make it quite safe enough for the careless, the brazen, the naive, and the arrogant.

And even if we could have turned Yellowstone into something totally safe and risk-free, would most people have stood for it being that way? I like to think not. Instead I suspect that one of the things that makes Yellowstone so loved and adored is that it *does* have risks and the unexpected. Yellowstone and its backcountry are one of the few remaining places in the continental United States where a person can feel humbled by a force greater than himself.

20

I had to be seeing things. How was it possible that a smoldering three-hundred-acre forest fire had spread to 4,700 acres in only a few hours? And since when did fires burn through thousands of hundred-foot-high trees as though they were blades of grass?

I looked at Curt Wainwright, the helicopter pilot. His long pale face bore as much incredulity as I was sure mine did. Both of us had seen a lot of fires over the years, but certainly nothing like the one below.

As the smoke rolled and spurted fitfully further and further into the dense pine forest, tree after tree—sometimes several at once—literally exploded into swirling torches of fire.

"Dan! Straight ahead."

Curt was pointing eastward into a deep river canyon that lay directly in the fire's path. In a wide part of the canyon, on the opposite side of the river, sat the bright metal roof of the historic Calfee Creek patrol cabin.

"Make a fly-by and turn to the fire," I said into my helmet's microphone.

Curt nodded. Canyon and cabin rotated beneath my feet. I stared again at the twenty-thousand-foot-high smoke column of the Clover fire. Its white and gray wall was so thick I couldn't see anything behind it. But the fingers pushing out from it couldn't have been more than three quarters of a mile from the cabin.

The forest canopy between the widening fire front and the cabin was ragged and mature—perfect fuel for the fire to skip across.

We would have to act quickly if we were going to save the historic old ranger cabin. We had an hour or two at best.

I turned again to Curt.

"Do you think you can land a crew down there?"

He peered through the bubble window beside his right shoulder.

"Sure!"

That was all I needed to hear. If Curt thought it was possible, then it was as good as done. He had flown me in and out of all sorts of terrain and weather over the past three years. I knew the ex-Vietnam chopper pilot was as skilled and cool as they came.

I ignored the incessant radio chatter spilling from the speakers in my helmet and sized up the situation. The fire was moving much faster than it had when I flew over this morning. It was being prodded by the southwesterly winds that prevailed in the park. It looked as though the main front would pass just to the south of the cabin, heading in an easterly-northeasterly direction. Very likely there would be some lateral down-canyon movement to the north toward the confluence of Calfee Creek and the Lamar River, where the cabin was.

I turned to the other passenger in the helicopter, Dick Bahr, the park's air operations supervisor. Curt had been taking Dick and me to a fire strategy meeting in Grant Village when a call from a backcountry ranger had diverted us to this blaze. He had reported that the Clover fire was on a rampage, and that visitors might be at risk in an outfitter's camp up along Miller Creek. He'd wanted us to fly into the outfitter's camp to warn everyone there that they were in the fire's path.

Dick Bahr scooted forward on his little fold-down seat as if to hear me better through his helmet's intercom.

"Dick, what do you think?"

"About saving the cabin?"

I nodded.

"I think we'd better hurry. And I also think we're going to need help."

The cabin was in a remote and rugged backcountry area of the park: forty miles from Mammoth, where the help would have to come from. By the time any fire crews could be assembled and transported or hiked into the area, it could be too late. We were going to have to do it ourselves.

"We have a team only about three miles from here. They're clearing some trails for the upcoming backcountry visit by Vice President Bush. I'll radio them that we're coming to get them for the cabin work," I explained.

I pointed to a rocky ridge about a mile northwest of the cabin.

"Do you think you'd be safe there? Okay. We'll drop you there with your radio. You'll be the lookout."

I turned back around in my seat. The fire below had me more concerned than any I'd seen yet in my nearly three years at Yellowstone. It was beginning to behave like a Yellowstone forest fire does under extreme drought conditions, unlike the eight others burning in the park. Normally when lightning ignited a fire in Yellowstone, it stayed small and soon burned out on its own. The area's long, snowy winters and short, often wet summers were not normally conducive to such conflagrations. But we'd had a drought all summer: It hadn't rained significantly in a month.

I took a deep breath and looked out the window at the growing ridge just ahead. At this time yesterday afternoon the fire had been of such low priority that we on the fire management committee at headquarters hadn't even considered it worthy of on-site fire monitors. But what a spectacular change since then!

As the helicopter headed for the ridge, I got busy on the radio. John Dunfee, of the crew working on the trail, said he and the others, Jane Lopez and Kristin Cowan, were available to help and would be waiting at a clearing for us to pick them up. I told him we were on the way, then called Mammoth and requested that firefighting equipment such as hoses, pumps, and chain saws be brought to the Lamar ranger station. That way the gear could be brought into use more quickly by helicopter.

We dropped Dick off and headed for the others while I did some quick calculations as to our chances of fireproofing the cabin area before the fire reached it. It was going to be touch and go. On our side was the lateness of the afternoon. With the sun going down, the fire should slow as the temperature dropped and the

207

humidity increased. Even if a firestorm swept down the canyon's sloping two-thousand-foot west wall, I was sure the river would reduce the intensity. A one-hundred-foot-wide band of water was as good a firebreak as anything around. It might even stop the damned thing. But if the flames did jump the river, there should be only inconsistent spotting in the trees near the cabin.

The two young women and Dunfee were waiting right where he had said they'd be. They clamored into the idling chopper on my side after lashing their gear into a wire basket on the helicopter's skid. In their fire-resistant yellow shirts, green pants, and fluorescent-orange hard hats they filled every bit of the rear passenger space. They had to be hot with the mid-July sun's rays slicing directly through the clear sides onto them. But they chattered away as though we were off to a dance.

Dealing with forest fires is very much a paramilitaristic thing; there are rules, strategies, and a definite unchallenged chain of command. As the helicopter approached the target area, I let the crew know that the suppression work at the cabin was going to have to go like clockwork.

"Our only goal," I explained, "is to save the cabin. Get rid of anything near it that is flammable. I will be giving each of you your specific duties once we're on the ground."

They nodded their sweaty red faces anxiously.

By the time we were back over the cabin the fire was within a quarter mile. Fingers of flames were zigzagging down the opposite side of the canyon and threatening to join. If they did I knew the power they'd generate would be very hazardous.

I looked at my watch: 4:30.

"Curt, we've got to get as close as we can to the cabin. There's not a minute to spare."

"We're going in," he yelled back with his eyes riveted to a large meadow about one hundred yards north of the cabin.

The ground quickly blossomed as Curt's long fingers expertly worked the control sticks. I tensed and reached for my web belt under the seat. Attached to it were a water canteen and fire shelter pouch.

All at once we were rocking and pitching violently. There was a sickening howl against the small craft's metal and Plexiglas sides.

"Windstorm," Curt shouted disgustedly. He fought to stabilize the craft.

I glanced back at the others. Their eyes were staring wildly at the thick grayish smoke and large embers swirling madly by. I tried not to think of the stalled rescue helicopter that years ago had brushed past my face and exploded into flames at the bottom of the 3,200-foot vertical face of Yosemite's El Capitan Peak.

My throat was shoved into my guts as the helicopter lurched upward and away from the chaos. I felt as if I had just escaped a whirlpool below an invisible waterfall.

Curt shook his head angrily. His hands were gripping the controls as though they might blast off.

"No way, Dan! The winds—they're too erratic. I've got to reduce our load or we'll land too heavily."

"What if we drop off one of the crew?"

He nodded vigorously. "Let's give it a go."

The engine whined angrily as we charged to a large green meadow atop another ridge five miles away on the east side of the river. As the *thump-thump-thump* of the blades overhead mimicked my heart, I glanced at the numbers being swept past by the second hand of my watch and knew the fire was doing the same to the trees behind us. It was going to take some sort of miracle to win this battle.

Five miles north of the cabin I had Lopez scramble out. The downdraft pounded her crouched figure. She turned to retrieve her pack from the side of the helicopter. I waved her away; it was tied beneath the others and would take too much time to get out.

"Leave it! There's no time," I yelled. "You'll be safe here. The fire front's about five miles away, there's all this meadow around you, and you have a radio."

She looked so alone and vulnerable, as if we had dumped her a million miles from civilization.

"I'll come back to get you if the fire gets too close," promised Curt.

She stumbled backward and in seconds was shrinking into a dot as we darted away to the smoke columns.

In the few minutes we had been gone, the landscape around the cabin had become smothered under a low cloud of dark smoke. We sank into the strange light of a somber gray world filled with murky forms. Again the powerful convection winds howled and slapped at us.

Curt pulled away, glanced around, and flew to a gravel bar at the river's edge. I flung off my harness and helmet and dropped to the rocks. Pebbles, air, water, and fire churned about me as if I'd plunged into a cauldron. I grabbed my hard hat and web belt. The fire shelter pouch and canteen flopped against my legs like a pair of six-shooters.

"Let's go!" I shouted to those in the back.

"I can't stay long!" Curt yelled to me over the others' scrambling figures. "If the fire gets much closer I'm going to have to escape by flying downriver!"

"Keep the engine running and go like hell if necessary!" I yelled back.

He laughed and flashed a look of soldierly encouragement. For a second I was back in Nam. But only for a second. I turned, and said to the others as I ran past: "I'm going on ahead to size up the situation. Grab your gear and meet me at the cabin."

I walked quickly to the cabin with scarcely a glance to either side. Strange flashes of light and shadow mixed and remixed in the hazy air of the woods. From somewhere unseen sounds like those of an angry ocean surf pounded my ears. At the cabin's covered porch, I paused long enough to call headquarters on my walkie-talkie and request a fire retardant drop between the cabin and the fire as soon as possible. Then I unlocked the padlock on the door and retrieved shovels and anything else I thought could be useful to stop the fire.

The cabin was surrounded by fir and lodgepole pine. There was also split firewood stacked on the porch and in the side yards. It was a tinderbox just waiting to explode. Small swirls of smoke, where hot embers had ridden the winds to the ground around the cabin, hinted that disaster was very near.

The firewood needed to be scattered, the trees needed to be burned so they did not become part of the main fire, and a scratch line had to be dug around the cabin to hinder ground flames. And though I felt the fire would reach the cabin, I decided we were going to stay on the site through it all. If we left in the helicopter it would be hours before we could return because of the smoke, and in that time an errant ember or two might be all that was necessary to start the pine log walls flaring. I felt we would be safe, and there was no reason to leave the cabin to chance.

The others stumbled from the trees carrying saws, packs, and other assorted gear. I had them pile everything on the ground in front of the cabin, then follow me to the meadow in which we'd tried to land. The first rule in any firefighting situation is to establish an escape route and a "safety zone," a place to flee to and wait out any firestorm, should one happen to sweep over us.

A damp place in the meadow's knee-high grass became our safety zone. If we needed to rush back here, our plan was to lie down on the damp grass and cover ourselves with the fireproof aluminum foil tents in the pouches on our belts.

We returned to the cabin and quickly went to work. Wood went flying everywhere. Sticks and pine needles were piled around the trunks of those trees closest to the cabin and set afire with fusees. It was important to "starve" the main fire when it reached the area by having any fuels around the cabin already burned away or removed. That way it would go around, to where there were still flammable materials.

Ironically, when I stuck one of the hissing fusee flames into the kindling around the trees, nothing happened for a minute. The humidity was rising now that the sun was setting, and the smaller sticks had just enough moisture in them to resist burning. But the problem was short-lived, as the main fire flared suddenly closer and whatever moisture there was began disappearing.

As small flames crept up the trees' scaly bark and into their branches, they *whooshed* into a cacophony of crackling and popping that reminded me of a gun battle. Mixed with the *whoomph!* of those trees nearer to the main fire reaching tinder point and exploding, it sounded like a war was breaking out.

211

For several minutes chaos ruled overhead: Everything was imploding or exploding, the air was growing darker with smoke, grit was raining onto my face and peppering my tongue, gases were stabbing at my tear ducts, and the trees were shaking eerily from the wind and heat.

"Dick, what's the position of the main fire?" I asked into the walkie-talkie.

"It's across the entire drainage . . . can't be more than six hundred feet from . . ." came the weak, static-filled reply.

"Dan!" It was Curt breaking in on the walkie-talkie. "Dan, the trees are shaking all around me. This place is about to go. I can't stay any longer or the smoke will be too thick."

"Go, Curt," I advised. "You need to leave before the fire retardant drop anyhow."

"You coming along? I'll wait."

"Negative. Get out while you can. We'll be fine."

"Seven hundred-Fox, this is Helicopter One departing Calfee Creek Cabin," Curt's voice informed the communication center at headquarters.

I turned back to the others; they were furiously hacking and scraping out a line around the cabin.

Suddenly a gust of wind fanned some storm embers lodged in several tall pines beside the horse corral. As if a huge fireball had suddenly rolled down, the crowns of the trees boiled in orange, yellow, and red. The fire leapt from limb to limb as though they were the rungs of some hellish ladder. There was a flash, then another, as trees nearby also burst into spectacular orange towers.

"Let's get out of here," I yelled.

Embers and flaming branches were falling everywhere. The tree crowns along the east side of the meadow dissolved one by one into torches. To the west, across the river where the main fire was, was a seething black wall coming at us like an immense tornado.

At the safety zone I decided to deploy the shelters for practice, to be ready when and if the firestorm hit. Though I knew that as a rule the shelters were never used unless it was a matter of life or death, I also knew that when the main fire did hit, there would be only seconds to act. We had to be sure that the shelters were in good shape. It was likely the flames in the tree crowns to our east would be sucked upward toward the main wall when it reached the river and we would have a fire bridge flaring right over our heads.

I quickly pulled a tightly folded bundle of foil-and-fiberglass cloth from the yellow pouch on my belt. After a good shake it billowed out into what looked like a floorless pup tent. Supposedly it could withstand heat up to 1,400 degrees Fahrenheit.

Cowan and I flopped onto our stomachs in the grass and covered our backsides with it. We held its sides and ends tightly against the ground with the toes of our boots and our gloved hands. I was relieved to find that we could both fit under it. Dunfee had his own shelter.

The three of us emerged from our shelters only to hear a powerful roaring like that of a 747 jet engine. Louder and louder it grew. Puffs of black smoke started shooting out horizontally through the trees across the river followed by fireballs, as if a great invisible dragon were coming. Then came the winds of oxygen being pulled from our suddenly tiny space into the furious beast.

We dived right back under the shelter. Tensed and waiting in its darkness, I could tell from the rumbling in the ground that the main wall itself was right at the river, just 150 yards away. I tried scrunching lower into the comforting grass. Our foil membrane seemed so fragile.

It sounded as if there was a swirling vortex right above our backs, sucking more and more oxygen into an endless funnel, like a black twister in a farm child's nightmare.

Our shelter shook, ash pelted it, and all about us raged a tempest as tiny voices called to me on the walkie-talkie—asking if we were okay, telling me that the retardant bomber had had to turn away because of too much smoke, and that Curt was departing too, for oxygen and fuel. I replied as best as I could, hoping they could understand me above all the background noises.

I dared not lift the end of the shelter to peer out: It was possible that the meadow was ablaze too. So many hot fragments were raining around us, and though the tips of the grass blades were green, they were like paper near the roots. As the oxygen beneath our shelter became slightly acrid with smoke, my imagination toyed

213

with the image of two ghostly shelters poking like silvery body bags from an otherwise black and dead landscape.

I sought to keep Cowan calm by talking to her. Always in the background, however, were the mocking voices of the storm: the terrible roar of tree crowns being snatched by the fire, the sharp crack of limbs being ripped off and slammed to the earth by the fire's own gale-force winds, and the distant reports of boulders shattering into innumerable shards under the blast-furnace-like heat.

Cowan began coughing.

"We're going to be okay," I reassured her. ". . . We're going to be okay."

"Have you ever been in a fire like this before?" she wondered.

I chuckled. Highly erratic wildfires were nothing new to me. I'd fought many. I was an expert on fires. But even experts could learn something new.

"Sure. That's why I know we're pretty safe right here," I replied. "How about you?"

It was her first fire, she said. She'd had all the basic firefighting courses, but she'd never actually been on a fire line before.

"Well, you sure picked a good one to break yourself in on," I kidded.

It was her turn to chuckle.

I knew I should have been more worried; only yards away billions, if not trillions, of BTUs were being released—enough to heat thousands of homes for a year or to crisp us in a second. But a wildfire normally did not frighten me nearly as much as it did others. Perhaps one reason was that I had personally burned hundreds and, in some cases, thousands of acres in conifer forests in other parks. The objective then had been "prescribed burning," or the carefully planned and managed burning off of accumulated deadfall and diseased trees that might otherwise add to the intensity of actual wildfires. It was not a practice at Yellowstone because of the relative sparseness of *burnable* vegetation on the forest floor and the normally cool moist summers at the high elevation. It took extremely dry conditions to get the forest to burn at all.

Another reason that fire was not so frightening to me was that

I did not think of it always as an enemy, or "destructive." As perverse as it may sound, I actually liked to see a fire burning in the overmature stands of wilderness like that around us. As I have said, every ranger or environmentalist worth his or her salt knows that in nature fire is a natural and important process. If it is an evil, then it is a necessary evil.

But this fire was disconcerting in how quickly and voraciously it was spreading, I thought, as I listened to it moving relentlessly to the north. And too much fire, like too much of anything, could be harmful. Every one of the eight fires currently burning inside the park was in dense timber and had the potential to burn into a major conflagration.

I was sure that not many outside of the Yellowstone area were even aware that we no longer fought any naturally caused forest fire in Yellowstone. That practice had ended in 1972. We let them burn out on their own, except for those fires that threatened lives or buildings, or endangered animals, or threatened property outside the park's boundaries.

Putting fires out, as was the rule in the first century of the park, had caused the forests to grow more diseased and decrepit. Fires created a mosaic of different-aged trees and vegetation that helps to prevent the dominance of such parasites as the mountain pine beetle and dwarf mistletoe. As when a farmer burns off his fields, nature's fires kill the old growth and decompose its stubble to make room for a new crop. And fire establishes new meadows, which results in far more food for the animals.

Letting nature again take over and burn the forests, as it had been doing ever since the last ice age, was simply another logical step in the ongoing attempts of the Park Service to return the park's ecology, as much as possible, to its original state.

So far the new fire policy had proven a success in Yellowstone. Despite the fact that in the park as many as 10,000 lightning bolts may strike the ground in a single summer storm, hardly any of those ever actually cause a fire. Indeed there had been in the last 16 years only 235 lightning-caused fires. Most of them had burned less than an acre. Only four had actually gone over 1,000 acres—the largest consuming 7,400 acres. All of them together only added up to

215

around 34,000 acres. That's less than 2 percent of the park's area
—not even a flicker in its tens of millions of trees.

The roaring outside had passed. I heard only the snapping and
crackling of individual small fires feeding on the firestorm's residue.
Cautiously I lifted the end of the shelter. Hot air and a thin finger
of gray smoke wafted in on the dim light. The smell of burnt wood
and grass was almost overpowering.

Where earlier had been an almost unbroken wall of green pine
trees around the meadow, there were now dozens of charred skeletons and flickering spot fires. A spooky fog of smoke hung in the
air, as if it didn't know where else to go.

After some forty minutes the three of us walked back to the
cabin, past coal-black trunks smoldering and twisted upon the
ground.

Many trees had been knocked over by the winds, some
wrenched completely out of the ground. Their roots still clutched
the soil that had held them for the past century or so. The large
mounds of fire-leached soil between the trees' roots protruded from
the forest floor in irregular rows, like crumbling tombstones in an
ancient burial ground.

Amazingly the cabin was only scorched. Even the elk antlers
hanging above the front porch were barely touched. I had expected
to find a ruined shell; loud popping noises at the height of the fire
had made us think the cabin was burning.

I stepped up to the heavy plank door and opened it. The cabin's
interior exhaled hotly. I searched through the metal food pantry
cabinet for something to eat or drink. Finding several cans of fruit
juice I brought them outside and took them to the river for the icy
current to cool. I returned to the sooty structure and put Cowan
and Dunfee to work putting out any spot fires smoldering near the
cabin. In the meantime I checked the smoking tree limbs overhead
to make sure none was about to fall on the cabin or on us.

When we finally went to the river to take a well-deserved rest,
the fruit juice was so cold against my parched throat that it was
like drinking liquid ice. I savored each drop.

Dark flecks of ash floated past on the Lamar River. I watched them swirling and jiggling on the fast-moving current. It was almost as if the cutthroat trout hidden in the eddies and short falls of this stretch of the river were shedding the black spots that covered their bodies. I wondered how many of the fragments that had fallen onto the water from our little battle at the cabin would make it all the way to the Lamar Valley, or perhaps even in some form or manner to the Atlantic Ocean. If they did, they were in for an incredibly wild ride through hundreds of rapids and falls and, ironically, the same firestorm that had created them.

I smiled. Cycles . . . death and rebirth . . . Wasn't that what nature was really all about, when you got down to the basics?

"Dan?"

I looked over to the black-smudged and sunburnt face of Dunfee. His eyes were shining again and a big smile was sitting where only a few minutes earlier had been a tightly drawn set of thin, cracked lips.

"This was really some fire. Don't you think?"

I nodded and answered with a big smile of my own.

"I've been in five large fires before this, but none was ever so intense," he added.

"It is a mean one," I assured him.

I had been struck by how suddenly and thoroughly it had attacked the trees. It was as if they had been primed and waiting for the fire to happen. The more I thought about it, the more I was awed not so much by the size of the firestorm, but by the *way* it had burned. It had attacked everything in its path with a ferocity that is more common in places as dry and brittle as Southern California. Fires in this part of the country just weren't supposed to burn so harshly until August and September, when the sun had had a chance to really dry things out.

Did it mean there was something else going on that we weren't taking into account? We were in a drought because of the low snowfalls over the past seven years. It was not so much the spring and summer rains that supplied the park's plateaus with their moisture, but the snowpacks in the mountains. The last several years the weather had been totally bizarre at times and extremely hard to predict overall. While the winters had been unusually dry and mild, the springs and summers had been abnormally wet, sometimes reaching 200 to 300 percent of normal rainfall even in July. And yet, all in all, weather experts were saying that the period up to this year was rapidly becoming the driest since the dust-bowl years of the 1930s.

Could 1988 be the year that all the crazy weather came to a head? The year for the big fires that the park's scientists said historically tore through the area every two hundred to four hundred years? I didn't think so. Nevertheless, they were past due. The tree rings in the older conifers pointed to about the early 1700s as the last great fire season in the region.

I, along with others on the fire management committee, had reviewed the latest fire danger projections and had found them not all that different from some previous years, especially 1979 and 1981. May had brought to Mammoth double its average rainfall and snow. And overall precipitation in the park that month was 81 percent above average. There had been a sharp decline in moisture after May, but I was confident that the rainfall would again be back to normal, maybe even back to the above-average amounts of the past several years. It had rained enough last week to reduce most of the fires burning then to smoldering spots. And, I assured myself, it would be raining again any day now.

Still, there were some, even on the fire committee, who thought we should be starting containment work on some of the fires. I didn't blame them for being worried. Sometimes, when I thought of how back in February a forest fire had burned 1,600 acres in a blizzard northwest of the park, of barges running aground in the Mississippi River, water being rationed in California, and corn crops in Iowa shriveling, I felt there was more to the situation we should be taking into consideration. It was eerie—as if revolving around us was a colossal time bomb waiting to be set off.

In the back of the fire cache building at Mammoth was a metal kiln that was used to measure how much moisture was in the park's wood and duff. It had been reading fairly normal levels of around 16 to 22 percent in the medium and larger sticks until four days ago when the levels had suddenly plummeted into the low teens. Presently they were hovering at the 12 percent level, a highly volatile situation—as witnessed by the half dozen new fires that had cropped up the past five days.

I looked at the trees around me that the firestorm had spared. They obviously hadn't been as dry as the others. But for how much longer? One more day? Two? Sudden dramatic drops in the moisture levels of the park's vegetation were quite common, because the air was thin and dry and not much of a barrier against the effects of the sun and wind. Still, I told myself, if the jet stream brought in even a light rain tonight, those moisture readings would jump right back up. And in Yellowstone the history of the weather patterns the last one hundred years indicated that rain always fell in July and August.

I just couldn't panic right now. The fires' ecological value was simply too great for us to extinguish them just because we were a few weeks overdue for our monthly rains.

And, besides, historic park data seemed to indicate that a large fire for Yellowstone was usually around ten thousand acres.

I could handle that. Even a couple or three.

21

The unthinkable happened: The rains didn't come. Only hot, dry, fierce winds. And more lightning. And more fire.

Nature appeared to have become her own worst enemy. For the first time in the park's written history *all* of Yellowstone came under siege and was threatened. So much so, in fact, that the natural-burn policy of the past sixteen years was suspended and was now being condemned from almost every quarter. It didn't seem to matter that fully two thirds of the fires' blackened acreage had been caused by fires that started *outside* the park and that had had nothing to do with the park's natural-burn plans.

I grabbed a copy of the latest fire map sheet from a table in the fire cache's crowded radio room and exited through the back warehouse. Weaving and ducking my way past dozens of yellow-shirted firefighters who were hastily gathering packs, hoses, drip torches, and axes from long rows of tall shelves, I stepped through a doorway into what seven weeks before had been a garage for ranger vehicles. Even though it was barely midmorning, the Mammoth fire command post was already buzzing. Rangers and other staff on the fire incident command team were huddling before large wall charts and topographical maps. Computer operators' fingers were punching at banks of keyboards. Telephones were ringing, computer printers clattering. And somewhere outside and above the wire-festooned ceiling pounded the twin-engined Chinook helicopters ferrying more soldiers-turned-firefighters into battle.

I stepped out of the way of a messenger rushing somewhere with a box of papers and studied the fire map sheet in my hand.

GUARDIANS OF YELLOWSTONE

The black splotches marking the burned portions of the park were so large they covered nearly half of its area. Only two months ago, on July 15, when the park offices printed the first of these maps, those evil-looking ragged patches had been mere dots.

YELLOWSTONE FIRES. *September 7, 1988, 8:00 A.M.* proclaimed a large bold headline just beneath the map. It was followed by:

> Since mid July more than 2,000 (and currently, over 9,200) firefighters have been actively working to contain or suppress the different fires in the Yellowstone area. This summer the park is experiencing a drought along with high daytime temperatures, low humidity, and strong, gusty winds. These conditions cause fires to grow and burn actively. They make it difficult to contain or suppress the fires.

I turned the sheet over and read the neatly typed paragraphs on the back. Their summarized statistics were as shocking as ever. They read like a war report.

> To date, over 663,000 acres in Yellowstone National Park and over 1,066,010 acres in the Greater Yellowstone Area have been affected by fire. However, only about half of the vegetation has burned within many fire perimeters. Through the summer, 52 different fires have been started by lightning. Of those 52, eight are still burning inside the park. Firefighters are working to control them. Any new fires will be suppressed as quickly as possible.

663,000 acres. Just a week ago it had been 550,000 acres. What would it be next week—a *million* acres?

Had anyone ever told me that someday I would watch nearly half of Yellowstone burn, I would have thought they were nuts. After all, the worst previous fire season in the park's 116-year history had been only *20,000* acres!

Not so very many weeks ago I had thought the 4,700-acre fire sweeping toward the Calfee Creek cabin was a major blaze. What was it now? I looked at the fire summaries. It was the first one listed: *Clover-Mist fire*—238,000 acres.

This summer was a never-ending nightmare. How much longer could this go on?

I thought back to mid-July, when the fire at Calfee Creek had managed to become such a monster. It was something I had run through my mind a lot. No sooner had I left the Calfee Creek cabin area on that fateful July 14 than it was apparent to me—and soon to the entire world—that nature had gone completely berserk in and around the park. When I returned that night to Mammoth, I called together to the fire cache building the key members of the park's fire staff. We decided that the sixteen-year-old natural-burn policy was no longer feasible in Yellowstone for the 1988 fire season: The behavior of the fires was too erratic; there was too much potential for them to burn into developed areas such as Grant Village and onto the adjacent national forest lands; and there were just too many fires burning intensely inside and outside the park. As of that night suppression action was to be taken on all new fires—natural and man-caused—as long as there were equipment and firefighters to put on them. And as long as it didn't appear that the fire would burn into, or be overrun by, an already existing fire.

It had been no little thing to cancel a fire policy that had worked flawlessly for so many years, that all of us knew was vitally important to the long-term health of the park's ecology. Some on the fire committee had wanted to let the fires go a little longer unrestrained, were sure the summer rains couldn't be far away. But the drought conditions and the fires' refusal to die or diminish had hinted too strongly that a crisis was looming. One that might find the park's limited firefighting resources stretched beyond their capabilities.

The time had come for quick, firm action. There was no sense in being philosophical about the suspension of the natural-burn policy. Too much was happening too fast. We were, in a sense, "off to the races."

The next morning I informed Superintendent Barbee that we

had established an "incident command team," with myself as the incident commander and Steve Frye as the operations chief. Rather than simply monitoring each fire's progress, we would be actively planning strategies and tactics to suppress or contain it within natural boundaries such as mountain ranges. Whereas before, the staff and I had met once a day informally in my office, from then on we were to meet twice daily in a fire command post inside the fire cache building. Everything, in effect, was more regimented and long-range, rather than day-to-day, wait-and-see.

A small lightning-caused blaze along the park's southern border that was named the Falls fire became, on July 16, the first lightning-caused fire to be attacked with the intent of being controlled.

Unfortunately, those of us who were hoping rain would come and bring the fire situation back to normal were not to have it so. Instead, again and again, gale-force winds came from seemingly nowhere in the following weeks, on a scale never known before in Yellowstone Park, and fanned fires such as the Clover into ever bigger blast furnaces.

Almost effortlessly the Clover spread to 10,700 acres on July 22, joined forces with another fire called the Mist, became a 47,000-acre beast on July 27, and then, as if to highlight a tour of the park by a very worried Interior Secretary Donald Hodel on July 27, exploded that afternoon to 68,000 acres—almost four times the size of the previously largest fire *ever* recorded in Yellowstone.

While flying with the secretary over the fire-ravaged sections of the park, I explained to him how we had decided two weeks before to do away with, at least temporarily, the natural-burn policy. He approved of our decision. When he reiterated his approval in the afternoon news conference, it was erroneously reported by the news media that *he* had suspended the park's natural-burn policy as of that day. In actuality, park headquarters did not receive any such "official" decision from Washington to suspend the natural-burn policy until late August.

I shook my head and looked again at the September 7 report in my hand. Scanning the fire updates, I could understand why the media was calling this a war, and why some scientists joined me in classifying the summer of '88 in Yellowstone as the ecological event of the past three hundred years.

Clover-Mist fire: 238,000 acres. Mist fire started July 9. Clover started July 11. They joined on July 22. The fire could reach Pahaska today. 1,352 firefighters, 35 engines, 7 bulldozers, and 3 helicopters

Fan fire: 23,325 acres. Started June 25. 25 firefighters, 1 helicopter

Hellroaring fire: 57,470 acres. Started August 15. Tuesday night this fire joined with the Storm Creek fire. 628 firefighters, 5 helicopters

Huck fire: 56,345 acres. Started August 21. Caused the evacuation of Flagg Ranch. Spreading SE into Teton Wilderness and N across the Snake River into Yellowstone National Park. Fire has pushed around Pinyon Creek into Gravel Creek. Fire exhibiting erratic behavior. 640 firefighters, 6 engines, 5 helicopters

North Fork: 145,800 acres. Started July 22 by human. Split from Wolf Lake fire at Gibbon Falls. The fire has spotted to within ¾ mile of Old Faithful area. The area was evacuated this morning. A major run to the NE occurred in the Mt. Holmes area. 1,608 firefighters, 39 engines, 22 bulldozers, and 6 helicopters

Snake River Complex: 205,800 acres. Red fire started July 1. Shoshone fire started June 23. Joined August 10. Falls fire started July 12. Red-Shoshone fire joined the Mink fire on August 31. 703 firefighters, 16 engines, 6 helicopters

Storm Creek fire: 65,000 acres. Started in June and allowed to burn as a natural fire. Suppression action taken starting July 3. A spot fire has moved just N of Silver Gate. Fire also is within one mile of Cooke City. All non-essential fire personnel and all area residents have been evacuated. No structures were lost overnight. Hwy 212 from Tower Junction to the Sunlight Basin Cutoff (Hwy 296) is closed. 1,236 firefighters, 48 engines, 4 dozers, 7 helicopters

Yellowstone Lake at sunset *(Michael Pflaum)*

Bull bison in midwinter along Yellowstone River *(Steven Fuller)*

Lower Falls, Yellowstone River (*Michael Pflaum*)

Lower Falls, frozen over (*Michael Pflau*

Bunsen Peak, looking into Mammoth (*Michael Pflaum*)

Looking east into Yellowstone at the North Fork fire *(National Park Service)*

"L" Loop burning, Grant Village campground *(National Park Service, Jeff Henry)*

September 9 night fire run on Mammoth over Bunsen Peak *(Jane Green)*

Columbine (*National Park Service, Bob Barbee*)

Calypso orchids, Hellroaring Creek (*Michael Pflaum*)

Bighorn sheep lamb (*Michael Pflaum*)

Red fox in Canyon Meadows (*Steve Fuller*)

Black bear *(Michael Pflaum)*

Helicopter rescue operation *(Michael Pflaum)*

Bison with calf at Old Faithful *(Michael H. Francis)*

Bull moose at Yellowstone River (*Michael Pflaum*)

Elk in meadow with fire in background
(*Boise Interagency Fire Center*)

Flowers in 1988 burn area near Tower
(*Michael H. Francis*)

Bull elk at sunrise, Steamboat Point (*Steven Fuller*)

Steam coming from Hayden Valley geyser
(*Steven Fuller*)

Black bear cub, Mammoth area (*Michael H. Francis*)

North Fork fire, south of Mammoth *(Michael Pflaum)*

Fireweed near Tower Ranger Station, one year after the fire *(National Park Service)*

Wolf Lake fire: 61,200 acres. Originally part of North Fork fire. Divided from North Fork fire at Gibbon Falls on August 25. The fire is advancing NE in Carnelian Creek and in the area of Dunraven Pass and Mt. Washburn. Lines on the S held well. Lines around Canyon Village also held. More engines arrived from California. 675 firefighters, 30 engines, 3 helicopters.

Coordination and communication between us at Mammoth and the U.S. Forest Service supervisors of the national forests surrounding Yellowstone National Park had become a top priority. So from July 23 on, the overall distribution of the outside firefighting crews, equipment, and supplies had been delegated to a group of fire experts brought into a temporary command post set up in West Yellowstone. Called the Greater Yellowstone Unified Area Command (GYUAC), it was placed under shared leadership representative of the various jurisdictions in the Greater Yellowstone area —Yellowstone and Grand Teton national parks; Bridger-Teton, Custer, Gallatin, Shoshone, and Targhee national forests. In all, almost twelve million acres.

As the chief ranger of Yellowstone, I still had the responsibility of coordinating the development of the strategy for fighting fires inside the park. I worked very closely with each of the incident commanders of the fires and with the area command. Bulldozers, for example, could not be used inside the park without my first being informed and, ultimately, not without the approval of Barbee. The superintendent was the only one who could override my decisions. However, he rarely did; both of us were strong advocates of "minimum impact suppression" tactics and the natural-burn— or as the public liked to say, "let-burn"—policy.

In the beginning we had thought that the Yellowstone staff could stay abreast of the fires. But when they grew literally by leaps and bounds and began to threaten the park villages, we realized they were beyond our resource capabilities.

The North Fork fire began on July 22, in the Targhee National Forest, from a smoldering cigarette butt left by a woodcutter. Though spotted within an hour of its start, it was already too big to stop with the limited number of firefighters and equipment Targhee had available. The winds that day—as they had all summer —were blowing strong; the fire started three hundred yards west of the park boundary and moved quickly toward Yellowstone's western boundary.

It was soon over seventy-five acres in size.

Smoke jumpers were sent by the Targhee staff to fight the fire inside the national forest, but the winds were too strong for them to jump. The fire continued to burn at will and spread into Yellowstone. The next day, bulldozer cuts were made along its back side inside the national forest. Inside Yellowstone, however, dozers were not allowed. Barbee and I knew the scars they'd leave would outlast anything the fire did. In forty to sixty years the visual impact from the fires would be gone, but the scarring of the land by a bulldozer blade would be around for hundreds of years. That was something we definitely did not want as a legacy of our administration. Our light-on-the-land tactics dictated that only hand tools and chain saws were to be used off the roads. This was to minimize the damage to the topsoil and plant life, which were very fragile in an environment as high and dry and rocky as Yellowstone's.

Even had bulldozers been used in the first twenty-four hours, there still would have been less than a 50 percent chance of stopping the flames: Hundreds of spot fires had already started in front of the main fire.

And so the North Fork fire had spilled into the park. We thought at the time that the usual summer rains would be coming and that the fire itself would help to rejuvenate some of the old forests on the Madison Plateau. Furthermore, even if there weren't any rains for a while, we had the Firehole River and a main road to stop the fire from spreading into the park's interior.

Old Faithful was fifteen miles to the east.

The more imminent peril at that time was Grant Village, and that battle was demanding every resource we had.

But just two days after it started, the North Fork fire was within nine miles of the Old Faithful complex and its thousands of visitors and four hundred buildings. By July 25 it was at 2,500 acres, on

July 26 at 8,2090 acres, and on July 27 at 9,700 acres. Then just as suddenly it calmed down, until August 1 when it made another leap from 12,700 acres to 17,700 acres and seemed more intent than ever to get to Old Faithful and its seventy million dollars worth of development.

If there was anyone in the world who hadn't heard of the Yellowstone fires by August 1, then they would soon enough. As it became apparent that one of this nation's most important historical structures, the Old Faithful Inn, was in danger of being burned, the media rushed to the park in ever greater droves. By the time Larry Caplinger, a newly appointed Type I fire team leader—the most experienced kind—who had been in charge of the North Fork fire in the Targhee National Forest, arrived to direct the first defense of Old Faithful, there seemed to be as many journalists in the park as firefighters.

Since the Forest Service had used bulldozers in the attempt to control the spread of the North Fork fire in Targhee, Caplinger was anxious to do the same inside Yellowstone. But Barbee and I again held firm against the use of bulldozers. Maybe it was okay in the scrub brush of Southern California to bulldoze firebreaks around million-dollar homes and communities, but we were not about to see the park's wilderness violated. U.S. Forest Service policy, too, was against bulldozers for initial attacks in wilderness areas, especially if the nearest buildings were fifteen miles away.

Caplinger was forced to rely on retardant drops, hand-dug firebreaks, and large backfires. He succeeded in stopping the advance of the fire toward Old Faithful by having a series of large back burns made just five miles west of the complex. That completed, he turned his attention to the fire's intense north flank. There on August 5 he had a three-mile-long backfire started. It might have worked, too, except that sudden high winds drove a finger of the backfire northward. To everyone's dismay that fire tore across the Madison Plateau as if there was no mercy to be had anywhere. On August 11 it jumped the Firehole River and then on August 15 swept northward over the Madison and Gibbon rivers into Madison Junction itself.

Once again we were evacuating visitors and campers and fighting to save structures. And wondering whether nature was ever going to return to some semblance of normality.

The North Fork, Fan, Clover-Mist, and Red-Shoshone fires were making park history. They refused to follow any of the usual rules of a wildfire. They didn't respect fire lines. Meadows, rivers, canyons, and roads, continued to be no obstacle to their progress.

So many populated areas—Grant, Lewis Lake campground, West Thumb, Old Faithful, Madison—had fallen under the fires' shadows that I wondered how the summer could possibly get any worse.

Our decisions at headquarters were based on projections being made by the nation's top fire experts. On August 2 a committee of such experts—including Dick Rothermel, known as one of the country's top fire-behavior gurus—had sent out a report from the GYUAC that said Yellowstone's fires would grow no more than 25 to 50 percent if they were left alone. The committee members were convinced the rugged mountain ranges and lakes would naturally contain most of the fires.

At that time 150,000 acres—between 7 and 8 percent of the park area—had burned. The committee's projected burn total of 187,500 to 225,000 acres was high but not unacceptable to us in the administration: It would have resulted in between 9 and 11 percent of the park area being burned.

Most of us saw the North Fork fire, already diverted from Old Faithful by Caplinger's firebreaks, as never reaching Madison Junction. Don Despain, a research biologist in Yellowstone and an ardent supporter of wildfires, felt there were too many young trees in the way. His records of past fires in Yellowstone showed that fires normally died out amid such young trees.

By August 15, the fire acreage in the park was up to 260,000 acres, 75 percent over the 150,000 acres at the time of the GYUAC's prediction. In the ten days the North Fork fire alone took to spread to Madison Junction it ballooned from 19,250 acres to an incredible 66,500 acres. Freed from the confines of the two rivers that flow through the Madison area, it had a clear shot at any of the other main fires.

We were no longer in control of the situation. It was obvious that no village in the park was immune any longer to the wildfires—not even Mammoth.

And as if to drive that point across to us, on August 20, "Black Saturday," there roared out of seemingly nowhere the worst fire day in Yellowstone's history. Gale-force winds of up to seventy miles per hour pushed the park's fires fiercely toward the northeast. Over 164,000 acres in and around the park went up in smoke as men and their machines had no choice but to retreat and let nature have her own way. Nearly five times the amount of acreage that had burned in the entire sixteen years since the natural-burn policy went into effect was burned that afternoon. The Clover-Mist fire alone burned 46,000 acres that day.

On that nightmarish weekend, the Norris campground and museum became the North Fork's next hostages. Flames twice as high as the trees swept in behind a thick gray smokescreen and got to within 150 yards of the museum, where they were stopped by the general barrenness of the surrounding geyser basin. Undeterred, however, the fire simply swept onward in the following days to Canyon Village. That complex also was saved, but then the fire roared on to the north and over Mount Washburn.

In the days to follow, so many of the park's campgrounds, villages, roads, and entrances would be threatened, closed, re-opened, and reclosed that I could hardly keep up with it all. Frustration was high among many of the firefighters, rangers, concessionaires, employees, and visitors. Spirits sank especially low when Grant Village and the picturesque Lake Hotel were shut down early for the summer—Grant because of continuing fire danger, and Lake because of the dwindling number of park visitors and the thick pall of dark smoke that encased it and Yellowstone Lake each day.

Smoke columns in the park became visible from as far away as five hundred miles, in places such as Casper and Cheyenne, Wyoming. Ash fell over one hundred miles away in Billings, Montana. The first of what would eventually be thousands of U.S. Army soldiers were called in to help the civilian crews. And as those convoys of soldiers and firefighters crisscrossed the park in their large green military trucks and huge helicopters, there was more of a sense of war than anything else in the entire area.

With the moisture level in some logs falling to much less than 7 percent—and to around 2 percent in the twigs and grasses, it was apparent we were in for a long and probably hopeless struggle. Even young and healthy vegetation was burning with ease.

So we completely revamped our firefighting tactics. No longer optimistic that we could contain any of the fires, except for the very newest and smallest ones, we directed all fire bosses to shift their resources and attention to protecting the communities inside and outside the park. New fires would be aggressively attacked, but backcountry fires already burning and not threatening buildings would be left alone.

There wasn't one of us who hadn't been humbled by the tremendous display of nature's power. If anything it served to remind us that after 116 years of running Yellowstone, man was still little more than a bit player. When our projections that the fires in Yellowstone could spread to over one million acres, or half of the park, were made public, it was as if we had admitted for the first time that we really didn't know what the hell was going to happen.

The cool dry front outside the command post this September Wednesday was bringing more than smoke and ash. It was carrying the possible destruction of Silver Gate and Cooke City, Montana, by the Storm Creek fire that started in the Custer National Forest; of the Crandall area of Wyoming by the Clover-Mist fire; and of the icon of the park, the Old Faithful Inn, by the North Fork fire.

By some miracle, no life had yet been lost in the Yellowstone fires. Tonight, however, that could change. The fires, it seemed, had saved their worst until everyone was most fatigued and discouraged.

If the Old Faithful Inn, which some claimed was the largest log structure in the world, or any of those towns or any of the hundreds of firefighters and soldiers defending them were destroyed, then God help those of us who had been the advocates of the park's natural-burn policy. Even though Old Faithful and the nearby town of West Yellowstone were being threatened by a man-caused fire that had originated *outside* the park, the media were covering it as if it were our responsibility. And most Americans were mad enough at us as it was for "allowing" even this much of the Yellowstone area to burn.

This summer was still weeks from its finish, but already it had become a public relations disaster unmatched in all the park's years. And the culprit, of course, was the Park Service, for not putting the fires out when they were young.

To the firefighters, already suffering low morale because of the way the fires were overrunning anything and everything put in their way, seeing the Old Faithful Inn become a giant inferno would be the worst emotional letdown yet. And to a public whose attention was presently focused on it by a large media corps, it would probably be the last straw. As the numbers of those who became convinced the park was destroyed went up, so would the credibility of those of us who said the fires were good for the park be diminished.

None of the park's villages had ever been evacuated because of fire before this summer. Emptying three thousand visitors and employees from Grant Village at the height of the season had had a major impact on the concessionaires. The need to evacuate had shaken many in the park administration. Nevertheless, one evacuation had not made us feel we were losing control of the fire scene in the park. But now we had to evacuate again.

Only a couple of hours ago, all six hundred guests at the Old Faithful Inn had been evacuated from their rooms. They had been sent back out onto the park's roads in their cars and tour buses to make sure the battle to save the inn and the complex's four hundred other buildings didn't trap them in the middle.

I looked once more around the busy room, saw that everything was going smoothly, and headed to the administration building. I needed to get back to the main communication room, where I'd have a more direct link to all the rangers in the park and an available telephone, too. Should things go crazy at Old Faithful, I wanted to be able to speak to the rangers there at once. A wildfire as large as the one threatening Old Faithful was more than flames and heat. It was also fireballs, howling hot winds, and thick deadly smoke that could drop a person in seconds.

The buildings at Old Faithful were old and wooden, with highly flammable shake roofs. If the fire did get a hold on the inn, the result would be unforgettable. The lobby was a natural pyre; it was a massive balconied cavern that was open all the way to the roof eighty-five feet overhead. Fire would eat its way up the exposed knobby log ribs and seemingly endless miles of pine railings.

Nevertheless, we, like the new fire incident commander at Old Faithful, Denny Bungarz, believed strongly that the Old Faithful complex was a highly defensible area. The cinder lawns around most of the buildings and the huge parking lots offered plenty of safety. The hundreds of firefighters, nearly twenty fire engines, and half a dozen fire retardant bombers and water-ferrying helicopters assigned to its defense should have enough muscle to deal with any errant fires. Furthermore, the fire crews there had removed most of the deadfall from around the complex, trimmed the lower branches from the trees so they couldn't act as ladders for any fires on the ground, and could turn on in a second the sprinkler systems on the inn's huge roof and observation deck.

Still, we already knew from bitter experience that the fight would not be an easy one. At Grant Village, back on July 25, over 280 firefighters and a small fleet of retardant-dropping bombers had turned back the Shoshone fire threat at the very end, but it had been nothing less than a heroic effort. The firefighters and their engines had lined the main road only a quarter mile west of the village to try to stop the advancing wall of flames, only to have it leap over their heads. Again and again they had knocked the flames out of the tree crowns just yards away and behind their positions, as embers the size of a man's fist landed in the complex itself. Incredibly no one was seriously injured. Everything man-made had been undamaged except for the rest room that was burned.

No less dramatic had been the saving of the other park villages threatened. About the only time there wasn't the fright of flames leaping over heads and embers pelting wooden buildings was also in July, when the Fan fire to the west of Mammoth went after the Church Universal and Triumphant's most sacred ground, their "Heart of the Inner Retreat" valley. Some said it was God sweeping over everyone's heads.

In a scene that could have been taken from a biblical tale, CUT's leader, Guru Ma, had led 250 of her followers to a meadow a few miles from the 16,000-acre fire's front, had them raise their arms at shoulder height toward the flames, and chase it away chanting at high speed all night and all day: "Reverse the tide. Roll them back. Set all free. . . ."

Whether the credit belonged to the slight rain that fell oddly enough only in that area, the one thousand firefighters and helicopters ferrying water, or to Guru Ma, the stopping of the fire at the park boundary was another of the handful of little victories that had helped us to stay optimistic that maybe, just maybe, we would soon be stopping the fires.

If conquering the fires were simply a matter of numbers of men and equipment, everyone would have been home by now. True, the buildings had been saved, but in the forests themselves we had known nothing but defeat. No decent rain had fallen since Memorial Day, and the land was primed to explode into flame. No matter what firefighting tactics were tried, the fire was uncontrollable.

No firebreaks—whether dug by hand or by bulldozers—slowed the fires.

There were voices in my own ranger ranks clamoring to have the park shut down. Why not concentrate all our energy and time on the fires? Why put the visitors at risk?

For one thing Barbee and I felt that such an awesome fire drama offered the public an educational opportunity too valuable to be denied. Perhaps not for another two or three centuries would anyone again have the opportunity to see and *experience* so directly fires on such a scale. What was happening around us was something people would be talking about centuries from now; it would have been unfortunate to allow only a few scientists and firefighters the chance to experience it.

And then there was the less romantic side of our reasoning— politics and economics. Too many people in the perimeter communities and inside the park too depended upon the park's visitors for their livelihood. To shut the park down entirely would have been devastating to all those merchants, park concessionaires, and thousands of employees. As it was, the two major businesses in the park, TW Recreational Services, Inc., and Hamilton Stores, Inc., were estimating they had lost many millions in sales and hotel reservations. For them and others, this year was hopelessly in the red, no matter how the rest of the summer turned out. The majority of the small vendors in the gateway communities, however, were doing a booming business selling supplies to the firefighters.

The number of visitors in July was down more than 7 percent, in August, 30 percent. With less than a quarter of the rooms in the park's main lodges occupied this past week, it was a foregone conclusion that thousands of employees would be getting their last paychecks any day now.

Still, enough visitors were coming that most merchants could at least keep hoping. The millions being spent by the firefighters and the media for lodging, food, supplies, and the occasional souvenir helped to offset some of the lost tourist dollars.

We wanted to do what was best for everyone. No decision could ever be made without our first stopping to consider its impact on both the land *and* the people of the Greater Yellowstone area. Yet we were keenly aware that one wrong decision in a summer like this could result in a horrible tragedy.

How nice it would have been to have had only the fires to worry about, I thought with a sigh as I climbed the stairs to the second floor of the administration building. Whenever I learned of a fire front edging up against another stretch of road, I thought not only of trees crashing onto the roadway, but also of cars and vans filled with visitors and their wide-eyed children passing only yards away from those flames.

For weeks now all of us had been getting along on far too few hours of sleep and far more adrenaline than calories. Common sense told me our nerves had to be wearing in places, even as I was amazed at how well we were still working together. But the fires were so ungodly huge that it seemed the requests for help or supplies of some kind were as constant as the odor of smoke.

The hours passed too slowly on the large white face of the wall clock in the communication center. As the morning of September

7 changed to noon and then to afternoon, the voices of those on the fire teams at Old Faithful squawked from the cramped room's switchboard and radios. Their short, crisp replies and requests seemed to indicate that all was in order and that they were not about to be ambushed by the rapidly approaching fire.

Still I was uneasy. After all that had happened the past two months, only a fool would have been arrogant enough to think there was absolutely no way such a huge and spread-out complex was going to be totally spared by the North Fork fire.

The fire had proven its tremendous might by stretching from that simple cigarette butt in some pine needles to over fifty miles and millions of trees. Over twenty miles wide in some places, it now had the park cut in half, yet there seemed to be no end to its appetite.

I was tempted at times to compare the power and intensity of the North Fork fire with what I had experienced as chief ranger of Hawaii Volcanoes National Park in 1983, when the mighty Kilauea Volcano sent fountains of dazzling orange lava over eight hundred feet into the air. The rivers of lava that oozed down from the giant crater in the following months were completely unstoppable. Then as now nature was making all the decisions and in total control. I was able to quench the small grass fires the lava flow produced, but as for the main body, that had to be conquered by something far larger than the volcano—the Pacific Ocean.

So large had the North Fork become that it was no longer classified as one fire but two. Its north half, which had swept on past Madison Junction and burned through the Norris and Canyon Village areas, was now known as the Wolf Lake fire. The North Fork half was at 145,800 acres and the Wolf Lake half at 61,200 acres, for a total of 207,000 acres. That was second only to the Clover-Mist fire's 238,000 acres, which had started almost two weeks before the North Fork, and which was *still* burning.

What size the North Fork–Wolf Lake fire would reach was anyone's guess, but one thing was clear: It had the capacity to cover nearly the *entire* interior of the park. And all around it were nearly a million acres of forest just as vulnerable as those which had already burned. All that was needed were continued droughtlike conditions and more winds like those of Black Saturday. The black-white mosaic on my fire map could easily become a solid black square any day now.

It seemed only a matter of hours before the eastern perimeters of the North Fork–Wolf Lake fire could be joining forces with the western edge of the Clover-Mist and the north edge of the park's next largest fire, the Snake River Complex, which itself totaled nearly 206,000 acres.

Hardly more than a dozen miles now separated the North Fork–Wolf Lake fires from the others. With the right conditions that distance could be bridged in a day or less. We had plenty of examples of other fires covering that kind of distance in that short a time. A fire appropriately named the Hellroaring advanced a mile an hour for eight hours on Black Saturday, while on the same day the Clover-Mist fire went sixteen miles and the Storm Creek fire north of Silver Gate and Cooke City ran for ten miles—against the winds!

And then there were the great fires of 1910. In that summer over five million acres burned in western Montana and the Idaho panhandle, three million of them during a single forty-eight-hour period! Those fires eventually burned themselves out, but not before they killed eighty-five people. If it happened once, it could happen again.

Sometime just before four P.M. the traffic on the radio in the communication center increased tremendously. Most of the voices belonged to the Old Faithful rangers. From the urgency in some of the voices I knew the front of the North Fork fire had finally crested the low ridge to the west and south of the Old Faithful Inn. It wasn't difficult to picture the scene: the sky dark with smoke; the sun barely visible, a dim fireball the size of a dime.

And then the even greater darkness, like that of the night, until at last the fires reared up a stone's throw away, and roared forward spitting firebrands and embers.

Voices and engines of every kind would add to the chaos: off to the sides the hissing of fire hoses trying to save the wood-shingled roofs and shake walls of the numerous buildings.

Trees that only seconds before had seemed safe would be quickly overheated by the fire's breath and flare into torches. The thick smoke and whipping ash would assault the lungs and eyes of humans and animals alike.

I could imagine the scene all too easily, because I'd been through it myself before. Our main concern now was the safety of the employees and visitors still at the Old Faithful complex. Would they panic and think the fire was going to burn right through the air to them? I knew it would certainly look that way.

There were reports that buildings were indeed burning, that a fuel truck had exploded, that the fire had surrounded the entire complex and was on all the ridges. I was able to contact Joe Evans, the West District ranger, who was right in the middle of it all at the little ranger station. It was true the fire was burning more ferociously than anyone had anticipated, he said in his low, calm voice. But as far as he knew no one was injured. There was some panic, even crying, among the concessionaire employees, but at least all were safely huddled in the open areas around the Old Faithful geyser.

The winds were howling, ripping madly through the area, he said. Embers the size of golf balls were being whipped everywhere, and spot fires were springing up all around. But the firefighters were holding their ground.

By the time I left the communication center, night had finally fallen over the park's many smoldering galaxies. I was as exhausted as if I had been in the middle of the fire lines at Old Faithful.

The Old Faithful Inn had been saved, thanks largely to the sprinklers on its cedar-shake roof. But, again, the margin between victory and disaster had been razor thin.

Winds of up to eighty miles per hour had whipped the blaze with such intensity that the firefighters dousing the buildings with foam and water were forced to retreat. Trees were described as "popping like matchsticks." Weather forecasters had predicted strong winds, but the actual velocity was beyond anyone's most pessimistic expectations. One eighteen-inch-thick lodgepole pine near the inn had snapped as if it were little more than a twig.

About one hundred visitors were trapped inside the area when the winds shifted and pushed the fires around them. The heat had become intense everywhere, but fortunately no one was killed or injured. It disturbed me that anyone except firefighters had been in the complex when the fire rolled into it: All visitors should have been cleared out. But, then again, no one had expected the fire to arrive that quickly; for days the winds had been undecided, and had given no clue as to where and how fast they would blow.

The most experienced fire bosses had described it as unlike anything they'd ever seen. They felt that had the wind shifted even a little more to the south, the Old Faithful Inn would have burned. As it was, over sixteen cabins and a storage shed were destroyed, while an employee dormitory, several storage buildings, a water tank, TV transmitter station, and five vehicles were damaged.

The peak of the firestorm had occurred around 4:30 P.M. It lasted an hour. While the cabins and sheds in Old Faithful were burning, so were other buildings just outside the park's eastern boundary. For the first time this summer, private properties had become victim to the Greater Yellowstone fires.

Over in Silver Gate, a backfire set on Forest Service land to fend off the Storm Creek fire had jumped the lines and gone the wrong direction. Racing more than three miles down the north side of the canyon, it destroyed four cabins in Cooke Pass and a shed in Cooke City. And in the Crandall area, the leading edge of the massive Clover-Mist fire burned three cabins, a small store, and a dozen trailers.

Now the only question was: Which community would be next?

22

The orange glow from its forest fire made Bunsen Peak resemble the volcano that it had been in prehistoric times. Though it was almost one in the morning, those flames 2,300 feet above Mammoth's rooftops were as active as if it had been the middle of the day. Reflected against a low and heavy ceiling of uneasy clouds and a wall of smoke blacker than the night, they looked as if they could hardly wait to sweep down from their mountain host to devour the village's three hundred buildings. A strong wind from the south could shove the fire front onto everything in less than an hour.

I stepped off the veranda of the administration building and turned toward home, my attention still riveted to the fiery spectacle overhead.

The last two days since the North Fork fire's southern section had swept past Old Faithful—and since the near disasters at Silver Gate and Cooke City, and the destruction at Crandall and Cooke Pass—had seemed as if the world were falling in around the park. President Reagan had become so alarmed that he dispatched a cabinet-level delegation to assess the damage.

Now the North Fork's northern front was right at Mammoth's own south edge. Some were saying that one more spell of strong winds was all it would take to have these same flames licking at Gardiner's edges, too.

Unfortunately, strong winds were exactly what the weather experts had predicted for today after sunrise.

My fire staff and I were no longer sure just how large the North

Fork fire really was; so much smoke was spewing from Yellowstone's heart that it appeared the entire park was one huge convection cloud. Breathing the air around Mammoth and Gardiner, where ash was falling like snow, was as bad, air quality experts were saying, as smoking four packs of cigarettes a day. Yesterday the sun had been little more than a red dot, with visibility less than two hundred yards at times.

I walked a little faster and tried not to think about how the park was sinking ever deeper into controversy. It was, some would say, poetic justice for those of us who had refused to put some of the fires out at the start.

I passed a parked lime-green fire engine bearing California license plates. It had to be worth a quarter-million dollars, and it was one of about twenty fire engines in the village. At least as many others were due to arrive by morning from other parts of the park and Wyoming. Most of them were probably driving here right this moment, over winding cliff-hugging roads and through choking smoke.

Mammoth was the newest top fire priority in the region. With winds of twenty to forty miles per hour due the next two days, and possible gusts of sixty miles per hour, it was a certainty the North Fork was not going to stay put on Bunsen. Would it make it to Gardiner?

The fire on Bunsen Peak had put on an impressive and disquieting show as night was falling. I doubted there was anyone who saw it who wasn't worried daybreak might bring the worst day yet in this incredible saga. At a town meeting in the Mammoth elementary school yesterday evening I'd tried to assure everyone there was no cause for imminent alarm. But even I was beginning to listen to myself with more than a little skepticism. How could I expect others to believe me or my fire staff anymore? Every prediction we made about the fires seemed to go awry. Hadn't we said not all that long ago that the headquarters was too far removed from any of the fires to be threatened?

If the fires did explode down Bunsen Peak, we certainly would be ready for them. About one and a half miles separated Mammoth village from the flames, and I had plans for at least fifty fire engines, three hundred firefighters, and several retardant bombers to try—weather and smoke permitting—to beat them back.

All told there were 230 fire engines on duty throughout the Yellowstone area and nearly 10,000 firefighters as of this Saturday, September 10. And from all indications we were going to need every single one to keep this Saturday from surpassing the destruction total of August 20, Black Saturday.

Sunlight Basin and the Clarks Fork area in Wyoming were directly in the path of the still-growing Clover-Mist fire. The homes and resorts there were scattered in so many trees that I doubted they could escape some damage. Cooke City and Silver Gate were in that same area and still being threatened by the Storm Creek fire. Thus they'd been evacuated again.

But those areas were outside the park and therefore the responsibilities of others. What we were facing in the park was daunting enough.

In addition to the danger here at Mammoth, several other of the park's complexes were in the possible paths of huge fire fronts: Lake had another arm of the North Fork fire, as well as the Clover-Mist and Snake River Complex fires nearing it; Canyon and Tower were right beside the Wolf Lake fire, which had nearly overrun Canyon a few days ago. Anything could happen, as had become evident yesterday afternoon when an arm of the same flames on Bunsen Peak swept seventeen miles in four hours east to Tower Junction and joined the Wolf Lake fire.

Gardiner, too, was as crowded with fire engines and firefighters, and had a list of contingency plans should it have to be evacuated. And above Gardiner the little gold-mining settlement called Jardine had already been evacuated, because it had only one escape route through the mountains.

I still wasn't sure whether I should evacuate all of the non-firefighters in Mammoth. There was a definite possibility it might be necessary. Still, I was going to put it off as long as I could; the evacuation of the headquarters would send out the worst signal yet in this fight against the park's fires. I wanted to delay until I had no choice. And keep hoping that the cold front moving in had some precipitation in it.

If it was necessary to evacuate, telephone calls would be made to each person or family, and rangers sent to each household that didn't answer our calls. I doubted that there were more than 150 non-firefighters still in Mammoth. And from the packed look of most of the cars parked outside the residences, it appeared many of them were thinking of leaving, too.

I turned down the little walkway to my residence. The red metal roof on my home was bright from the light of the North Fork fire. A believer in premonitions might have seen it as a warning of imminent doom. At the back door I took a deep breath, then grimaced at the odor of carbon seemingly attached to every molecule of oxygen. The stuff was even on my lips. I expelled the filthy air noisily. Whatever happened to the usual poetry of a high-country summer night—the cool pine-scented breezes, the twinkling bands of stars, the cries of the coyotes? I couldn't wait for the summer to end.

The screen door's hinges creaked and gave me a slight scare. Tana eased up to the carbon smudges on my yellow firefighting shirt. She looked a little like a tired angel with her wrinkled white night robe gleaming softly in the fire's light.

"I'm worried," she whispered, as if the denizens about might be encouraged by the fear in her voice.

Who wasn't worried? It seemed all I did was think about fires.

"Tana, I need to rest for a few minutes." I sighed.

I put my arm around her shoulders, and we went inside the house.

As was so often the case now, I felt as if we were almost strangers. We saw so little of each other because of the tremendous amount of extra responsibilities the fires had brought to me and my staff. Ever since the middle of July, when I'd jumped out of the inferno at Calfee Creek, I had become little more than a creaking sound in the wee hours of the morning—coming in around one or two and leaving before the first sunbeams had faded any stars.

I cleared my throat. "Listen—"

She put up her hand. "Dan, you must be exhausted."

For the first time in two days, ever since the fires had started surging toward Mammoth, I allowed my shoulders to sag. It felt nice for a change not to have to explain myself.

"I am," I said simply.

I followed Tana into the bedroom. I sat on the bed's edge and telephoned some of the other incident commanders and Area Command in West Yellowstone. I wanted to confirm that all the fire engines I'd requested were on their way. We needed them by daybreak, I emphasized. The fire at Mammoth's edge was threatening to take off anytime. I sympathized with their worries that their men were dead tired and shouldn't have to drive all night to get to Mammoth. But I had to stress to them that any delay at all could be a terrible mistake: The tighter the fire closed around Mammoth, the harder it would be for them to get in.

At last I lay back and closed my eyes. Just last night I had rushed in my car to the Indian Creek campground to set a back burn around it to save its scenic stand of pines from the North Fork fire. Indian Creek was eight miles south and the last developed area between the fire and Mammoth. I'd gone to it filled with frustration. I'd grown so tired of watching the black on the fire maps grow and grow each day as if none of us were doing anything.

Last night had been the anniversary of my marriage to Tana. For weeks I had been hoping that the fires would slow down enough that I would be able to surprise her with an evening at a little romantic hideaway in the Paradise Valley called Chico Hot Springs. I wanted to let her know that I loved her dearly and that I deeply appreciated all the family matters she had had to take care of on her own ever since the fire season exploded.

I knew I should be getting some sleep. But I couldn't let myself do so. At least not now. There were still too many concerns on my mind.

I wondered if those fire engines being sent from the other fires would be enough. And would they even be able to get through? We were surrounded by fire and smoke on every side but the north. Also, would there be enough time to evacuate Mammoth and Gardiner if the winds suddenly picked up? And what kinds of stories and pictures would those hundreds of journalists who had rushed here from Old Faithful be sending out next to the world? So far their accounts had been largely slanted to the dramatic, inaccurate about the extent of the damage to the park, and nearly always simplistic and devoid of scientific data. The Associated Press, whose news items were repeated daily by thousands of newspapers and radio stations, had said most of the park was blackened. It, like the rest, never mentioned that over half of the vegetation in each burn area was *not* burned, or that five of the major fires had started outside the park, even though those points were made right on their reporters' fire map handouts each morning.

I thought of the rows and rows of TV satellite dish trucks from all the network and cable news crews parked outside the Mammoth Hot Springs Hotel. They were like a cluster of hornets—each waiting for the slightest disturbance to buzz into action. Tomorrow, if most predictions held true, they were going to be buzzing madly indeed.

"Dan?"

"Hmmph?"

"What are you going to do?"

"About evacuating?"

"Yes. Are you going to do it?"

I listened for a few seconds to the crackling of the fire on Bunsen, audible through the window a few feet to my right.

I knew we were going to have to evacuate. But *when* depended on what the fire and wind did, what the temperature and humidity were in the next few hours. Hopefully the fire would settle down, but right now it was still unpredictable.

"Yes, I'm going to evacuate. But for now I'm going to rest my eye for about twenty minutes. Then I'll decide as to when," I finally mumbled.

I rested the back of my right forearm across my good eye, as I was in the habit of doing each night. With my left hand I groped for Tana.

For days now my incident management team and I had been planning for the possible evacuation of headquarters. I was worried that with so many fire engines and support vehicles coming into such a small area as Mammoth we were going to be too crowded.

244

If and when the fight to defend Mammoth did begin, the trucks and the hundreds of firefighters would be racing every which way. With the engines darting to the fires and the families trying to get out, there was a chance of serious accidents.

To be on the safe side, we'd recommended that those not directly involved in the firefighting or running of the park leave before the weekend. In the meantime everyone else in Mammoth was to scatter their firewood at least fifty feet away from the sides of their houses, clear away all dead limbs and brush, and spray their houses' roofs and sides with water from their garden hoses. We'd even taken down the Thomas Moran paintings in the visitor center museum and put them and some of the more valuable documents from the archives in safer spots.

We'd also closed to the public all the campgrounds and remaining lodges, including the huge Mammoth Hot Springs Hotel and all interior roads. It was the first time the entire park had ever been closed to overnight visitors because of fires. But with such huge fires now covering much of the interior, and with every ranger occupied with the firefighting, Yellowstone was simply no place for visitors.

"You haven't slept at all, have you?" I asked.

"I can't. I made the mistake of looking out before I went to bed. When the fire popped up from Bunsen's back side and spilled over the crest, it was just so incredible, Dan. I sat there on the picnic table for the longest time, thinking of how close it was to our home, and to us. How helpless I felt. All I kept thinking was, The kids and I should be gone already. We shouldn't be here."

I'd seen the fire then too. The glow from its sudden strange flare-up had brought many in Mammoth out of their homes. They stood around in hushed groups, the parents in night robes and the children in pajamas and surgical masks as protection against the smoke that had been plaguing us for weeks. It was an awesome sight: red flames springing from behind the peak almost as if from a flamethrower, then racing briefly down the Mammoth side of the thickly forested and steep mountain. I had even been able to hear the crackling of the larger trees torching.

I'd tried to telephone Barbee at midnight, to warn him things

245

were looking progressively worse. But his line was busy. I'd tried again several more times over the next half hour with the same result. At last I figured he must have had the telephone off the hook. He had been through a lot and no doubt needed sleep as much as the rest of us.

Tana squeezed my hand. She spoke in a dreamlike tone.

"As I sat out there watching that fire coming closer, I wondered where you were. I kept hoping that you weren't somewhere up there on that mountain. I . . . I have to confess that in the middle of all the confusion I hopped on a bicycle and went looking for you. I went everywhere in Mammoth. The elk and firemen were every-where . . . but I couldn't find you.

"Then I finally gave up and came home, to try to sleep. But I couldn't. How could I when I didn't know if the fire wasn't soon going to be at our house? I . . . worry about you."

I pressed my lips together. We'd been through this several times before. She couldn't understand why I insisted on visiting the fires personally, whether on foot or in a helicopter, why I didn't just stay put at the command post. And why, as on more than one occasion, I fought a fire personally, as at Calfee Creek and Indian Creek.

I suppose I could have stayed with my desk and charts every day as some commanders did, but these fires were virtually rewriting the book on firefighting. And I, like everyone, was trying to make some sense out of what was going on. I'd decided that planning anything based entirely on paper predictions or on second-hand information was just too risky in such severe conditions. I told myself: I know this park, so—damn it!—why can't we get a hold on these fires?

It was almost as if the park had a mind of its own now. Anything to do with the fires seemed to go wrong. Even something as simple as a fire siren test couldn't go well. Thursday evening at the daily village meeting in the Mammoth elementary school, I had said that on Friday noon there was going to be a test of the fire siren; we would give it a couple of ten-second blasts, I said, to make sure it was working.

I told everyone not to worry; if there was an actual evacuation everyone would be either telephoned or notified in person by one of the Mammoth patrol rangers. And if the wind should suddenly go wild and a major firestorm erupt before calls or rangers could be sent out, the fire siren would emit a steady long wail and everyone was immediately to get in their cars and move them either to the ball field beside the elementary school or to Gardiner. A long siren blast was nothing less than a life-and-death matter!

As luck would have it, about ten o'clock one of the park radio technicians was giving the siren some final maintenance checks before the noon test, and the siren not only started blaring but became stuck. I'd been in the middle of a fire briefing with Barbee. The wailing from the siren was the sort given off by the old air-raid sirens: loud and spine-tingling.

I rushed outside to see if the mountain was suddenly throwing fireballs into the middle of Mammoth, for that was what the ear-piercing wail instilled immediately in all our minds. But to my surprise the mountain and Mammoth looked no different from before. For over twenty minutes the siren had kept up the nauseating howling, driving nearly everyone half mad.

I turned onto my left side and looked at Tana.

"What did you do when the siren went off this morning?" I asked.

Her eyes opened wide. It was as if the siren were still blasting clearly somewhere in the back of her thoughts.

"I was out in the yard, putting the kids' bikes away and planning what I should do in case I had to evacuate. The fire alarm ripped through the air so suddenly that I about jumped out of my skin. I was thinking, This can't be happening! They said there would be a lot of time. This must mean the fire has really taken off and snuck up on them and is going to come down on us any minute. I really have to get going!

"Oh, my heart was racing so madly, and I was running around trying to grab Trevor, putting things in the van, getting ready to pick up Brooke at school."

"And then?" I asked.

"Well then someone came over and said, 'Do you think it's a false alarm?' And I said no. But he thought it was."

"And of course you called and found out?"

"Why yes. But tonight before I put Trevor and Brooke to bed, I just left everything in the car. Dan, I tell you it was such an eerie afternoon—so dark and with that brown smoke so thick I couldn't even see your office or the chapel."

I rolled onto my back and stared at the ceiling, mulling over how the fires completely dominated our lives. It was almost as if there wasn't anything else that mattered. I went to bed with them on my mind. I woke with them on my mind. I spent all day plotting and planning about them—seven straight weeks of twenty-hour days. There was no way to get around them. No chance even of striking up a conversation in which the fires didn't get mentioned.

"You know, Dan, I did learn something very important in all the confusion."

"What's that?"

"I learned that there are very few things we own that are *truly* all that important. When the alarm was silenced, I looked to see just what it was that I had put in the car. I was amazed to find it was little more than Trevor, Brooke, the family photos, some clothes, the quilt Grandma made, and of course Snowball."

I laughed, then stretched. I wanted to say something funny about that large white ball of unkempt fur that was the children's guinea pig. But as the words were making their way to my lips they were ambushed by sleep.

My eyes popped open. I stared nervously into the blackness of the bedroom. Something wasn't right.

I rolled over and focused on the alarm clock's lighted numerals—3:30. I'd been asleep for . . . what, fifteen minutes? That seemed too short a time for anything drastic to have happened. Yet I sensed that the night outside was far worse than when I'd dropped off to sleep. What was it that had awakened me?

I listened closely. And before long I was aware that the fire's crackling was louder than before.

I pivoted onto the bed's edge and bounded up and away from a restless Tana. Into the kitchen and out the back door I rushed to look at the fire on Bunsen. It sounded much closer.

The North Fork fire had indeed moved closer, as well as further along the ridges on the east and west sides of the village. The tall old pines on Sepulcher were sending orange and yellow flames straight into the sky like jets on a gas burner. There was a definite stirring in the air.

More rest was impossible. I had to return to the fire command post to start the evacuation preparations. If the fires circled around to the Gardner River canyon, our only escape route would be burning too.

I hurried into the house and made for the bedroom. Tana had the light on and was sitting on the edge of the bed. Her eyes were wide. I went straight to the bathroom and splashed water on my face.

When I entered the kitchen, Tana was making something for me to eat. I sat on a chair and slipped on my boots, saying: "The fire's gotten worse. We're nearly surrounded, so I'm going to go ahead and evacuate."

She put a sandwich and a banana in my hand. "Should I wake Brooke and Trevor now?"

I paused at the door. "No, not just yet. I think it would be best to let them sleep a little more.

"You don't think that will be too late?"

"No," I replied in what I hoped was a convincing tone.

On the way to the incident command post I noticed that most of the windows on the old officers' quarters to my left and the old canteen to my right were alive with reflected flames. The surfeit of dancing yellows and oranges at every side of me and the brightly lit sky above made it look as if I were hurrying through a burning ring.

At the administration building I headed around to the back, where my ranger car was parked. There were still a couple of hours before dawn, and I wanted to check the situation at the fire front before I did anything. I unlocked the car, tossed my walkie-talkie radio onto the dash, and slid in behind the steering wheel.

On the way to the south edge of the village I passed the Mammoth Hot Springs Hotel, the dining hall, and the Hamilton General Store. The wooden buildings, as well as the dozens of vacation cottages and the three-story employee dorms to their rear, were clustered so tightly together that I imagined flames leaping rapidly from one of their wood shingle roofs to another. It was as if the planners of the complex had refused to believe that fire would ever strike Mammoth.

A short distance later I came upon the haunted-looking limestone mass of the hot springs. The tree skeletons and mineral protrusions poking from it loomed larger than life in the fire's glow. The red glints of cow elk's eyes around the base of the terraces added to the surrealism.

In the low area below the village's drinking water reservoir, where the wooden dormitory and cafeteria buildings of the Youth Activities Conservation Corps camp were located, the fire wall was less than a mile away. I inched the car through smoke as thick in places as fog. Everything outside the windshield looked ghostly, elusive, even the firefighters passing before me.

I backed into a space between two idle fire engines and headed again for the main road.

At the main road I turned left and headed south to above the hot springs, where after two miles I ran into the fire. I quickly turned around.

In Mammoth I went directly to the fire command post in the fire cache, where I found Steve Frye, the very man I wanted to consult with. The slender, blond-haired North District ranger looked more tired than I'd ever seen him. He too had been up most of the night thinking about the coming firefight and the need to evacuate the remaining families from Mammoth.

We huddled over some maps and coffee. After several minutes we decided to notify all residents at five o'clock. Everyone would be given until after daybreak to leave. We didn't want any unnecessary rush or panic.

"I'll alert my patrol rangers," he said when we parted.

I headed for Barbee's home to let him know of the decision personally. I felt sadness at the thought that for the first time in its long and illustrious history Fort Yellowstone was being evacuated. If the buildings could talk, I wondered what they would have said.

In passing the old canteen building, I noticed the lights inside it were burning brightly. Its workers, too, must have been swamped. Weeks before, the little gymnasium inside had been partitioned into separate office areas to handle such things as public affairs, finances, and workmen's compensation. If someone wanted to rent out their fire truck, or bulldozer, or even a chain saw, they went there to take care of the transactions and paperwork. It was all very efficient, just as the great majority of our firefighting operations had been to date. And yet even with such professionalism and so much manpower, money, and other resources, we had been utterly helpless in stopping the fires.

Could we have killed the North Fork at its beginning and thus prevented this from ever happening? Should I have allowed bull-dozers inside the park to slow the fire or try to stop it? So many questions were flying through my head. It was as if the evacuation was a confirmation of what a lot of critics had been saying: We had acted too slowly at the beginning on the main fires. But hadn't the North Fork and others started outside the park and been ag-gressively attacked right from the start by the Forest Service's teams? And yet still they'd raced out of control. How could anyone have stood a chance against the drought conditions and high winds that had characterized the entire summer?

I told myself that now was not the time for doubts and second guesses. There was a village to be saved, and that had to be my first consideration.

Not half an hour after the evacuation notice was given, the cold front's winds picked up and prodded the fire closer to Mam-moth.

As Mammoth's remaining families, including mine and Frye's, streamed north like refugees from a war front, a chilly breeze buffeted the village from the southwest with infuriating steadiness.

I met with the fire team leaders in the command post. Outside, the media and firefighters scrambled about taking up positions for the coming assault. The battle everyone had been waiting for was finally upon us. Nature was bringing us into direct combat with one of the biggest fires in history. There would be no room for mistakes from here on.

"Today could be the worst of the summer," I warned the grim mix of faces around me in the glare of the command post's fluorescent lights. "We had been hoping for some moisture in this front, but now the meteorologists say it may not come until Monday, if at all. So don't count on Mother Nature for any relief. We're going to have to do it all on our own."

"Is there no end to these fires!" a fire crew leader muttered disgustedly.

"Someday. Believe me—someday!" another offered.

Laughter broke out all over. Styrofoam cups were lifted to lips and everyone tried sipping more energy from their strong, bitter coffee.

I continued: "As you know, the North Fork has spread around both flanks of Bunsen Peak, as well as up the back side and over the top. If it gets a strong enough wind at its back, which is exactly what is supposed to happen today, it'll come roaring off there and down through the side canyons like a blowtorch. It's burned through two hundred and thirty thousand acres so far and looks like it wants to go through a heck of a lot more. And it just might, if nature doesn't give us a break."

"What about water and retardant drops?"

I shook my head slowly. "I don't know. We're hoping to have reconnaissance flights made this morning, but the inversion from the cooler air in the front is probably keeping the smoke too thick around Mammoth to allow flights of any kind."

"You mean we have a whole fleet of choppers sitting just a rock's throw away, and there's not a damned thing they can do for us?" someone moaned.

I held my hands up to show I was just as frustrated. "We'll have to see if enough of the smoke disperses by the time the main winds hit. But don't count on it. This whole valley has a tendency to hold in the cooler air. We could be using flashlights to see who's next to us by midafternoon."

A lot of eyebrows arched high. By denying us the retardant drops, the fire had effectively denied us one of our most important firefighting tools. We were going to have to stop renegade walls of fire with hand tools and fire hoses. Even the most optimistic among us would have to admit that all the signs, except one, pointed to another disastrous day.

"If it will make you feel any better, our lookout on Mount Sheridan reported rain, hail, and snow fell in his area last night at the high elevations. So what he got could reach us today, if it doesn't peter out or veer away. And, I've been told there's been a significant increase in the moisture in the air at Mammoth the last few hours. On Black Saturday when we had one hundred and sixty-four thousand acres burn the humidity was two to four percent. Today it's supposed to be over forty percent."

"That hasn't stopped the North Fork yet," a fire crew chief offered through a mouth of pipe smoke.

"Nor will it today. With all the heat it's generating, it's as if it's in its own world. But, the humidity might keep it moving slowly enough that we can defend against the fire piecemeal rather than having to deal with it all at once. And then maybe the rain at Mount Sheridan will reach it, before it reaches Mammoth proper."

Just before noon the wind suddenly and dramatically picked up. A darkness settled onto Mammoth that resembled night. Everyone covered their faces and looked apprehensively to the south to Bunsen and west to the swirling chaos on Sepulcher. The smoke was pouring off them and avalanching into Mammoth so thickly that streetlights and headlights came on everywhere.

I dashed to my car and drove through the brown smoke toward the YACC camp. My gut feeling was that the fire was making its main thrust.

At the YACC camp hundreds of firefighters were hosing down the buildings that had not been sprayed with fire retardant foam, as well as the ground around the buildings. Some of the crown fires were less than fifty yards away. The engines were lined up like tanks, their crews spraying their water ammunition toward the fires as if everyone's life was hanging in the balance.

The heat was blistering, the smoke nearly overpowering. Dust was whipping about madly; it tore at my car's paint and the men's bandanna-covered faces. Some firefighters staggered when stung by the flying dirt and tree parts, or when smothered by the noxious smoke. Most, though, kept their heads down and grimly refused to budge.

Fortunately, most of the buildings had been foamed by now, for the firestorm was spitting embers by the thousands. Spot fires flared wherever the grass and pine needles hadn't been wetted down, but were immediately stomped out under the boots or shovels of firefighters.

So much smoke was rising from so many spots that the entire area appeared to be percolating the stuff. I felt as though I was trying to breathe in a room in which someone had left the damper in the chimney closed. When the crowns of trees only fifty to one hundred feet away from the buildings started bursting into giant torches, it seemed only a matter of seconds before everything else in the camp was going to do the same. From a side canyon that fed the village's water reservoir, downdrafts pushed out flame and embers. A huge new cinderblock vehicle-maintenance building, presently being used as a cafeteria and a shelter for several hundred of the firefighters, shimmered in the heat as flames unfurled like little flags at its foundation.

I thought of the trees throughout upper Mammoth and the Mammoth campground. Most of them were well over a century old and sitting beside wooden buildings. My own house was at the edge of the chapel grounds, where there were probably a couple dozen very tall and stately old pines. If the fire ever did reach my neighborhood, it would have a feast. Nearly every building was old and wooden.

I drove my car around to the north side of the camp, past the rows of small trailers and campers that belonged to the seasonal rangers and firefighters. A group of firefighters rushed past my car, heading in the same direction. I stopped and jumped out to see what was happening. And I saw exactly what I had feared: dozens of spot fires cropping up in the meadows that swept down past the old cemetery and horse corral into Mammoth.

I hurried back to the car and restarted its engine. The ash on the windshield was thick. I squirted it with some windshield washer fluid and turned on the wiper blades. They streaked across the glass, smearing the black flecks. When I could see through it, I turned off the wipers and started to put the car into gear. Something on the windshield, however, caused me to pause.

I stared at the glass more closely. Tiny clear blips were popping up everywhere, by the hundreds. I couldn't believe it. Rain!

My hand slapped the dashboard. At last, the one thing we needed more than anything to defeat the fire had arrived.

I rolled down my window and stuck my head out. Shutting my eyes, I let the misty drizzle fall onto my skin. Every drop tingled. In the back of my mind a voice whispered that every leaf, every needle, every inch of bark that wasn't in the flames' grip was receiving the same drizzle. A few hours of this, and everything would be too wet to burn.

Laughter reached my ears above the car's idling motor and the growling of fire engine pumps. I opened my eyes. Firefighters who only moments ago had been rushing around looking grim and frantic were now smiling. Some were slapping each other on the back.

Flames were still tearing at the camp's edge and looking as if any second they would gain on the camp's buildings. But suddenly I no longer thought they would make it.

I put the car into gear, flipped the windshield wiper knob on again, and headed toward the main road.

The wet weather was the one big cold front I had kept expecting since early August. Much of the park that afternoon and for several days afterward received light rain and a dusting of snow. Some of the peaks received several inches of snow. We finally had a real chance to gain the upper hand.

The moisture that fell on the ground in the lower elevations was not all that much—less than four hundredths of an inch in Mammoth. But it *was* moisture. And what was important was not how much snow or rain fell, but that the humidity rose significantly. The rise of just twenty percentage points did more to squelch the fires than all the tens of millions of dollars and equipment and men we had thrown at them over the past two months.

It was extremely frustrating to know that if the rains and snow had come to the Yellowstone high country in August, as they normally did, we would have been spared most of the summer's conflagrations without hardly having to lift a finger. Still, I was very happy that they had finally come. For a while everyone had been wondering if the firestorms were going to last into October and even November. If they had, there would have been a lot more than just trees and meadows and the occasional cabin burning.

By the next morning after the front reached Mammoth, I decided any imminent danger of the fire burning into the village was past, and I had the evacuation order rescinded. My family and the others were telephoned at their motel rooms in Bozeman and Livingston and told they could return. By Monday morning most had done so, including Tana and the kids.

For those of us at the fire command post, however, the drama was hardly ended. We were still under the gun: One more sunny, windy day anytime soon, and much of the area could be in flames again.

I drove straight from the YACC camp fire up to the Swan Lake Flats to make sure that other parts of the fire front were also being cooled by the moisture. On the open plateau just above Mammoth that certainly seemed to be the case. And the cooler wind was clearing out the smoke considerably. I rushed back to Mammoth and was soon heading by helicopter to other parts of the front to check them out.

While the North Fork and Wolf Lake fires were bearing down on the Northern Range, it had been difficult for us at the Mammoth fire command to tell just where and how extensive the fires' fronts were. Each time I had gone out in a reconnaissance helicopter, the pilot had been forced by the tremendously huge smoke clouds that hung above the fires to fly low to the ground. It was the worst sort of perspective—along with being more than a little frightening when one thought of the peaks looming on every side in the murky air. Many times when we thought we were above a front, it turned out we were merely above a cluster of very smoky spot fires.

Several times as the North Fork raced toward Old Faithful and then Mammoth we were fortunate enough to have detailed digital and photographic images of the park's fires taken by NASA to help us in our planning. Flying at sixty-five thousand feet in an ER-2 jet, an enhanced version of the U-2 spy plane, and in a C-130, a medium-altitude, propeller-driven, cargo-type plane, the NASA pilots used infrared and thermal sensors to photograph the North Fork's fire's front. The two planes were crammed with remote sensors that could see through the smoke to all the hot areas. Their highly sophisticated instruments could spot fires in the backcountry that were impossible to see by traditional ground methods. The images on the scanners on board the planes were recorded on videotape and delivered to the Area Command at West Yellowstone for use by the field commanders.

As I flew toward Tower and Roosevelt that Saturday afternoon, I was able to see clearly for the first time in ten days the majority of the North Fork's northern front. I couldn't get over how many thousands of spot fires were burning both behind and in front of the main fire. And yet there was just as much *unburnt* vegetation in the scene below as there was burnt. It was one of the best examples of a mosaic burn pattern I'd seen anywhere. As always, I marveled at how one tree was reduced to ashes and yet another one exactly like it just yards away was hardly singed. It was like the damage done by a tornado going through a neighborhood, where one house is totally destroyed and the next one is hardly scratched.

I'd expected to see spot fires, but not so many. It was frightening to imagine how ferociously powerful the fire had to have been at its height just a few hours before. To think that we had tried to battle it with our meager jets of water and with sprinklers placed on roofs and beneath power lines! It just didn't seem possible that we had escaped it. But looking now at all those spot fires billowing their smoke across the landscape, I knew this was no time to be complacent. Everything downwind of that horde of spot fires was still very much in danger. And it was possible they might spread outside of the park into the thickly forested mountainous expanse of the Gallatin National Forest.

By the time we had turned the helicopter back toward headquarters, I was already planning for the next round of the fight. It was extremely important to take advantage of the lull in the fire's movement and intensity to shift all our resources into positions where the fire would be at its strongest.

Much of the manpower throughout the park was weary and weakened; increasingly, the firefighters and soldiers were lining up for sick call.

Fortunately two battalions of marines arrived on September 13. One of the battalions—eight hundred men—was stationed at Mammoth. So many of the longer-serving firefighters were able to get the rest they so badly needed.

Ironically, the greatest influx of men and resources occurred in the days right after the rain and snow began falling, after the climax of the firefighting. During the rest of September, the areas along the edge of Mammoth became like scenes from M*A*S*H. Pup tents, mess halls, marines in baggy fatigues and muddy black boots, and military troop trucks crowded into the area. Still more helicopters, from Blackhawks to large troop-carrying Chinooks, rumbled overhead and rattled every window several times each day.

By September 17 the number of military personnel in the park was around 4,200. The army soldiers, from Fort Lewis, Washington, had been around since late August and most had been involved with mop-up operations, though some did see direct combat on the fire fronts. The marines, as anxious as they were for action, arrived at the tiny West Yellowstone airport in cold, pouring rain, and had to be content in the weeks to come with mostly chasing down and stomping out lingering spot fires.

For me the marines were an especially welcome sight. When I addressed them upon their arrival at Mammoth, I felt as if I were again with my men in Nam. The many stories the burr-topped officers and I shared each evening helped me forget the fires.

Perhaps indicative of how quickly and completely the weather conditions in Yellowstone could change, some days in the following weeks found many of the military and civilian firefighters *making* fires in an effort to stay warm, as the snow and rain continued and temperatures crashed into the teens!

It took until mid-October before all the fires were 100 percent contained. And the last fire to be contained was the horrible North Fork. Pillars of smoke would still be visible until winter in the backcountry, but they were from spot fires that stood no chance of surviving the tons of snow that would soon be drifting over them.

Fortunately no one working on the fires in the park had been killed or seriously injured, though one chopper pilot was quite embarrassed when his craft flipped over while dipping water into a giant bucket, and dropped upside down into the lake. Unfortunately one young firefighter was killed outside the park, when a tree whose roots had been killed by a fire toppled over on him as he waited to be picked up and returned to camp.

For the park's rangers, the dousing of the fires did not mean a time to relax. What followed at once was the monumental task of doing all the reports and regular duties that we had had to ignore during the firefighting. Just as the summer had been the busiest ever for everyone, so the long, long winter promised to be.

For Barbee, me, and others such as John Varley, the chief of research, there was to be the oftentimes unpleasant continuation of the political and media matters. Congressional hearings were called, detailed reports were demanded, and many reporters seemed still to believe that the fires were going to be formally blamed on Barbee or me any day. For months reporters continued to call to try to get the "scoop" on whose head was going to the chopping block. The reporters didn't want to hear about ecology, but about politics and possible scandals. It was as if they couldn't bring themselves to believe that wildfires were mostly nature's doing, not some administrator's.

An accusation made more than once by critics of the park's administration was that we had purposely hindered fire suppression efforts. Those critics pointed to, among others, four occasions during September when firefighters from the Clover-Mist fire were denied entry at the East Entrance and when we did not agree with that fire's incident command's desire to use bulldozers inside the park.

On September 2, Barbee and I had denied the use of bulldozers inside the park on the fire's southwest flank. On September 8, one of the incident command's crews trying to come into the park through the East Entrance had been delayed at my command. On

September 10, I again saw no need for the use of bulldozers on the fire's south flank. And then on September 12 yet another of the firefighting crews was held up at the East Entrance.

Perhaps eager to stir up controversy, the reporters who covered those denials or delays to the Clover-Mist firefighting crews portrayed them as signs of a breakdown in communication between Mammoth and their incident command team, or even as evidence of a conflict of personalities—Mammoth versus the Clover-Mist incident command leaders.

That there were communication problems there was no doubt: The Clover-Mist command team had two camps in Wyoming, in the Crandall and Pahaska areas, which were fairly remote, 100 miles apart, and often difficult to reach by radio and telephone. And there were definitely tempers raised at times. But it was not because of opposite personalities. Rather it was more a case of us in Mammoth knowing the park better than that incident command's leaders. To them the place just to the west and north of the East Entrance where they wanted to carry out their firefighting plans was just another map feature. To us, the Pelican Valley was the most important grizzly bear habitat in the entire Greater Yellowstone ecosystem. Not only is it exceedingly beautiful and pristine, but also filled with numerous hazardous thermal areas that those firefighters wouldn't have been familiar with. We knew its boggy terrain would have been easily and permanently scarred by any vehicles or bulldozers, and that the large amount of nonnative—"exotic"—plant seeds that might have been brought in on the firefighters' clothing and tire treads would have harmed the local ecology forever.

I sympathized with the others' wishes to attack the Clover-Mist from every angle, and if what they wanted to do would have actually suppressed the fire, we would have let them in with the bulldozers. But we felt the actions they were proposing wouldn't have had the least effect on the fire: The dozer cuts were to be in spots the fire was unlikely to pass through. The planned dozer lines were upwind from the fire's path, and even if the winds did turn and push the fire their way there were numerous natural barriers

—mountain ranges, meadows—that should have been adequate to stop the fire.

As to the crews delayed at the East Entrance, they had come without first seeking prior authorization and coordination from the park. As a result, they were unaware of the extreme ecological importance, and dangers, of the backcountry area to which they were headed. The crew that was stopped on September 8 was allowed in as soon as a ranger who knew the Pelican Valley area could be found to accompany them and discuss their plans with them. One of the first things the ranger did was to inform them there was a very big female grizzly with cubs feeding on a bison carcass right on the access trail they had planned to walk down!

When the second request for the use of bulldozers was made, on September 10, Barbee told me that we were going to have to let them do it. The secretary of the interior back in Washington, the superintendent explained, was under immense political pressure to have the fires put out at any cost, and President Reagan was involved, too. If we didn't say yes, then someone else higher up would.

Barbee agreed to let me get the request for the use of bulldozers directly from the incident commander, Larry Boggs. I called Boggs and asked if the bulldozers were absolutely necessary. He thought they were, but acknowledged he had not personally seen the area in question. His teams had planned to have the bulldozers in action no later than six A.M. But Boggs agreed to discuss the matter with me at a meeting scheduled the next morning in Grant Village for all the incident commanders.

That next morning, Sunday, September 11, it snowed three inches where the bulldozer lines would have been. The snow made the use of bulldozers totally unnecessary. The request for their use was dropped. And the Pelican Valley was spared more damage than any fire could have done.

Though we at park headquarters had not actually said no to the use of the bulldozers that September 11, we were accused of doing so by some. Certainly someone on the Clover-Mist incident team left no doubt what he thought: On the cover of their secret report to the regional forester he scrawled in large thick letters: "They said NO!"

Perhaps nothing flared tempers more among the firefighting teams brought in from outside than the issue of using bulldozers. Though eventually some thirty-two miles of bulldozer lines became part of the scars left by the firefighting teams, had we been more lenient, I am convinced there would have been ten times as many miles of bulldozer scars left. Better, we had decided from the start, that there be burned trees, which would eventually crumble away, than the gouges of bulldozer lines wide enough for six-lane freeways scarring the wilderness for centuries. Furthermore, as we watched the fires eventually blow across every bulldozer line put in the national forests, where they were permitted, it was clear that had we allowed the dozers to be used at will, Yellowstone would not only have burned anyhow, but also been as horribly hacked up as some of the surrounding national forests. If rivers couldn't contain the fires, certainly no bulldozer lines would have.

As the fire battles in the park wound down and entered the mundane stage, several of those reporters who hung about in Mammoth appeared to refuse to believe that their great moment as "combat" reporters was over. Still hungry for excitement and sensational headlines, they pounced on any rumor that came along. One of the uglier ones was that on the last major day of the fires, over two thousand elk had perished in the North Fork fire on the south side of Bunsen Peak.

I didn't believe any such thing had happened. But to be certain the park sent a team of rangers into the field to take a count of all animal carcasses. As it turned out, elk had died in that especially cruel part of that fire. The number was not in the thousands, however, but around four hundred. And the elk had not been roasted alive, as some reporters said, but were asphyxiated.

Those elk had—like the reporters, the fires, and the summer—run their course. Enough is enough, Mother Nature had said.

The process of life and death was going to carry on, no matter what any headlines said.

* * *

Steve Frye, whom I turned to more than anyone else during the fires for advice and assistance, estimated that had the park's fires been left alone they might have burned only an additional 10 to 20 percent of forestland.

Furthermore, those fires had been too big, too unpredictable, and too unlike anything ever experienced before to be affected by our firefighting methodology and equipment. To have a thousand fire engines spraying their water loads onto something as huge as the North Fork or Clover-Mist fires was like trying to save a burning house with a garden hose. It wasn't that the brave men and women who worked twelve to sixteen hours a day on the fire lines had been bad at their jobs—quite the opposite; it was just that nobody, no matter how expert, was going to stop fires that moved faster than a man walked and were spitting embers two to three miles ahead like a hail of bullets. Keeping people in front of such storms for very long at any time would have guaranteed sure casualties.

In the early stages of some of the main fires we had entertained thoughts of throwing everything we had at them and trying to put them out before they grew past their then moderate sizes. Options were presented to Barbee and me by the incident commanders on the Clover-Mist and North Fork scenes. The Clover-Mist plan prepared by commander Curt Bates called for three options: a) monitoring the fire and allowing it to burn to the natural mountain breaks, at a cost of $52,000 and a 60 percent chance of success; b) forty firefighters fighting for a week and mopping up for another week, with helicopters used to transport them at a cost of around $377,000 and an 80 percent chance of success; and c) using six hundred people and appropriate equipment at a cost of $2 million and a 90 percent chance of success. The North Fork plan prepared by commander Larry Caplinger had also called for three options: a) letting the fire alone and just making a stand at Old Faithful, at a cost of $500,000; b) turning the fire away toward the north of the park by helicopter water drops and then attacking it aggressively at the Madison River cliffs, if it got that far, at a cost of $2 million;

and c) putting a bulldozer line around the front of the fire, inside the park, at a cost of $4 million and probably some lives.

Our decision in the Clover-Mist fire was to go with a modified version of steps *a* and *b*—mopping up the fires along the boundary, and setting back burns to deter the main fire from spilling over the park's eastern boundary. That appeared to be the least expensive option, since there had been a slowing of the fire's burn rate just before then, and the feeling was the natural boundaries would hold it inside the park. In the North Fork case we went with the second option, since it seemed quite feasible, and because of our gut feeling that the rains just *had* to be coming. But, as they say, the rest was history.

The criticism that rained down on Barbee's head as the fires upset again, and again, and again every prediction, had to have been the harshest a Yellowstone superintendent ever weathered. In places such as Gardiner, Cooke City, and particularly West Yellowstone, where the smoke was thick much of the summer and the tourist dollars were thin, the atmosphere at times resembled that of a vigilante lynch mob. Signs popped up in all three places, saying things like WELCOME TO WEST YELLOWSTONE BARBEE-QUE. And at the town meetings, where our initial decision to let the fires burn had convinced the townspeople we had a cavalier attitude, words like "arsonist," "liar," and "communist" were slung at the man everyone seemed most intent on getting rid of.

But unknown to most people who were not on the park's fire command team in Mammoth was that Barbee trusted me and my staff to make almost all of the final decisions about how fire operations should or shouldn't be managed. I, Frye, and the others on the fire command staff were, after all, wildfire experts and had more experience in fighting fires in Yellowstone than anyone else. Barbee was not one to usurp the authority of those on his staff who knew about the workings of a particular subject. He greatly respected our knowledge and experience, and for that trust we were determined never to let him down.

He could easily have deflected the criticism by revealing that he had simply approved decisions made by his chief ranger. But that was not his style. When politicians began calling for his head and saying, as Congressman Ron Marlenee of Montana did, that the park policy was one of "ruin and ashes," Barbee still accepted all blame, even to the point of saying point-blank to the reporters that he had no regrets at the way things had been handled.

Barbee was not simply trying to be a hero to his staff. He truly believed, as did all of us on the park fire command, that the long-term picture of the park's health had to have priority over any quick fixes. So he trusted us, even when to the outside world everything seemed to be falling apart.

23

The October air flooding through the pickup window brought smells of mountains and moisture and trees to my nostrils, and had me thinking of adventure. I breathed deeply and forgot the chatter of the tires against the rough pavement, the creaking of the horse trailer wagging along behind, and the rain clouds gathering in the south where I was heading.

The blur of wild water tearing down a dusk-shrouded stream on my left swept my thoughts even further from the road. But then there was a loud gasp from my passenger and I looked ahead just in time to see a coyote dashing across my path. Quickly I applied more attention, and less gas.

"So, how is everything going at Lake?" I asked ranger Mary Taber in a way that implied I had been in firm control all along.

Mary relaxed her grip on the seat and replied with all the enthusiasm of a seasonal ranger who hoped someday to join the ranks of the permanents.

"Very well! And it's so beautiful here I can't help but like my job."

I stole a glance out the corner of my eye at the friendly face beneath her ranger hat. Mary's eyes were staring straight ahead, showing no hint of sarcasm or humor. Evidently she meant what she'd said, despite the fact that the forest we were passing through looked as though it had been a testing ground for napalm bombs.

"You don't think the fires have ruined the park?" I asked in a friendly way.

266

Mary looked at me suspiciously. "Why no! If anything it will be even more beautiful. Don't you think?"

"Oh, you bet. In fact I wouldn't be surprised if with so much of the forest cover gone, we have the prettiest wildflower show ever next year."

"Well, there should certainly be plenty of fireweed."

I laughed at her little joke. Yet it was very, very true. The dense pink spires might well outnumber all the other flowers in the park by next fall. They were usually the first to thrive in a newly burned area, and they spread like crazy. I'd seen them grow so thickly in some burned forests that I had been reminded of a pink wave washing against the black pilings of a rotting dock.

"It probably wasn't one of your favorite summers in Yellowstone—especially with all the confusion down in these parts," I ventured.

I knew Mary had spent a lot of the summer assisting with evacuations and traffic. She'd also helped form a roadblock at Bridge Bay, between the Lake and West Thumb areas, where she'd let motorists coming south from the East Entrance road know when it wasn't possible to continue on to the South Entrance or Old Faithful. I figured she'd had her fill of angry and distraught drivers.

Mary shrugged her shoulders. "I suppose it would have been a lot less hectic without the fires, but I still feel pretty lucky to have been here this summer."

"Why's that?"

She shifted uneasily. "Well, I just think that history was being made, and—and I got to be right there, seeing and experiencing it in person. That's something that a lot of people don't get to do—"

"Nor apparently wanted to do," I interjected.

"You mean the park visitors?"

"Yeah." I thought of the steep drop in visitation in August and September during the height of the fires. No doubt the word had gotten out that many of the park facilities were shut down, and that deterred many, even those who had wanted to come.

Mary thought about that for a minute. "I suppose that was

true for some. But when they learned that the fires were not actually burning as much as the media claimed, and that fire was actually helping the plants and animals in the long run, they didn't act so upset." She threw up her hands, adding: "Actually a lot of visitors asked where they could go to see the fires up close."

I nodded and smiled to myself. She was right. Once the public had been weaned away from the misleading Smokey the Bear rhetoric that said *all* wildfires were bad, and found out that wildfires were normal and necessary for Yellowstone to renew itself, they became supportive, as well as curious.

Now that there was time to evaluate the way we in the park's administration had handled the fires, I saw several things that could have been done to lessen the confusion in the public's mind about what was *really* happening in Yellowstone. We had, quite simply, been grossly unaware of how little the general public and the media actually knew about the workings of the Park Service and Mother Nature. We had trusted the media, especially, to be professional and accurate and up-to-date on the science of ecology, and most had failed miserably on all counts.

I downshifted as the truck left the turnoff to the now empty Grant Village behind. We climbed toward the plateau on which the Red Mountains and Heart Lake sat on. The transmission's gears groaned, reminding me of how often we in the park administration had done likewise the past summer each time the TV news presented its version of the burning park to the public.

To be sure, only a dead man would not have been awed and frightened by the tall walls of flame and the ferocious windstorms of the summer's fires. And how could anyone not have been cognizant of the mystique the name Yellowstone had added to the fires? But even so, I thought it was sad that in all the excitement of the battle the media had somehow left everyone thinking the park was dead or dying. For in reality the park was only shifting into what might well become its most splendid phase in decades.

There was, I felt confident now, a reawakening taking place. Not at all the funeral that so many other voices—far more powerful than mine—were claiming. And it was partly because of my desire to get an intimate look at the beginnings of that awakening that I was making this trip to the Heart Lake trailhead. From that lonely little turnoff along the road to the South Entrance, I planned to strike out alone on horseback across the entire southeast corner of the park, from west to east, to the depths of what had been one of the hardest-hit backcountry areas. It should be spectacular, I thought. And it should also be inspirational. For as Mary had said: Not many got to see up so close the making of history.

Gently I swung open the tailgate on the horse trailer and stepped up inside and past its occupant's swishing tail. Shibida turned his head to me and gave a thankful look. I stroked his powerful thick neck and with a slight tug at his lead rope pulled him around to the open end. He stepped down as if he had been waiting for this moment from the second we'd left headquarters.

Though it was overcast, and I knew I had no chance of getting to the Heart Lake patrol cabin before dark, I was still glad to be on my way. Today had been another of a very long string of extremely busy days since the fires had ended: Committees formed for this and that had been needing more information; reporters had called wanting to know if such-and-such rumors were true; maintenance workers had found still more fire damage; scientists had wanted to get on the growing list of research projects; and rangers had reported yet another day of heavy traffic of the curious.

With the fight against the flames finished, there was now the even more daunting task of trying to preserve the integrity of the natural-burn policy that had allowed some of those fires to burn in the first place.

Even though it was almost a month since the fires had ceased to rage out of control, some in Congress were still making predictions that some of the administrators in Yellowstone and the Park Service would lose their jobs. One western senator was claiming the Park Service had done nothing to stop the fires, that there would be a high-level review both looking for facts and looking for blame, and that "some of the people sitting in Mammoth will be replaced." I was happy just to be going somewhere where such antagonism was not likely to be reaching my ears.

I threw the saddle and saddlebags onto Shibida's back, slipped my boot into the stirrup, and heaved myself up onto the horse. He remained as calm as a statue while I fidgeted with my revolver holster and then my ranger hat. I knew I could depend on Shibida in any situation. If only the same could be said about the relationship between many of those politicians in Washington and the Park Service.

I nudged the horse ever so lightly with my spurs. He headed down the trail with all the self-assurance of a steed much wiser than his five years. He had been raised on the plains of eastern Montana, and hadn't been a trail horse for very long. I'd taught him everything he knew about handling himself in the forest, fording swift rivers, and crossing bogs, and I was still somewhat in awe of how quickly he had picked up everything. He was as intelligent and calm as he was strong—an almost perfect patrol horse. Still, he was largely untested in the really rough backcountry.

I twisted around and looked back at Mary Taber. She was just pulling herself into the driver's seat. Her expression said she'd have gladly traded the truck and her chores back at the Lake ranger station for the horse.

"Drive carefully," I said.

She waved and said back, "Enjoy yourself!"

I looked forward over the horse's bobbing head and smiled. How could I not enjoy myself? So what if it was going to rain or snow, and it was nearly dark, and I could hardly see where I was going? I loved being out on horseback in Yellowstone's backcountry.

I stroked Shibida again along his lush mane. We had a lot of territory to cover—eight miles to the log patrol cabin I was going to stay at tonight, and seventy miles to the end of this ride. And with still more meetings looming back at the office in two days, I couldn't make this as long an adventure as I would have liked.

I watched my saddlebags bouncing lightly against the horse's flanks. There were hardly more than a couple strips of jerky and some granola bars in them, as well as the usual survival gear. But that was okay. The first four miles would be on an easy upslope, and the cabin would have all the food and warm bedding any traveler could need.

The last four miles to the cabin figured to be challenging, since they were in thick forest, and it would be pitch black. But I had a flashlight, and Mernin had assured me over the telephone that the trail into the cabin was cleared of deadfalls.

Only a few miles to the west of here the Shoshone fire had been born on June 23 and the Red fire on July 1. Both had later gone on to threaten the Grant Village and West Thumb areas. They were the earliest fires to explode into major conflagrations, and also two of the very hottest.

The cool air was still ripe with the pungent odors of smoke and seared vegetation. Even though the park's scientists had said over the years that the young and very green forest I was passing through would not burn, it had done so with a vengeance. True, it was not all black and charcoal-colored, but it was more so than anyone could ever have foreseen. And I knew from my overflights that the most intensely burned areas were still miles ahead.

The summer of 1988 would be remembered as the time even the marshes and swamps went up in fire, I thought, as the ground slowly rose and the trees crowded in more closely. Willows, aspen, anything that had limbs and leaves and roots had turned out to be as vulnerable to fire as the oldest deadfalls.

The thin outline of a low-lying branch popped up before my face, and I swatted it aside. With a snap that ripped loudly through the still forest, the branch broke and fell to the ground. I looked at the black streak it had left on my palm. How many of the other boughs reaching out at me were similarly dead? Many still had their needles, but that didn't mean they weren't slowly wasting away inside from the effects of the fires' heat on their roots and trunks. Eventually the beetles were going to have an easy time of it, I thought.

"Whoa, Shibida."

He stopped and stood still while I sat and looked long and hard around me. I was trying to establish my night vision. Though there was the flashlight in the saddlebag, I thought it would be best if I tried not to use it. It was just a small one and wouldn't last more than a few hours.

As I sat trying to discern details in the almost black surroundings, I saw the trail was not nearly as cleared as I had been told.

271

There were several large trees lying across it, both ahead and behind me. They had probably fallen since the crews came through. I realized Shibida must have very good night vision, for he hadn't been spooked at all by the previous snags. He had maneuvered around and over them so smoothly I'd not noticed.

We continued on, a little more slowly. I was going to have to be extra watchful. One poke of my good eye by a sharp branch could be disastrous in such a maze of limbs, trunks, and rocks.

As my eye and ears became fine-tuned to the forest, I grew aware that I was surrounded by a deep stillness of the kind one would find in a graveyard on a cold midwinter's night. It was so complete that each time an owl hooted, or a fire-killed snag broke loose from the scraggly pines and crashed to the earth, their noise shot through the darkness. There was never more than one sound at a time, and in between—absolute nothingness. Still, Shibida remained as steady as iron.

I was nearly as dependent now upon my smelling and hearing senses as a blind man might have been on his. When the odor of sulfur crept into my nose, I knew from having been this way before that I was halfway to Heart Lake. For at that point were some hot springs. Then, a half hour later, when a cool draft and the sounds of splashing teased my right shoulder and ear, I knew I was beside Witch Creek, and that just on the other side of it was Factory Mountain.

At a spot where the creek sounded as if it was spilling over a small waterfall, and the trail sloped steeply down, I had Shibida halt. Rain was beginning to fall. Leaning to my left, I untied my raincoat from the saddle. I dismounted and pulled on the ankle-length garment.

Shibida suddenly seemed uneasy. I grabbed his rein and looked around nervously. We were in an area used heavily by bears. With the creek and the rain masking our smells and sounds, there was the possibility that a bear was nearby checking us out.

The time had come for the flashlight. I wanted to lead the horse down the slope to level ground, and I had no intention of blundering into a set of grizzly claws. When I retrieved the flashlight, however, I found its batteries were extremely weak. I felt around in the saddlebags for an extra set of batteries. Though they were new, they turned out to be bad, too. I'd gotten them from the fire cache, and there was no telling how long they'd been stored there.

Against my better judgment but having no choice, I continued into the night with barely enough light to see ten feet ahead. Always preceding me was a dark wall. So as not to surprise any bears that might be lurking ahead, I carried on a long—very long—conversation with the horse.

It was well after ten when the cabin finally materialized. I was wet up to my thighs from having to ford the creek in three different places where bridges had been destroyed by the fires. The footing had been anything but easy. Several times I had sunk way past my ankles in the bogs along the creek and stumbled. Fortunately Shibida was strong enough to keep from doing likewise. It was amazing to think such a wet area could have burned so fiercely.

Coyotes serenaded me as I relieved Shibida of the saddle at the horse barn, brushed him down, then treated him with a feed bag of oats from a metal bear-proofed bin in the barn.

I was mighty hungry too, and went straight to the old restored log cabin. Once inside, I lit the mantle of a Coleman lantern and invaded the pantry. In hardly any time I had a pot of canned chili bubbling on one side of a camp stove and a pot of water for washing the dishes boiling on the other side.

Before turning in, I went back outside to lead Shibida to the lake's shore for a drink. As I stood there in the great calmness the large lake exuded, I felt as if I were in some unlit church. Had I not known better I would have thought the world about me had hardly changed from the one I'd known in years past. There was still the faint musky scent of the thermal basin just to the west, at the bottom of Mount Sheridan, not far from where I'd soaked away many a worry on midwinter ski trips along Witch Creek. Still the sweet and invigorating coolness of a mile-high autumn night, still the hoots of the solitary owl, and still the blessed gleam of the cabin's window. Maybe it was just coincidence, but when a lone

273

star peeking through a hole in the clouds at the other end of the lake caught my attention, Shibida looked up, too. It was as though we were both making wishes on that teeny speck of fairy dust.

I took Shibida to a meadow a quarter of a mile away, where the grass hadn't burned. Along the way I made a lot of noise—this time whistling and jingling a horse bell—in case any bears had been attracted by the chili odors. It was the time of the year when the bears were fattening themselves for the long winter hibernation, and they would be extra antsy. In a place where the air was so pure and thin the chili odors would carry for miles; I just knew there had to be a grizzly or two not far away in such a rugged setting.

At the meadow I pounded a metal stake into the ground with the flat part of an axe and secured Shibida to it with a forty-foot-long rope. He wasn't pleased with the wide leather strap I buckled around his front left ankle, but he quickly forgave when the aroma of the grass swayed his head downward.

"See you in the morning," I said with a rub of his massive back.

He shook his head, as if to give his tacit approval.

Back at the cabin I did the dishes and retired to the bed. It was past midnight when I dropped off to sleep.

Morning brought me a sense of freedom. For perhaps the first time since spring, I could lie there under my covers without anything urgent on my mind.

In due time I eased up onto an elbow and then made my soles travel the rough, cold floorboards. I scampered over to the camp stove to make some coffee. That done, I bounded back to the refuge of my wool blankets and sipped the coffee. Then I quickly dressed, went out to lead Shibida back to the cabin, and returned to a breakfast of canned peaches and more coffee. There was nothing like a hot cup of fresh coffee on a cool, damp morning in the woods to make a man feel just plain *good*.

I went to the door and opened it. A blast of fresh air greeted me.

Seating myself just outside the door on a stump, a few yards from the patient Shibida, I watched the sun come up over the Continental Divide with all the majesty of a god.

274

It was a perfect morning, but it could not disguise the blackened mountainsides in my view. Looking to my right, to the faraway simple stone fire-lookout on top of Mount Sheridan, my eye had to skim over a swath of burned forest. At the end of August, I'd flown onto that same mountaintop in a helicopter to rescue the lookout's ranger. The smoke and flames from the Red fire that afternoon had been so intense that the rescue had been very risky. The entire mountain had roared like a ten-thousand-foot high bonfire, and up there at its apex was the lookout with a propane tank just outside it.

I stretched the muscles in my legs and arms, sprang to my feet, and made my way to Shibida to brush him and load him with the saddle once more. Looking around me at the stands of unburnt pines still slightly soft-edged with mist, I felt a surge of optimism at what the day would be holding for me. It was easy to see that both near and far there was far, far more beauty than desolation.

Nevertheless, from now on every place I visited inside the park would have memories of smoke and fire connected with it.

By the time I was back on the trail, it was past eight o'clock. The sun was in my eye and making some attempt to keep my nose and ears warm. Shibida's and my breath billowed out ahead of us like small geysers while we made tracks to an area that had been the scene of a major fire in 1979.

By going through the old burn area I could see plainly what a lot of Yellowstone was going to be like in ten years. And what I saw was highly encouraging. The pines that had grown up to replace the burned ones were already six feet high and bushy with health. The flashes of feathers in their boughs hinted they were alive with more than needles. Some day the area would be as beautiful as any forest anywhere—no longer the old, dying, beetle-infested forest it had probably been when the fire struck it down a decade ago.

If only I could have had the critics along, I lamented. Maybe they would have been convinced that the fires were not entirely a disaster. That this was how nature intended it to be.

Those who would "protect" the park from "disaster" overlooked the fact that Yellowstone is beautiful and mystical *because* of its violent past. Had there not been the tremendous upheavals of the earth's crust there would never have been beautiful Yellowstone Lake. Had the Yellowstone River not gouged relentlessly at the volcanic rhyolite and conglomerates beneath its path, there would not have been the grandeur of the park's Grand Canyon. And had there not been the cycles of fire and regrowth every two hundred to four hundred years since the last ice age ten thousand years ago, there likely would not have been half the animals in Yellowstone that there are today. For their habitat would have become an ecological desert of lodgepole pines tangled upon plateaus too shaded and robbed of nutrients ever to bear much green.

Yellowstone is poetry because of cataclysms—many of which made the latest fires mere child's play.

Yet how far did most critics seem willing to look into the future? Only as far as the next dead tree apparently.

Typical of the shallow outlook on the fires' importance to Yellowstone was an article I'd seen in a late September edition of *The Des Moines Sunday Register*. PARK OF IDYLLIC BEAUTY NOW AN UGLY LANDSCAPE the headline read. "What once was one of America's most beautiful places has been transformed into a landscape that can best be described as an awesomely ugly forest fire theme park," warned the opening paragraph. Then, in a later paragraph: "Only a few weeks ago, visitors to Yellowstone could enjoy a pristine, timber-ringed river valley famous worldwide for its blue-ribbon quality trout fishing and its hordes of full-antlered elk and other game animals. Now, 'black snags'—burned but unfallen trees—are all that remain. No living thing walks there anymore."

What a story! Though the acreage that had actually been burned inside each fire area was still being ascertained by scientists, it was apparent that it was going to be far lower than originally estimated. High-altitude and ground surveys revealed a mosaic of fire activity and intensity patterns throughout the Yellowstone region. Substantial areas of moderately burned, lightly burned, and totally unburned forest were found within the perimeter of the nearly one million acres of fires that had burned inside the park. Some scientists were saying that only half or even less of the area within the fire perimeter had burned, and that even in those burned areas, almost all were only lightly or moderately burned, so that

276

roots, tubers, bulbs, and the seedbed below the soil surface were undamaged. Barely one tenth of one percent of the park's soil was severely damaged.

I couldn't think of any valley as completely destroyed as the article described, and I had seen almost every acre of fire damage by now from either a helicopter or on foot. Obviously the writer had incorporated a lot of imagination and emotion into his reporting. Or else he, like even the most experienced firefighters and rangers, had been overwhelmed by the magnitude of the fires.

While a burned forest or meadow is ugly to the human eye and seems lifeless, nothing could be further from the truth. The very second that a fire passes, animals and plants begin their recovery and reestablishment. Insects go to work recovering the nutrients released by the fires. The roots of many plant species, protected by the soil from the heat, start resprouting. Other plants like the lodgepole pine even use the heat to force open their seed pods or cones. Surveys done at the fire sites by the park's biologists showed lodgepole seed densities on the ground of from fifty thousand to one million per acre. Those seeds are not only a food source bonanza to the birds and the smaller mammals, but their very number virtually guarantees the return of the forests.

All the talk about Yellowstone coming back to life as if it were in its grave was pure silliness. The park was merely in a change—for the better.

Within a few years almost every inch of the burned forest floors in the park should be a mat of grasses, flowers, and shrubs. Animals will be attracted to the new food sources in large numbers, and in the springs to come there will be an abundance of wildlife that should make what we had before the fires look sparse. Ironically, the most serious problem to come out of the fires in the long run might be *too much* wildlife. Within lodgepole stands that have burned in the past decades, a threefold increase in the species of plants and small animals has been seen.

The increased vegetation will provide sustenance for some of the largest wildlife population increases ever.

Surveys carried out thus far discovered that a surprisingly small number of animals had died as a direct result of the fires. Some four hundred of the park's thirty-two thousand elk had been found killed by fire, while in the same period five bison, a black bear, a handful of deer, a couple of moose, and numerous small mammals had likewise perished. With a few more areas still to be surveyed, those numbers would probably increase, but I doubted by very much.

Many of the small animals such as the pocket gophers and voles burrowed or lived underground and so would have survived all but the most intense of ground fires. What was most critical to the survival rate of those smaller animals was not the fires, but what was left afterward. Animals will migrate to where the foods they prefer are still plentiful. Some species will drop in number and others will increase, but none will be exterminated. Studies from earlier burns have shown that for the next several years there is an even greater diversity of wildlife in those areas that have been burned.

To all who spouted gloom and death, I could only point out that even the most severe fire left islands of unburnt vegetation and trees that served as havens in which mammals could reproduce and spread back into the recovering burned areas. Some of the small mammals would have several litters a year. Nature knows quite well the tricks of survival.

The animals I had observed during the fires behaved very differently from those often portrayed in film and popular literature. Unlike the classic scene in *Bambi* where the young deer and his father, the Old Stag, fled a forest fire in sheer terror, the large mammals I watched were incredibly calm. Far calmer, in fact, than some of the firefighters Rather than running or acting confused and disoriented, the animals mostly grazed calmly at the fires' edges. They appeared to be a lot more concerned about their stomachs than their hides. Some even used the fires to their advantage: Sometimes dozens of hawks and eagles—all mixed together and whirling high overhead in the smoke like a dark cloud—could be seen feasting gluttonously upon the many helpless small mammals fleeing at the head of a fire. And others ventured into the burn areas even before they had cooled: Bluebirds and black-backed three-toed woodpeckers went after the agitated, homeless insects and mice; gray owls plucked gophers scrambling across the black to a spot of green; bison licked the ash as if it were candy; coyotes slunk around for roasted carrion.

There was a lot of concern about the grizzly bears, since the fires had swept over much of the park's bear habitat. But even they seemed hardly disturbed by it. Those bears we tracked through their radio collars exhibited a habit of simply moving a short distance out of a fire's path, then moving right back into their old territory. And they didn't even seem in that big a rush when they moved!

But there were very sad stories about some of the wildlife in the fires. Terry McEneaney told of going out on Yellowstone Lake in August to see the effect of the fires on the lake's birds, and coming across a wall of very intense fire bearing down on a nest of osprey fledglings. From his boat he watched as the mother of the birds, who were just days from being old enough to take their first flights, grew increasingly worried but refused to leave her young. In time the wall of fire's heat was so great Terry could feel it out on the water. Yet still that mother made herself a barrier between the flames and her children in their ragged jumble of large sticks.

The father, meanwhile, made several passes at the fire, as if he thought he could fend it off like some other beast of the forest that would prey on his family. But then seeing that he could not, he headed out over the lake's water, dived hurriedly for a fish, and sped back to the nest with it. He gave the fish to the female, who passed it on to the young while he again went for fish. Faster and faster the parents worked to get all the fish they could into the little ones' beaks, as the flames kept up their relentless approach. Even when the flames were just fifty yards away and towering well over the centuries-old pine, which was ready to explode from the massive heat, the parents were still getting all the food they could to their frightened fledglings. And though the young ones were old enough to eat the fish on their own, the mother hurried them along by cramming it into their throats herself. It was, Terry thought, a desperate attempt by the parents to get the young birds to quickly—*immediately*—grow up, so they could flee too.

It was the male who retreated first when the heat reached the intolerable level. The female held on a little longer, and even made several brave swoops at the fire as if attacking it. But in the end she too had to back away, leaving her babies to the inevitable. The last Terry saw of her, she was still circling her burning home.

A part of Terry had wanted very much to go ashore and rescue the little ospreys, but he was as aware as the rest of us that the policy was to let nature run its own course as much as possible in every situation in the park. He knew that though the ways of nature are oftentimes not all that sensible or agreeable to our way of thinking, nature has a habit of balancing things out in the end. And maybe in the next spring the parents would have not two chicks, but three or four.

Two animals severely hurt by the fires had to be destroyed by humans. In early September a black bear with severely burned feet appeared outside the park near the road at Cooke City and was put out of his misery by a Montana state highway patrolman. And then just a few days before I had authorized my rangers to put down a bull elk with terribly burned hooves near Mammoth.

Shibida picked his way carefully down to the bank of a lively little stream that originated just up ahead, near where the Continental Divide again crossed my path. From the thick young pines we descended to where the frost was heavy on the shaded grass and willows and the dew just as abundant on the sun-stroked blades and leaves and the finely spun veils of spider silk. In the freshness of the morning I saw many forms of wildlife, from ducks and geese to elk. And had I been a little quieter perhaps I might have even gotten to see the owner of a pair of very fresh bear prints that fell into my sight.

I loved deeply the way time sat thick and heavy in such places. I dismounted and scattered a few million of the diamond dewdrops with the tips of my boots. *Who knows, perhaps I am the last one to see all this before winter buries it again,* I thought.

The high, ringing notes of a bull elk's challenge tumbled down from Overlook Mountain just ahead. They spread from horizon to horizon with such clarity that I stopped and awaited any replies. Out of the recesses of the forests around me they rose, one by one, to play upon the soft land.

This land belonged to those elk, the deer, the coyotes, and

bears, and every other furry and feathered creature in between. It was not man's alone, no matter how vainly he bickered and argued and debated over it. We were only a part of the very dirt and rocks and trees we thought we possessed.

A still, misty body of water bordered on its north and east sides by meadows greeted Shibida and me halfway up the rise to the divide's back. I recognized its shallow and highly reflective face as that of Outlet Lake, and the small mountain at my right shoulder as Overlook Mountain. My being between them signaled that I was seven miles east of Heart Lake, and thirty-one miles from the cabin on the park's eastern boundary that was my destination for the day. I looked at my watch. Though the going thus far had been filled with more downed trees than I'd been expecting, I was making good time. I hoped I could make it to my destination before dark, for there was a mighty huge spread of forest and ravine-filled mountains awaiting me near the end.

I paused nevertheless to enjoy a flock of Canada geese whose idle banter had betrayed their suspended forms at the other end of the lake. Almost motionless, they might have gone undetected had they not spoken. But there they floated all the same, lords of this little-known castle of reflected clouds.

From the moment Shibida and I resumed our journey, I saw that the trail remaining was a horseman's nightmare. Dead, black, fallen trees were everywhere. Hardly a foot of the trail's path looked to be without some sort of potential hazard. Widow-makers, fire-killed trees that were still standing and could easily topple over on me, also looked to be numerous.

Shibida plodded on without the slightest hesitation. Like a true pro he calmly stepped over those deadfalls that were lower than his belly, and walked around those—the majority—higher than his knees. Like a good backcountry horse, he never jumped over any obstacles. I had trained him not to, because if I should ever be riding him and leading a packhorse and he jumped, he might well pull my arm out of its socket.

Steadily upward we moved along until the Continental Divide, or Chicken Ridge as it was called on the maps of this area, once more eased us to lower altitudes. The creek that was my guide on this side was called Grouse Creek. It is a mountain stream that gurgles and chuckles through every one of its tight curves as if it can't wait to get to the South Arm of Yellowstone Lake, two or three miles away at most. The numerous little trout in its pools darted every which way whenever my shadow flitted across their backs.

The stream's health was seemingly in contrast to the shocking appearance of the forest that had once shaded it. But I knew that the stream and its fish might have benefited from the burning of the forest. At such high altitudes the water in these streams is very cold, and the trees lining their banks only make it colder with their shade. A fire thins those trees, allowing the water to warm, which increases the oxygen and nutrients, which usually leads to greater spawning opportunities and an increase in the fish population. So, the fish of the park stood to benefit from the fires! In fact, with no fires at all, there might over time be a decrease in the fish in the park's lakes. While the erosion that sometimes results from rain and melting snow muddies the streams and lakes, the soils and ashes contain vital nutrients that will eventually settle in the water and rejuvenate the underwater plants and insects, which the fish feed on.

Better fishing in the years ahead because of the fires of 1988? It was very likely.

If Shibida could talk he probably would have blistered my ears for making him continue any further across the northern tip of the Two Ocean Plateau. From Outlet Lake to where the trail brushed against the southernmost point on Yellowstone Lake, the downed trees were the most numerous and chaotic I'd seen anywhere in the wake of the summer's fires. The forest had burned right down to the water's edge and left a graveyard of decimated tree trunks that looked as if both a hurricane and an atomic war had struck them. It had taken three and a half hours to travel the two miles from Grouse Creek to this spot.

I had Shibida rest a bit. Scanning the naked black jungle, I marveled that anything would ever try to live in it again. But I saw grasses poking up through the burn. Admittedly this was a meager greening, not at all as lush as the grasses already covering the burned forest floors in some other areas. But it was at least a start. I was confident that if I returned in a couple of years, the covering would be as thick as in most of the other places.

Just north of here was where lightning on July 29 had started a little fire we called the Continental. Too small to merit any attention, since the rest of the park was afire, it nevertheless became a classic case of how political pressures over the summer caused waste of money and energy in the firefighting scene.

Not long after it was reported by the lookout tower on Mount Sheridan, I flew over it and felt that it was not worth diverting any of our already overstretched firefighting resources to it. The prevailing winds from the west were driving the large Red and Shoshone fires, only four miles away, into it, and the only place it had to burn to was Yellowstone Lake. So on the daily fire analysis sheet handed out the next morning to the media, we said we were going to monitor it only, since it had nowhere to burn but into water. That didn't settle well at all; after all, only a few days before, the secretary of the interior had said *all* new wildfires would thenceforth be fought and extinguished.

So to assuage the criticism by the politicians and the media that we were not doing everything we could to "save" the park, I ordered a crew of twenty firefighters to be sent on a barge all the way down from the marina at the north end of the lake to fight the new blaze. There was no other way to get them there, because of the Red fire to the west.

The situation became too hot on shore for the crew on the barge to do much good, and after three days I had them pulled off the scene with basically nothing changed except that many thousands of dollars and manpower badly needed elsewhere had been literally wasted.

Much will probably be made in the years ahead of the costs to society of fighting the fires. So far the U.S. government had paid out over $120 million on the Greater Yellowstone area fires, with the average daily cost in the $3-million-a-day range. Over 77 helicopters and a dozen fixed-wing aircraft had flown 18,000 hours of support duties, with the average rate for renting each helicopter ranging from $300 to over $4,000 an hour. Some of the out-of-state fire engines and crews cost as much as $8,000 a day *each* to rent. Many fire departments were able to purchase new fire engines from what they made after a few weeks in the park.

Surely it would be years yet before every claim was finally settled. So the costs were bound to go higher.

It still numbed my mind to think that at the peak of the fires there'd been 9,500 civilian and military firefighters on the scene, and that over the summer more than 25,000 different firefighters worked in the Greater Yellowstone area. It was the largest fire suppression effort ever undertaken in the nation's history. Yet the Yellowstone chapter was but a small part of the overall fire fight in the West in those months. Overall there were 72,000 fires and five million acres that burned, with the total bill nearing the $400 million level. Still, 1988 was destined to be known as the year Yellowstone burned, because of the power of the park's name for the public.

I climbed back into the saddle and pointed Shibida toward the tall dark peaks rising from the east side of the park. Dark clouds were huddling around one giant called Colter Peak. I hardly gave them a second thought. For I knew where there were clouds, there were also eventually blue skies.

It was all a matter of patience.

24

The hunter knew he was going to get a kill. So did the Montana game warden leading them to the edge of the grazing bison.

Nearly five hundred other hunters in the past few months had been led to the same herd, and none, as far as I knew, had been denied a kill. How could anyone not be successful when they could get so close to their bison that they could practically hit its enormous humped figure with a rock? And, too, when the warden had a backup rifle?

From the very second the Montana Department of Fish, Wildlife and Parks notified him that the computer had drawn his name to participate in the shoot of Yellowstone Park's errant bison, the hunter probably had felt confident he was soon going to be the owner of a lot of buffalo steaks.

I stamped my cold feet against the hard ground and breathed onto my fingers. I wished the hunter would hurry up and point out to the thickly bundled warden which bison he was to cull from the ragged herd. Surprisingly they were walking past several large bulls that had to have wandered across the park boundary only recently.

I glanced at the others who, like me, had pulled over to the shoulder of the Livingston-Gardiner highway this February morning to watch these wayward park bison be shot. A lot of the watchers didn't look too happy. A couple were glaring at me, as if I were going to help pull that trigger. I figured they were some of the Fund for Animals protesters.

I was tempted to say something to them. To tell them that I

too wished the bison would stop their seemingly senseless exodus from the park's northern boundary onto this killing field.

I did care. I cared a hell of a lot. So did every other ranger in Yellowstone. It wasn't for nothing that the gold badge on my shirt front and the patch on my sleeve featured, along with the words "National Park Service," a mountain, a tree, and a bison.

I understood fully why what was happening was upsetting so many people in and outside of the park. There was a sense of the bizarre, of the circus, about this hunt. Towering peaks, the bloody snow, reporters, TV cameras, spectators, the traffic jam, the bison chewing their cud as calmly as if death was the least of their worries . . . I had trouble believing it was all really happening just a couple of miles from an entrance to Yellowstone Park.

The bison was one of this country's greatest wildlife conservation success stories and had always been the symbol of the agency I worked for. Yet here, nearly within sight of the mountains that less than a century ago had harbored America's last remaining wild herd, bison were again being shot down as routinely as in the days of Buffalo Bill Cody. I doubted that so many in one herd had been killed since those bloody times of the last century.

Here was a creature that had numbered around 40 million only 150 years ago, but was hunted by America's settlers to less than 550. And though there were now 70,000 nationwide and bison were probably no longer in danger of extinction, hadn't the poor beast suffered enough at man's hands? Furthermore, some of the bison in Yellowstone bore the distinctive badge of being descended from the last wild ones. Who was to say that the bison about to be killed wasn't one of those?

This latest bison shoot was legal, even reasonable in the Park Service's eyes, as a way for Montana to control the bison that crossed onto private lands. But there was no getting around the bizarreness of it all—the daily "body counts" in the local papers, the protesters on television throwing blood and yelling obscenities at the gunmen, the worried letters from the schoolchildren across America, and—more than anything—the *numbers*. Just how high was the number of bison killed going to go? Six hundred? Seven hundred?

For weeks the bison in the park's northern herd had been

filtering through the boundary near Gardiner in numbers that had never occurred in the park's history. Before, it had always been a handful at a time, or at the most a few dozen. Never virtually an entire herd. Everyone was perplexed. Fortunately we had assurances from Montana that should all of the northern herd's nine hundred bison cross the boundary, a core of at least two hundred would be left unharmed to ensure the continuation of the herd.

Bison from the park's three herds had over the years mostly wandered across the north and west boundaries, but they had seldom caused many problems, since the wilderness areas and national forest lands they usually ended up on were unpopulated by man. That changed with the continued expansion of the northern herd's winter migrations.

During the severe winter of 1975–76, around eighty bison moved northwesterly down the Yellowstone River toward Gardiner, and in subsequent winters the movements had become more frequent, though never en masse. My first two winters as chief ranger had seen around 250 of the northern herd foraging in the boundary area near Gardiner. But that was nothing compared to what was happening now.

Were last summer's fires responsible in some way for the sudden wholesale migration? There was a tendency on a lot of people's part to say so. Or was there, as some scientists were suggesting, a strong primordial urge in the bison to recolonize their historical ranges outside the park?

Whatever was happening, it was causing a lot of bad feelings between many people and agencies, as well as attracting ever more negative comments on the park's natural regulation policies. As with those massive wildfires, a lot of people were saying that we in the park were encouraging destruction of the park's treasures.

Yellowstone is the only place left in the United States where bison are still wild and unregulated. Its herd is also the largest free-roaming one in the United States since the early 1880s. But that was not always the case.

Up until the 1940s those bison in the Lamar Valley had been fed, rounded up, corralled, culled, and vaccinated as if they were ranch cattle. Indeed there actually had been a "Buffalo Ranch" with all the usual barns and outbuildings, corrals, chutes, fenced pastures, and planted fields for supplying feed oats and hay.

As a result of such attention and care, the bison thrived. So much so that by the mid-1950s the autumn roundups and winter feedings ceased and by the mid-1960s all unnatural manipulation of the herd populations inside the park was stopped. Down went the fences, back came the freedom for the bison to roam at will over any and all parts of the park. With the bison healthy and numbering over 1,500, in 1966 it was decided nature could thenceforth handle her own more effectively.

Severe winters would take their heavy toll, but one thing bison are good at is making calves. By the time I came to Yellowstone, there were over two thousand bison in the park's three herds: in the northern herd in the Lamar Valley–Mirror Plateau region, the Pelican Valley herd, and the Mary Mountain herd between the Hayden Valley and the Firehole geothermal area.

The Mary Mountain herd expanded westward slightly but, except for a very few that crossed near West Yellowstone, Montana, they mostly remained inside the park. The northern herd was a different matter altogether.

The Yellowstone River north of Tower and the plowed road from Cooke City to Mammoth and Gardiner provided ideal winter routes for the northern herd to areas outside the park, and they seemed intent upon taking advantage of them. The trouble was that up to half of the bison were probable carriers of the *Brucella abortus* organism, a bacterium that causes domestic cattle to abort their young. After half a century of trying to eradicate the disease from their stock, the Montana cattlemen in 1985 had finally won the right to have the entire state declared brucellosis-free. They didn't want to face it again.

Though there was no documented case of brucellosis being transmitted from any of the park's bison to domestic cattle through the use of common pasture or calving areas, the park developed in 1968 a boundary control program to attempt to keep the bison inside the park. That seemed easier than trying to test all the park's bison and then killing all those with the disease. The cost and manpower required for such a roundup and testing would have been enormous, filled with risks to the personnel in such wilderness topography, and possibly wasteful given the lack of evidence that the park bison were a brucellosis threat. There wasn't any guarantee that such testing would eradicate the brucellosis for very long, since a host of other wildlife species inside and outside the park, from elk to coyotes to rodents, are also brucellosis carriers.

Among other things, the boundary control plan called for shooting individual bison that persisted in approaching specified boundary areas. For a while it was quite successful. Until the approval to shoot bison inside the park was rescinded in 1978, it was necessary for the park rangers to kill only five bison—three bulls in 1974 and one cow and one bull in 1978. There was the scare in the severe winter of 1975–76, when eighty bison moved toward the forbidden north boundary. Fortunately for them, they didn't quite step over that one invisible administrative line that would have led to their demise.

Or was it fortunate?

At the time such a large movement by the park's bison toward a specific boundary area was viewed by the park rangers and scientists as highly unusual. Hardly anyone thought it would happen again soon. But just in case it did, it was decided to attempt to restrict the bison to the park by using hazing tactics as an alternative to shooting.

Alas, bison are gregarious creatures, bunching up into large herds from time to time, and also have a keen sense of what is called "acquired knowledge." Once the herd leaders discovered there was a more promising-looking range to the north of their traditional grazing area in the park, they didn't forget it and the way there.

More and more, the bison of the northern herd ventured to the Gardiner area in the following years, until in the winter before I moved to Yellowstone all hell broke loose when Montana state wardens had little choice but to shoot eighty-eight of the wayward bison just outside the park. The same banner headlines and political scorn that the Park Service had sought to avoid by stopping in 1978 any more killing of bison by the park rangers was exactly what the state of Montana received—in big doses.

The Montana legislature answered the calls by hunters for a bison hunting season by giving them just that in the winter of 1985–86. It made sense that as long as bison were going to have to be shot, it might as well be done by actual hunters: Fees could be collected to help defray the costs and, significantly, the public's attention would be refocused onto others who were of their own ranks.

That first season, fifty-seven bison were shot by the new breed of bison "hunters." Of course hordes of journalists and television cameras descended upon the scene. For every bison hunter there seemed to be a dozen story hunters. Regretfully, what America got in its newspapers and on its evening newscasts were the scenes Yellowstone and Montana officials had been hoping would not happen: bumbling hunters taking several shots to bring down confused animals, orphaned yearlings standing over their dead mothers, magnificent bulls being shot down without the slightest effort, gunmen bragging about how much fun it all was.

The controversy only grew worse . . . and louder.

What followed was still more criticism, as well as a bevy of "solutions" by outsiders. Those included everything from shipping the excess bison to other places in the United States, to implanting birth control devices into the bison to keep their numbers down, to having the park's rangers return to their former ways of rounding up any extra bison and killing them inside the park. Almost all ended up being thrown out as too impractical, too costly, or unethical. No bison, for instance, from a herd infected with brucellosis could be legally transported across state lines without extensive testing and a long quarantine. And no idea was more quickly discarded than the suggestion that the public should be allowed to hunt the bison *inside* the park before they crossed the boundary. Though bison were hunted in other places like Alaska, South Dakota, and Utah on a limited basis, the idea of it happening inside Yellowstone was totally inconsistent with the philosophy that the park was a place where the ecology could unfold naturally and unimpeded by man.

The okaying of that first bison hunt outside the park resulted in a suit being filed against the park by the Fund for Animals protectionist group. In the suit the group said that the legislative mandate that required the park to protect the bison also meant they were to keep the animals in the park. Just as Montana officials liked to refer to the elk and sheep and deer that crossed from the park into their state as the *state's* animals (probably because they brought in a lot of hunting revenue), but the bison as *Yellowstone's* bison (because they brought only headaches and embarrassment), the protectionists' suit never mentioned the annual fall and winter migrations of the other animals. As Paul Schullery, the park's historian, put it, the Fund for Animals conveniently picked the bison out of its ecological context and made it a cause célèbre.

The suit was rejected by the courts, but during the affair the Fund for Animals founder, Cleveland Amory, accused the Park Service of having "cowards" in it who were not interested in doing their job of protecting the animals. The Park Service was also accused of "wanton, cruel, inhumane destruction of Plaintiff's national heritage" in regard to the bison being killed. Among the Fund's proposals to correct the problem were: capturing the trespassers and transporting them to other ranges in the U.S.; building a bison-proof fence along that part of the northern boundary where there were ranches; and driving the bison back into the park by chasing them with helicopters and snowmobiles, or on foot.

All those proposals no doubt sounded good to the public. However, they were likely to lead to larger problems in the long run. It would have been highly impractical, if not impossible, to round up so many free-ranging bison. Also, as I have noted, moving the bison to other ranges might have spread the brucellosis. And in the nation's other herds there was also the problem of overpopulation, since those bison are fenced into a set area. In places such as Badlands National Park and Wind Cave National Park in South Dakota and Theodore Roosevelt National Park in North Dakota, regular roundups and culling of the herds were necessary. Badlands took its captured excess bison on stock trucks to a nearby Indian reservation; those bulls too large and powerful to be trapped were shot and donated to Indian tribes.

Custer State Park in South Dakota went one step further in the culling process. From 1940 to 1974 it had a slaughtering operation and sold the meat to private buyers. It made its annual roundups easier by killing all bison over ten years of age. No such "cold-blooded" action could have taken place in Yellowstone without becoming big news quickly, and thoroughly horrifying the general public.

As for building a fence for miles along the boundary, there was the danger that such a barrier would also impede the historic migrations of the other ungulates such as the elk and antelope, as well as bear, deer, and bighorn sheep. That was the sort of proposal that gave true ecologists nightmares. In the rush to limit some bison's movements, we could have upset the entire ecology. It was yet another example of the difference in thinking between the animal protectionists and the park's resource managers. The protectionists were obsessed with the care of single animals, while we in the park had to look at the entire ecological picture. What was good for one animal was not necessarily good for the rest.

Further complicating any possible efforts to keep the bison in the park by physical barriers or by hazing was the simple fact that bison do not respect such things. As huge and stubborn as they are, a two-thousand-pound bison can and will go anywhere it wants to. As Dr. Mary Meagher, a research scientist with the park for thirty years and one of the foremost experts on bison in the country, testified in her response to the Fund for Animals suit: "Bison can be herded only where they are willing to go."

Actually, the park had been trying since 1976 to come up with some effective way to contain the bison within the boundaries. And all the money and efforts expended had ended up proving exactly what Mary said. The attempts to block or scare the bison over the years as they inched closer to the Paradise Valley worked temporarily, but did nothing to change their eventual arrival. Once their minds were set on getting to the new ranges, they would get there—sooner or later.

My second winter in Yellowstone seven other rangers, including Dr. Meagher, and I spent a November afternoon on foot trying to bluff a herd of fifty bison back toward the park's interior. About four or five of the animals were bulls and the rest cows and calves. The setting was mostly rolling hills. Rattling rocks in cans we managed to move them back to the east, but every so often they would dash into the folds of the hills and have to be flushed out. Bison, it was known, will usually cooperate once or twice, but that's about their limit. And as if to bring that point home to us that cold afternoon, the four bulls charged through our group from behind one of the hills. There were no trees or rocks for any of us to dive behind, but fortunately they missed every one of us. Though not by more than twenty or thirty feet.

Whether the park rangers tried by helicopter or on foot, it didn't seem that the bison were interested in turning back. They seemed to know they had a lot more speed and power than any ranger and his toys. It became obvious that to continue putting rangers on foot up against such unpredictable wildness could lead to someone being hurt or killed. So it was decided to end those attempts. The last attempt to use a helicopter to herd bison back into the park was in 1984, and resulted in some of the "escapees" returning and damage being done to ranch fences from frightened livestock. Besides, those that returned to the park merely hoofed it back out when the irritant in the sky left.

Other devices we had tried included the construction of a fence across the Yellowstone River trail route in the winter of 1975–76. Within two weeks the bison had figured out alternate routes around the blocked area. They went up other drainages and then made their own trails. They also moved to the plowed road between Gardiner-Mammoth and Cooke City. It became necessary to put a cattleguard along it. But again the bison found ways around it on both its north and south sides, including going across the very steep south-facing open slope of Mount Everts.

Two years ago, we tested many other means of hazing the moving herds. We used recorded wolf calls, flashing lights, sirens, cracker shells, tin-can rattles, streamers, and pain-inflicting devices such as rubber bullets. All of those, according to Mammoth Sub-

District Ranger John Donaldson, were effective once or twice at best, then virtually ignored thereafter. Some bison would even try to get closer to see what all the commotion was about!

There were those who suggested that we feed the bison hay, or whatever, to entice them to stay put. That too had been tried before. Baiting with hay was tried in the winters of 1977–78 and 1979–80, as was scattering charcoal on snow in the spring of 1978 to increase the melt. They were flops too. The plain truth was that the bison were being prodded by something even more powerful than their stomachs. Indeed, those bison examined after each previous hunt were healthy and had excellent amounts of fat.

Bison love to wander and are going to do so even if that means passing up perfectly good range along the way. Seven years of drought followed by a normal snowy winter with extremely cold temperatures, and the 11 percent of the northern range that was burned in the summer's fires, probably exacerbated the problem, but they were not the root of it at all. Bad or good range, cold or warm winter, fire or no fire, bison were going to move—period. The only way we could be sure of solving the problem would be to shoot every one of the bison that had any knowledge of the route to the Gardiner area! There was no solution that would please the public, the officials, and the bison.

As distasteful as it was, the cropping of the bison by outside hunting was the only real solution for the time being. That, with some limited harassment of the moving bison, wasn't going to change the bison's movements, but might slow them down.

The hunter knelt in the shallow snow behind a low boulder —not to be hidden, for that was unnecessary, but to steady his aim. I held my breath. He raised the rifle to his right shoulder, aimed it toward the old bison bull.

In my eardrums I heard the hunter's heart pounding. In my eye I saw the incredibly fine cross hairs of the scope sweep clumsily over the herd of other statuesque bison, then settle onto *it*. I thought his thoughts: *Steady now . . . don't breathe . . . one thousand and one, one thousand and—*

Craack!

The bull dropped to the ground as quickly and heavily as if a mountain had fallen squarely onto its back. The man and his friends hollered. His family cheered. He had his kill. A free-lance butcher's winch-lift truck crept forward. The bull, which probably weighed close to a ton, lay in the reddening snow, as still as the boulders.

I decided to return to the office. I didn't need to see any more. I knew that most bison shot were pulled up by the winch truck and gutted, then skinned and butchered and sent on their way with the hunters. I supposed that to some of the hunters here this was a sporting way to pick up a trophy head and a lot of game meat. That was their choice. Anyway, I felt it was better they did it than that the rangers had to.

I slid in behind the steering wheel, turned the ignition key, and steered the car around. Since the beginning of time, wildlife living in natural settings have had to endure winter. From a wildlife perspective, winter in Yellowstone and other mountainous wilderness areas means cold, barrenness, and death. The bison in Yellowstone had reached their upper equilibrium for the range available to them in the park, and they had somehow realized this. They had known instinctively it was time to move on. What they hadn't known was that the world outside the park was no longer theirs.

It would have been wonderful if they could have kept on going and filled in all their former ranges again with their great herds. Given enough time, I suspected they would have quite efficiently. But that just wasn't possible any longer. They were the prisoners of civilization, of cities and highways and shopping malls. To survive in this new world, they were going to have to learn to accept a much, much smaller role. For man had truly won the war against nature in their case.

Eventually the Yellowstone bison would force us to come to some solution. I only hoped that when we did, it would leave both them and the park no more "civilized" than it already was.

I looked in my rearview mirror at the people and cars receding into the bosom of the Paradise Valley. I shook my head. Why, I wondered sadly, was it more important to keep the bison from the cattle, and not the other way around? Those bison were feeding where they were because that land had once been a part of their natural winter range. They were only doing what was natural. Coming back to home, in a way. The cattle ranchers had driven them off to begin with, but now wanted to put all the blame on the park rangers.

The ranchers needed to face the fact: They were as much a part of the problem as were the bison.

25

A faint voice on the walkie-talkie radio hanging on my belt crackled up through the camping gear in my arms. The words "Man with a gun" snapped at my brain.

I dropped everything into the back of the pickup I had been loading, reached to my belt, and waved at Brooke and Trevor to be quiet. Disappointment spread across their faces. They stared at the walkie-talkie radio in my hand as if it were some dreaded party crasher: I had promised that this June Friday afternoon was to be for sailing on Yellowstone Lake and then camping, not for work.

Another splintered sentence jumped at my ears. The ranger's voice belonged to Bundy Phillips, a supervisor at Old Faithful. He was talking with someone about a man at the Old Faithful visitor center having a gun.

I turned up the volume. For several seconds there was only static. I hoped the incident was nothing more than a park visitor showing off a pistol or rifle to another visitor. That happened quite frequently, even though it was illegal to display any firearms inside the park. However, I then remembered that President Bush was scheduled to visit the park in a few days. He was coming to see how the forests were recovering from last summer's fires. Was something far more serious developing down there at Old Faithful?

Bundy's voice came back on the radio. "We have an apparent hostage situation."

I flashed an apologetic look at the children and immediately dashed back to the house. Along the way I instructed the dispatcher to get in touch with Debbie Bird, the ranger in charge at Old Faithful. "Tell her I'm on my way to the Comm Center, that I want her to call me when she gets to a phone."

As I did most mornings in the summer, I swung myself up onto an old gray mountain bicycle and pedaled directly to the rear entrance of the administration building.

As soon as I entered the communications center one of the three dispatchers there was waving at me to pick up a telephone. Debbie was on the line. She was calling from the Old Faithful ranger station.

"Debbie, what's going on?"

"We don't know much yet. Basically, that a park visitor named Larry Becker called the Comm Center on the nine-one-one line about five minutes ago to report a man with a gun in the visitor center. Since then, the assailant has released several women and children, and we're just now questioning them for more details."

"Do you have any idea how many people he's still holding? Has he made any demands?"

"No demands yet that I've been made aware of. As for the number of people with him I'd say there are at least eight. Apparently some people in the visitor center left as soon as he pulled the gun. And naturalists Ann Deutch and Tom Hougham, who are in the group of hostages, somehow got everybody in the back auditorium to safety."

"Have you had any contact with the man?"

"None, but Bundy is on the phone trying to call in. We did get a radio transmission from Ann saying that the man did not want to be able to see anyone through the windows."

"When did this all begin?"

"Approximately fifteen-hundred hours."

I looked at my watch. It was almost fifteen minutes past the hour. A lot could have happened in that time. Was he a mental case? A terrorist? Could this be something rehearsed and planned by a suicidal radical group with something against the government or Park Service? The possibilities were numerous and frightening. This might even be a diversion to get everyone from another more important target inside the park. We needed a much clearer profile of the man and the situation inside the center—fast.

"Debbie, tell Bundy to stay on the telephone with whoever answers. He must try to learn everything he can."

If we could learn the man's identity, we could begin to know what sort of person we were dealing with. Pat Ozment, the park's criminal investigator, was already on his way to Old Faithful, and once there could send the suspect's name by computer to the National Crime Information Center. By running it through their computers, they could find those driver's license holders in each state bearing the same or a similar name. From there it was a matter of getting his address off his license and contacting the police of his area for information on family and friends.

"Also, let's have all communications between rangers be on channels three, four, and five. It's possible the gunman is listening to the radio in the visitor center," I added.

The center didn't get those frequencies. So I would have the dispatcher in the communications center announce on all radio channels that until further notice emergency radio status was in effect, that all radio communication in the park should be on those channels.

"I've got rangers Campbell and Blair clearing out the visitors from the area," she said.

"Okay. I'll get our most qualified manpower rolling to the scene. In the meantime, you start establishing perimeters around the visitor center with the rangers you have. Put up a tight perimeter very close to the building, to prevent his escape and to provide immediate assistance to the hostages if necessary. Also put in place a secondary perimeter out of sight to stop anyone from accidentally wandering into the area."

"Right."

"And stay close to the phone or radio. You must be immediately available for any communications or new information."

I placed the receiver back onto the phone and reached for a button beside a microphone built into the dispatcher's counter. I pressed it and spoke firmly.

"Three-ten, three-ten . . . one-oh-three."

"Three-ten," replied a low voice barely discernible above the wailing of a siren.

"Joe! You're aware of the situation at Old Faithful?"

"I'm on my way there. Just past Madison."

"You will be the incident commander. When you get to Old Faithful, meet at once with Debbie and let me know you're there."

"Ten-four."

I stood up straight and ran a hand through my hair. The hostage taker couldn't have timed his action any better. Had he known that? With the summer vacation in full swing, the roads were in a virtual state of gridlock in places. Joe and every other ranger being called to the scene from across the park was going to be a long time getting there.

The door opened and shut behind me. I turned to find Steve Frye. He looked as if he'd sprinted from wherever he'd been. The news about the hostage situation had obviously reached him, too.

"Steve, you're just in time. We need you to help track down everyone we may need at Old Faithful and here."

He nodded. Steve had helped me in so many emergency situations over the years that he knew exactly the steps needed to get the necessary men and gear to Old Faithful. Together we telephoned several rangers I knew were excellent shots, including Jerry Mernin and Les Inafuku at the South Entrance ranger station and Joe Fowler at the Lamar ranger station, and told them to bring along their long rifles. That done, I rushed downstairs to the public affairs office. I knew that as soon as the word got out of the park that there was a hostage situation, the media would be calling in droves.

The public affairs staff went right to work rounding up extra people to help man the telephones the media calls would be directed to. We had sixteen telephone lines into the park, and I knew full well every one would be jammed soon with reporters calling from every corner of the region and nation.

While returning to the communications center I slipped into my office to call the nearest FBI office—Butte, Montana—for assistance: They had more expertise in this kind of crime than we did. The agent I needed to talk to wasn't in. I urgently requested that he return my call as soon as possible, then hurried on to Frye and the dispatchers.

As soon as I entered the communications center I noticed that every light on the switchboard was blinking.

"What's going on?" I asked.

"Every line has media trying to get in," the dispatcher explained.

Already? How could so many have known so soon?

"Dan! FBI."

I picked up the telephone the dispatcher pointed to. It was the agent I wanted. I explained the situation at Old Faithful and learned that the men who made up their SWAT team for the region were spread throughout the state. Each would have to be tracked down. And that would take quite some time. We were on our own for at least the next several hours.

"Dan, you won't believe who just called," said Frye as soon as I hung up the phone.

James Ridenour, the newly appointed director of the National Park Service, had called from somewhere in New England, said Frye. He had been watching the evening news, and one of the news pieces had been about the hostages.

I remembered Debbie mentioning something to me about a national network news crew being in her area filming material for the President's visit. They must have been at or near Old Faithful when the gunman took over the center. It was likely that they were the ones who had gotten the news out to the public so quickly.

"Dan, another call for you."

I took a deep breath and picked up the receiver.

It was Debbie.

"We have the suspect's name and age," she said.

His name was Brett A. Hartley. And he was only eighteen.

Bundy had gotten through on the telephone to the visitor center and learned that for some reason Hartley was talking to Ann Deutch, had even given her his name and birthdate, saying that he might as well since everyone would know soon anyway. He'd also demanded to have a ranger traded for each of the five civilian hostages he was holding. He told Ann it didn't matter who was hostage, since "People are people."

The ranger-hostage trade gave us the perfect excuse we needed to stall, to allow other rangers to get to the scene and into position around the center. There was no way such a trade would have been made, but Bundy had Ann tell Hartley that it would take a long time, perhaps an hour, to get the exchange rangers there, that there was a lot of traffic and the roads were crowded. To everyone's relief he agreed to be patient. In the meantime, we went to work feverishly to get a personality profile on him, to determine what sort of weapon or weapons he had, and where everyone else in the center was located in relation to him, in case an assault became necessary.

By asking Ann a series of questions that required only a yes or no answer from her, Bundy was able to learn plenty about what was going on inside the center and who was where. There were indeed eight hostages: five visitors, two rangers, and a Yellowstone Association employee who had been handling the book sales. All except Ann were being forced to lie on their stomachs on the center's floor. Ann and the YA employee were the only women.

By the time Joe arrived at Old Faithful and assumed the incident commander role, it was about a quarter to four and the situation appeared to be relatively stable. Hartley was his calmest yet, according to Ann, who was continuing to do an excellent job on the telephone with Bundy.

It was tempting to think that we might get through this yet without anyone being shot. But I couldn't be confident of that: In my years as a ranger I'd seen too many crazy or upset people shoot and knife others inside the national parks. I could pull out of my memory, particularly from my Yosemite days, dozens of such incidents. Though it had yet to happen to me in Yellowstone, I'd had more than one person confront me with a firearm or a knife.

"Dan, it's Joe on the line."

I told Joe to position his assault teams outside the visitor center's doors, ready to rush inside if necessary.

He informed me that based on the personality profile Pat Ozment was getting from the authorities in Hartley's hometown in Louisiana, it was likely Hartley did not want to hurt anyone. Most likely he was setting up a situation where he would provoke the rangers with his pistol and then hope the rangers would have to shoot him.

As soon as I hung up, I got a call from Barbee. He was in Omaha, Nebraska, at a meeting, and had heard about the hostages. I assured him we were moving quickly but cautiously.

The next time Joe called, he and his staff had formulated their plan of action.

"The plan is to try to stall and wear Hartley down, if possible. I've got two assault teams presently positioned outside the center's doors. One of those, the one under Mernin, has their door unlocked. Also I'm going to continue to beef up the outer perimeter, as more rangers arrive."

"What if you have to assault, though?" I asked. "What's your plan and code?"

"'Green Light' will be the code word to assault the building. Since Mernin is closest to the subject, his team will be the primary one. The second team, headed by Rick Bennett, will be for distraction. On the 'Green Light' command, an extra ranger assigned to Bennett's team will bang on the window by the winter entrance with a nightstick. Then Bennett, Jason Jarrett, and Rob Danno will enter the center through the east side auditorium doors."

"Are the lights on inside there?"

"Yes, they are."

"And what about Mernin's team?"

"He will count to two, then he, Les Inafuku, and Rob Chambers will enter from the west."

"What about Hartley's weapon? What have you determined about it?"

"Based on what Ozment has gotten out of Ann over the telephone, Pat thinks it's probably a thirty-caliber Ruger revolver with a six-inch barrel. The assault teams have been told it probably has five rounds in it."

Five rounds. Enough to kill several of those rangers or hostages, if for some reason the assault members couldn't disable him right away.

"What sort of medical help is standing by?"

"The ambulance from Lake is at Shoshone Point with three nurses. There's also the Old Faithful ambulance, and the Lifeflight helicopter is on its way to the Grant Village heliport. Dan—" There was a monetary silence, then: "Dan, I'll get back to you. Ann's reporting that Hartley is restless. He wants to know where the exchange rangers are."

I hung up the phone and paced back and forth a couple of times, trying to imagine what was going through Hartley's mind. Would he see through our game? Realize we had no intention of making that trade? That we were only waiting for the right moment to spring at him? And if he did, then what?

Hartley, according to what Ozment had found thus far over the telephone, was of above-average intelligence. He had studied at the Louisiana School for Math and Science, a high school for superior students. He was a freshman at Louisiana State University and had had a 3.2 grade point average in the fall quarter. But that was about all we had that was promising. The rest was scary.

Apparently he had attempted suicide four years ago when his mother had divorced and remarried. Then about two years ago he'd had a melanoma removed from his back. In recent months he'd been convinced the cancer had returned, despite medical tests to the contrary. Diagnosed as psychotic and schizophrenic, he had been having recurrent thoughts and nightmares about killing people and being killed.

The Baton Rouge County sheriff's office reported that Hartley had left home the first of May and was listed as a missing person. Just a few days ago, his mother had received a five-page letter from him. Postmarked in Denver, it was essentially a suicide note in which he discussed his dreams of killing himself and others, and said that he believed the cancer was back. Evidently Hartley had wandered on to Yellowstone, arrived this day, and in his wanderings through the crowded Old Faithful area had decided the center was the place to make his tormenting dreams come true.

Almost three hours after taking over the center, Hartley finally picked up one of the telephones and spoke directly to Bundy. Bundy started to talk to him about his family. When Hartley began to cry,

Bundy kept talking. Over and over he asked the increasingly distraught young man to lay his gun down and step outside. All the while the hostages, except for Ann, who was at the center's other phone, were still on their stomachs on the floor.

Then, without warning, Hartley suddenly blurted: "Everybody out!"

All eight hostages made their dash for freedom and were quickly led to the ranger station, where they were questioned. It was determined that there were probably no other weapons on Hartley, and this information was passed on to the assault teams. Also, the sun had moved enough by that time to allow us a clear view through the center's windows via a spotting scope we had placed in the geyser area an hour and a half before.

Our original plan to wear Hartley down remained in effect. Bundy stayed on the telephone with Hartley, and the conversation ebbed and flowed as the sun sank. Several times it appeared that Hartley was going to give up. But each time Hartley changed his mind at the last second. Bundy could hear Hartley nervously drop and pick up the telephone.

Bundy was exhausted, but somehow he kept Hartley on the line. Bundy had training in handling basic hostage situations, but he had never had to deal with a situation where so many hostages were involved. He had Hartley talk about food, the park, Hartley's family. Anything but death. The ranger watching Hartley through the scope could see Hartley lay his weapon down on the counter. But he never moved far enough from it to permit a safe assault.

Finally, five hours after pulling the Ruger from under his jacket in the visitor center and ordering everyone to get down on the floor, Hartley surrendered. He simply shoved the gun aside on the counter and strolled out of the center. Rangers Bird, Bennett, and Jarrett moved in swiftly. As they led him off to be questioned by Ozment and a couple of FBI agents who had just arrived, Mernin's team scrambled into the visitor center and secured Hartley's weapon.

By the time Old Faithful next erupted, Hartley was being whisked away to St. John's Hospital in Jackson, Wyoming, for a psychological evaluation.

Hartley eventually was found not guilty of his crime by reason of insanity. He was committed to an institution for safekeeping and treatment until he became, if ever, capable of reentering society. I figured it was but a matter of time before he'd be "cured" and released.

Hartley soon became just another memory. But one part of his drama didn't: the presence of guns inside the park.

That Hartley had a gun was not unusual in Yellowstone, or any of the national parks. A lot of the park's visitors do. There is really no way to know how many guns are tucked inside the tens of thousands of cars and trucks that pass the park's entrance gates each day, but I am certain the number is very high. The potential for deadly violence is there. And as all of us who have been in law enforcement know all too well, it doesn't take much to trigger it.

Two years before Hartley walked into the Old Faithful visitor center, there was an incident at the Fishing Bridge campground that made me think of the Old West. It too was the result of guns being brought into a place that was supposed to be a refuge from man's general mayhem.

A large motor home from Texas had pulled into a campsite just before midnight, and soon afterward the father of the family shouted for his little girl to find some firewood, so they could build a fire. Though most of the other people in the campground were trying to sleep, the RV group turned on their generator and all their interior lights, and made a lot of loud noise.

Afraid perhaps to go too far away from the RV in the dark, or maybe because there was no firewood near their campsite, the girl went to an adjoining camp and tried to take some firewood stacked beside a trailer. Its occupant, a man from Utah, caught her and yelled at her. She became upset and cried. Her father, who had been described by witnesses as drinking from a "Texas fifth," rushed from the RV. He demanded that the other man apologize to his daughter, or else he would "break his face." Very soon punches were thrown, and it was the Texan who got the worst of it. Cursing, their tempers at fever pitch, the two men rushed back to their respective campsites to fetch guns.

Several shots were exchanged. Many of the neighboring campers—mostly families attending a reunion—had spilled from their tents and campers during the shouting. The sounds of guns discharging had them scrambling now for safety. Incredibly, no one was hit by any of the bullets zipping through the area.

No sooner had the blasting stopped than a third man entered the fracas. He rushed in waving a .357 Magnum pistol, claiming at the top of his lungs that he was a police officer. When the RV driver called his bluff by demanding to see some identification, still another fistfight broke out.

It was soon afterward that the rangers arrived to see what was prompting all the 911 calls to the communications center. They found chaos and frightened crowds in what only fifteen minutes before had been a peaceful, sleepy setting. The weapons seized from the three parties included a Ruger .22-caliber revolver hidden inside a guitar case in one of the RV's closets, a .22-caliber semiautomatic pistol wrapped in plastic in a trailer's freezer, and the Smith & Wesson .357-caliber revolver inside a car.

The pistol in the freezer was the kind found for fifteen dollars in most pawn shops. The Smith & Wesson turned out to be on the National Crime Information Center's computers as a stolen weapon. When ranger Pat Ozment talked to the gun's rightful owner over the telephone, he learned the owner had checked out of a motel in Dallas several years before and had accidentally left the gun stuffed under the mattress. When he'd returned two hours later to get it, there were cleaning personnel in the room and the weapon was gone. The cleaning people had denied knowing anything about it.

In the end, the RV gunman was fined $1,000 by the park's magistrate and given two years' probation. The man whose firewood had been stolen was fined $150 and given a one-year probation. The police impostor who had the stolen weapon was not fined, but was handed one year of probation.

Anyone who thinks that a national park is a haven from the foolishness and crimes of society is sadly wrong. There will always be a percentage of criminals among any day's batch of visitors and the park's thousands of employees. Though our crime statistics are tame compared to the likes of a Yosemite, where the campers are more concentrated, and which is accessible to several large metropolitan populations, Yellowstone is still no angel. Such extremely violent felonies as rapes, armed robberies, and homicides occur in it every so often. In the last five years serious crimes averaged over 170 a year. All felonies and misdemeanors are closer to 3,000 a year, with over 90 percent of them occurring in the summer.

It would be nice if crime could be checked at the entrance gates, but that is never possible. Nothing is as unpredictable as the next man.

We still had no idea why Hartley had chosen to take hostages in Yellowstone, but it was possible he had decided the park would be an "easy" place in which to carry out his plans. For one thing it is legal to bring any firearms into the parks, providing, as I said, they are not displayed openly. The only stipulation is that the gun must be unloaded and stored out of sight away from the ammo. Ironically, while it is okay to have firearms in one's possession in the campgrounds and other heavily populated areas, they are not permitted in the backcountry.

Also encouraging to the criminal or mentally deranged is the fact that there are so many opportunities to commit a crime unseen by the law. There is usually one patrol ranger to approximately every one thousand persons in the park on a typical summer day. While that is actually a better police/citizen ratio than in most towns and cities, those same rangers are spread out over nearly four hundred miles of road and some two dozen developed campgrounds and tourist villages, in which there are fourteen bars or pubs.

It is impossible to provide more than a token, if any, presence in every place. Worse, that same ranger force is also expected to respond to crimes and incidents such as fires and medical emergencies in both the park and in some of the gateway communities such as Gardiner, whose main street is just inside the park boundary, and Silver Gate, and Cooke City. These are towns that were forged out of their rugged settings by a segment of society with a great fondness for guns, gambling, and whiskey, and many rangers have had to leave their area of the park underprotected as they rushed off to confront some fighting-mad drunkard at one of the towns' saloons.

Many road bandits are savvy enough to realize that the typical visitor to the park is going to let his or her guard down in such a place, and just as important, that the visitor will not likely know such basic things as how to get to a ranger quickly. Help is probably many minutes or even hours away at best. Usually by the time a camper or hiker returns to his or her car, discovers it has been broken into, and then manages to drive to the nearest telephone, oftentimes dozens of miles away, the offense is hours, if not days, old, and difficult to solve.

The violence and potential for death that characterized the Old Faithful and Fishing Bridge incidents were not isolated. They were part of what the law enforcement rangers lived with nearly every day in the park's busy seasons. It seemed hardly a week passed that a ranger wasn't having to pull his or her pistol in a threatening situation. Hartley and the campers at Fishing Bridge had made clear that we needed to continually upgrade our training and our own weaponry.

The rangers of Yellowstone have long resisted forming the SWAT teams and purchasing the warlike weapons now common in other police agencies across America. That sort of "siege mentality" has never seemed appropriate in a place as beautiful and peaceful-looking as Yellowstone. But then that is probably going to have to change: The animals in Yellowstone may seem the same from year to year, but certainly the humans don't.

26

I certainly hadn't expected to arrive at work to learn that the next twelve years of my life were going to be hell. But there it was—on the front page of the newspaper, under a headline saying something about bad karma.

Today was the day that the cumulative weight of mankind's sins from the past 25,800 years swirled down from the cosmos to earth and put the whole lot of us into something called the "Dark Cycle." The end of the world was not necessarily guaranteed, I read, but it wasn't too far off.

Guru Ma, it turned out, over at the Church Universal and Triumphant, had had another visit from her disaster-forecasters, the "Ascended Masters." And they had shared with her a lot of their tough-times-are-ahead warnings.

Until the year 2002, when the Four Horsemen would finally end their galloping around on earth, mankind was facing an upsurge of the usual economic collapses, wars, plagues, and massive earthquakes—with, possibly, a nuclear war thrown in for good measure. It was, Guru Ma said, the "debt bomb."

I took an extra long sip of coffee (it might, after all, be my last) and thought about how pessimistic some people were. And how hypocritical.

Less than a month ago Guru Ma had warned in CUT's newsletter, the *Pearl of Wisdom,* that the dark cloud of karma was swirling onto the world partly because of man's pollution and abuses to the land. And yet that was exactly what her flock had been doing—abusing the land—from the day they moved into the Paradise Valley in 1981. So much so, in fact, that there was hardly a neighbor of theirs who didn't see red at the mention of them. Particularly after what had happened in the past few weeks.

On April 10 CUT reported to Montana officials that a 20,000-gallon fuel tank buried at their massive bomb shelter complex on the north slope of Electric Peak had split and spilled 4,000 gallons of diesel into the ground beneath it. Then, as if that weren't bad enough, three days later on Good Friday (the first anniversary of the *Exxon Valdez* spill in Alaska), CUT called the state's water bureau chief just before midnight to report that yet another tank had somehow split and lost around 10,000 gallons of its unleaded gasoline contents, also into the water table. Then on Saturday came still more news of the same kind. At last count the total amount of fuel missing into the groundwater just yards from Mol Heron Creek was around 31,000 gallons. And, worse, there was a sheen on the creek itself.

For CUT the bad karma had already descended. For the rest of us who knew how beautiful the Mol Heron valley had been before CUT's arrival, something else was sinking over us—utter disgust.

For over a year CUT's members had been busily preparing for the calamities of the bad karma's full descent. Their chief of security had been arrested for purchasing $100,000 worth of assault weapons illegally. And they had been building their bomb shelters. Some, such as those in their Glastonbury subdivisions, were small and mostly for single families. But the one in the Mol Heron Creek drainage was the main shelter complex. With the capacity to hold 756 people underground, it was an elaborate conglomeration of huge corrugated metal rooms, aboveground grain storage silos, an animal corral, and 35 buried fuel storage tanks capable of holding 630,000 gallons of diesel and gasoline and 10 to 12 other tanks holding 300,000 gallons of propane.

Mol Heron Creek, one of only three Paradise Valley spawning streams for the Yellowstone River's cutthroat trout, had in the past week become polluted by those diesel and gasoline leaks. That abomination, added to the deep construction site mud, the noise, the fumes, the pits and trenches, and the huge earth-moving ma-

311

chinery, made a lot of people in Paradise Valley, Gardiner, and Yellowstone want to cry.

Such a tragedy. Such a horrible, horrible rape of the very spot that the church's publicity material had described to their members as their "consecrated shrine" and a "living cathedral."

The cleanup of the leaked fuel might take months, during which time there were no guarantees that more—lots more—of the missing fuel wouldn't find its way through the groundwater table to the creek. Then from there into the Yellowstone River—possibly during the trout spawn in the creek in June and July.

If the CUT people thought those of us in Yellowstone were upset by their treatment of their wilderness areas along the park's northwest boundary, they had better be prepared to be scalped by the local sportsmen and environmentalist groups.

As for myself, I felt mostly heartbreak. Didn't Guru Ma and her clan—many of whom were highly educated—care about how precious life is? Didn't they understand that environmental disaster is inevitable when such heavy-handed intrusions are made on something as sensitive as a high mountain meadow? In rushing to prepare for the disasters of the future, they had created one themselves, right now, in their own backyard.

As it was there were more than enough ecological challenges inside a park as huge as Yellowstone, without having others spill over from the surrounding lands. Some, like a recent request by a logging company to haul fire-damaged logs from Cooke City through the park to their mill in Livingston, we had been unable to foresee. Others, such as the accusation that the park was overpopulated with elk, seemed to have been with the park forever.

The park's northern herd of elk is the largest in the world, numbering somewhere over twenty thousand, mainly because of a succession of extremely mild winters. And some critics were saying that was five to ten thousand too many for them to live healthily on the park's northern range. However, we had extensive scientific data that said there was no such "overpopulation," that the elk and the range were in excellent health.

Normally around 5 to 10 percent of Yellowstone's northern

herd died naturally over the winter. But in the wake of the drought of the past seven years, the temporarily fire-damaged northern range, and the return of a normal snowfall, three times the usual number had perished the winter of 1988–89. Dead and starving elk became a common sight that winter after the fires, being found next to roads and in highly visible places like Gardiner. Once more the public started asking what we could do in Yellowstone to stem such wildlife loss. No ready, workable solution was forthcoming.

Why didn't we just feed hay or alfalfa to the starving elk? Though several people in Gardiner did just that, we wouldn't because we knew that in the long run it was not healthy for the herd. It was short-circuiting the natural processes that would normally weed out the weakest in the species and encourage the survival of the strong and fit. Also, causing so many of the animals to group together when they were their weakest was encouraging the rapid spread of diseases like brucellosis.

No one liked to see animals starving. But nature had its own ways of rectifying the situation. And nature was after solutions that were for the good of the whole, instead of just for individual animals.

Death, as cruel as it appears to man, is a necessity for the quality and the survival of the species in general. Nature's system is good, if and when it is allowed to work unhindered—something that is rare wherever man treads.

Yellowstone Park has been called by some "the Great Experiment." It is our society's attempt to have both progress and the wilderness. Maybe not side by side, but at least still there.

People have to realize that as in any experiment there are going to be disappointments before the right solution is found. We have to go slowly along the way, or risk ruining the parts vital to the answer we seek.

I rolled up the newspaper with the article about Guru Ma's Dark Cycle and tossed it into a wastebasket. I swiveled my chair around to some low filing cabinets and switched my thoughts to the main task for this day—addressing the newest group of summer seasonal rangers.

I pulled out a drawer and thumbed through its neatly filed papers. I had already scribbled out what I wanted to say about such things as policies, arrest procedures, and the latest controversies involving the park. But, as usual, I had waited until the last to decide what anecdotes I should use to make my points more effective.

In one of the middle files I found what I was looking for—a copy of a letter written in 1925 by the park's superintendent, Horace Albright. It was a form letter to anyone interested in applying for a summer seasonal ranger job. Throughout its five pages it spelled out in clear and sometimes stern terms just what the park was looking for in any applicant. I thought the rangers might have a laugh at some of the more dated statements, such as: "If you have the reputation of appearing unusually youthful or immature for a man of 21, don't apply. We want men who are mature in appearance. . . . We always prefer big men to small men."

I put it in the folder holding my speech outline, then hurried out of the office. The new rangers and their instructors would be assembling in a few minutes at the YACC camp's cafeteria, almost a mile away.

I got in my car and drove straight to the YACC camp. Inside the spartan cafeteria I came upon rows of new faces, as well as several familiar ones from the previous summer. Everyone was already seated behind the long gray tables. The air was buzzing with excitement and an unmistakable eagerness to get on with their training. All the energy made me feel like a new ranger myself, even though many of those before me were much older than I— being everything from schoolteachers to retired highway patrolmen during the other seasons.

I cleared my throat. The room became quiet.

Opening my folder, I began reading from the Albright letter. I read of the duties, and routines, and qualifications of a ranger in the park's early years. The veterans in the audience laughed and nodded when the letter emphasized that a ranger's job was anything but easy and glamorous. Quite a few eyebrows were raised, too, when I read that then a new ranger had to be a man, was paid a hundred dollars a month, supplied his own bed, could not attend dances or other entertainment more than two evenings a week, and was never to retire to bed any later than eleven o'clock.

Near the letter's end I read a little slower and with more emphasis. While much of the letter up to then may have seemed dated, what I now read about the characteristics of a good ranger was as true as ever. And exactly what I expected of each of the fifty-five men and women before me.

"There is no vacation about ranger work," I read with a nod. "The duties are exacting and require the utmost patience and tact at all times. A ranger's job is no place for a nervous, quick-tempered man, nor for the laggard, nor for one who is unaccustomed to hard work.

"If you cannot work hard ten or twelve hours a day, and always with patience and a smile on your face, don't fill out the attached blank."

I looked up from my papers.

"The basic requirements for being a good ranger in Yellowstone have always been demanding," I said with a glance at the instructors sitting off to the sides. "But nowadays they're even more numerous and time-consuming. On top of everything the early rangers had to be proficient at, you have to know about such things as emergency medical services, resource management, and stress management." Many chuckled at that. But I continued with more firmness in my voice: "Without question, the controversies the Yellowstone staff has to contend with are far more complex. More and more they are coming from, or spilling into, areas outside our jurisdiction. How, for instance, should we deal with the mounting evidence that if the Church Universal and Triumphant goes ahead and drills into the aquifer feeding the La Duke Hot Spring, they could possibly impact the Norris Geyser Basin, which as you know is thirty miles south of their property and *inside* the park?

"Or how do we win over the powerful proranching politicians who have vowed the wolf will never be allowed back into Yellowstone? And do we dare to give in any more to the growing list of special interest groups such as the environmentalists and gateway communities that feel *they* have a right to say how the park is run?"

I balled my hands resting on the podium into fists and shook my head at the idea of the park being made into something like a carnival park or an exclusive laboratory.

"No, we must not give in to *anyone* who would ever cheapen or violate the land and the animals of this park. For they are still the main reason so many travel so far to see this place."

I took a deep breath and went on, reading more from my heart than from the scribbles at my fingers.

"You know, though this is now my fifth year of welcoming the new rangers to Yellowstone, I feel every bit as excited as I did the first time.

"Even after all the controversies of the past several years, even with the promise of still much more turbulence ahead, I still think Yellowstone is the greatest place on earth.

"But we must not rest. The continuation of Yellowstone as a largely pristine wilderness should never be taken for granted. There will always be some who would not hesitate, if allowed, to use the park for their own selfish gain.

"With the improvement of transportation, the world is only getting smaller each day. The growing world population and the economic hardships it is causing have even some of the most ardent conservationists and well-meaning governments assessing the worth of such large tracts of wilderness.

"Fortunately, at least in America, the majority of society realizes, perhaps more than ever, the true value of places like Yellowstone.

"The human race, I believe very strongly, is only as rich as its desire to save its natural wonders for future generations to experience, enjoy, and learn from."

It was late that night when I finished my office work, switched off the desk lamp, and walked out the office door to go home. I had spent probably a little too much time at the training sessions for the new rangers today. But, I felt it was important to try to get to know all of them personally. I liked my rangers to be more than just names.

In the same hallway that I had rushed through this morning to get to my car, I paused to straighten my ranger's Stetson in a reflection in a display case. Normally I would have continued on past with little more than a glance at a nearby bulletin board brimming with photos, newspaper headlines, and maps of the 1988 fires. Heaven knows I had had enough of those fires to last me several lifetimes! But this time I stopped and really looked closely at it.

Some of the clipped headlines—PARK SIZZLES!, YELLOWSTONE FIRES RAGE, ALL-OUT ASSAULT—screamed for attention. But it was not them I was most interested in. Instead, I was drawn to a cluster of hand-drawings by schoolchildren. Their animals and mountains beamed with color and inspiration.

I smiled. If only everyone could show such concern and love, and hope, for nature. Every *really* good ranger, something told me, had a child's sense of excitement and curiosity.

On one lovely drawing that was unsigned there was a poem about the great fires that I thought was especially touching. It started:

> Like a canyon needs a river,
> Like a body needs a heart,
> Like the moon needs the sun,
> A forest needs the trees.

I zipped up my jacket and headed to the door, the child's words still echoing in my head.

The wind felt refreshing. As was my habit whenever I stepped outside after a long time indoors, I took a deep, deep breath and savored it.

The child need not worry.

It smelled of trees. Lots of trees.